Islam and International Relations

Global Dialogues:
Developing Non-Eurocentric IR and IPE

Series Editors:
John M. Hobson, Professor of Politics and International Relations, University of Sheffield
L. H. M. Ling, Professor, Milano School of International Affairs, Management, and Urban Policy, The New School.

This series adopts a dialogical perspective on global politics, which focuses on the interactions and reciprocities between West and non-West, across Global North and Global South. Not only do these shape and reshape each other but they have also shaped, made and remade our international system/global economy for the last 500 years. Acknowledging that these reciprocities may be asymmetrical due to disparities in power and resources, this series also seeks to register how 'Eastern' agency, in tandem with counterparts in the West, has made world politics and the world political economy into what it is. While this series certainly welcomes purely theoretically based books, its primary focus centres on empirical rethinking about the development of the world political system and the global economy along non-Eurocentric lines.

Titles in the Series

Islam and International Relations: Exploring Community and the Limits of Universalism, by Faiz Sheikh

Islam and International Relations

Exploring Community and the Limits of Universalism

Faiz Sheikh

ROWMAN & LITTLEFIELD
INTERNATIONAL

London • New York

Published by Rowman & Littlefield International, Ltd.
Unit A, Whitacre Mews, 26-34 Stannary Street, London SE11 4AB
www.rowmaninternational.com

Rowman & Littlefield International, Ltd. is an affiliate of Rowman & Littlefield
4501 Forbes Boulevard, Suite 200, Lanham, Maryland 20706, USA
With additional offices in Boulder, New York, Toronto (Canada), and London (UK)
www.rowman.com

Copyright © 2016 by Faiz Sheikh

All rights reserved. No part of this book may be reproduced in any form or by any
electronic or mechanical means, including information storage and retrieval systems,
without written permission from the publisher, except by a reviewer who may quote
passages in a review.

British Library Cataloguing in Publication Information Available
A catalogue record for this book is available from the British Library

ISBN: HB 978-1-7834-8457-7
ISBN: PB 978-1-7834-8458-4

Library of Congress Cataloging-in-Publication Data

Names: Sheikh, Faiz, author.
Title: Islam and international relations : exploring community and the limits of universalism / Faiz
 Sheikh.
Description: Lanham, Maryland : Rowman & Littlefield, [2016] | Series: Global dialogues: develop-
 ing non-eurocentric IR and IPE | Includes bibliographical references and index.
Identifiers: LCCN 2016012615 (print) | LCCN 2016013610 (ebook) | ISBN 9781783484577 (cloth :
 alk. paper) | ISBN 9781783484584 (pbk. : alk. paper) | ISBN 9781783484591 (Electronic)
Subjects: LCSH: Islam and international relations. | Islam and world politics. | Islamic countries--
 Foreign relations.
Classification: LCC BP190.5.D56 S44 2016 (print) | LCC BP190.5.D56 (ebook) | DDC 297.2/72--
 dc23
LC record available at http://lccn.loc.gov/2016012615

™ The paper used in this publication meets the minimum requirements of American
National Standard for Information Sciences Permanence of Paper for Printed Library
Materials, ANSI/NISO Z39.48-1992.

Printed in the United States of America

Contents

Acknowledgements	ix
Note	x
List of Abbreviations	xi
Glossary of Arabic Terminology	xiii

1 Introduction — 1
  Islam and Politics — 4
  Warming Up: The State versus the *Umma* — 6
  The Main Event: Liberalism versus Islamism versus
      Poststructuralism — 8
  Structure of the Book — 9
  Notes — 12

Part I: Critiquing International Relations

2 Islam(ism) and International Relations — 17
  Navigating Political Islam — 19
    Unique Politics in Early Islam? — 22
    Taking Issue with *Din Wa Dawla* — 24
    The Third Perspective: Normative Political Islam — 27
  Conclusions — 30
  Notes — 31

3 International Relations, Islam, and the Secular Bias — 35
  IR and Political Islam in the MENA, Sub-Saharan Africa and
      Southeast Asia — 37
    International Relations, Religion and the MENA — 40
    Marxist-Inspired Study of the Middle East and North Africa — 40

	Constructivist-Inspired Study of the Middle East and North Africa	42
	Theoretical Pluralism: Foreign Policy Analysis and Realist-Inspired Study of the Middle East and North Africa	45
	International Relations, Religion and the African Continent	50
	African Marginalisation in International Relations	51
	International Relations, Religion and Southeast Asia	55
	Southeast Asia, Religion and International Relations	55
	The Westphalian Narrative in International Relations Scholarship	58
	The Legacy of Westphalia	60
	Liberal Individualism, the Umma and Communitarianism	61
	Conclusions	63
	Notes	64
4	A Framework for Studying Religion in International Relations	69
	Epistemological Foundations	71
	A Note on Terminology	73
	Islam, Postcolonialism and Modernity	75
	Postcolonial Critiques of Modernity	76
	Poststructuralism and Islam: A Shared Agenda?	79
	The Study of Religion in IR	80
	Unpacking Political Islam Using Constructivism	83
	Problems and Limitations	86
	Conclusions	88
	Notes	89

Part II: Developing an Alternative

5	Sovereignty and Political Islam	97
	Political Islam and the State	100
	Islamic Philosophy and Political Islam	104
	Gnosticism and the Shi'ism of Ayatollah Khomeini	105
	Exotericism in Sunni Islam	109
	Exotericism and Politics	111
	Ibn Khaldun, Exotericism and Sovereignty in Islam	113
	Synthesising the Sovereignty of God and Exotericism in Normative Political Islam	114
	Deriving Political Sovereignty via an Exoteric Method	117
	Conclusions	121
	Notes	123
6	Accounting for Community	127
	Islam as Community? Islam as Citizenship?	129
	Liberalism and Communitarianism	133

	Communitarian International Relations	139
	Conclusions	149
	Notes	151

Part III: Pluralism or Polarisation? Poststructuralism and Religion

7	Value Pluralism and the 'International' of International Relations	157
	Communitarianism and the Clash of Civilisations	159
	The Foundations of the 'Problem' in IR	164
	Value Pluralism and IR	167
	Certain in Scepticism? Postmodernism and Islam	172
	Acknowledging the Truth of Islam, or Essentialising a Diverse Tradition?	175
	Bounding Expectations: Islamic Rationalism and Poststructuralism	177
	Conclusions	179
	Notes	181
8	Conclusion	185
	To What Extent Is an Islamic Notion of International Relations Tenable?	188
	Notes	190

Bibliography	191
Index	203

Acknowledgements

Seeing this book through to completion took long enough for me to meet, court and marry my partner, and for us to have our first child together. Either I write very slowly, or when you meet the right person, things move very fast. To Nelija I owe a debt of thanks for her love, patience and continual encouragement through the writing of this book. A quick word about my daughter, Maša: I say that there is no better way to deliver a book manuscript on time, than to know that you're racing against the due date of your first child.

To Clive Jones I express my gratitude for his mentoring and considered advice as I begin my career. Going to a panel that Clive was chairing at the University of Durham allowed for the chance encounter with John Hobson, the editor of this book series. To the editors John Hobson and Lily Ling, as well as the three external reviewers, I express my appreciation for their insightful comments and feedback, which helped shape the book into the form it is now. I also extend my thanks to James Piscatori, who organised and invited me to a workshop on the *umma*, allowing me to present my ideas and receive excellent feedback, which has enhanced the rigour of this work. James also had the misfortune of reading and engaging in full with the PhD thesis which was the precursor to this book, in his position as my examiner. His feedback and encouragement at that time and afterwards has given me the confidence to move forward with this project.

The writing of the book could not have been possible without the generous funding of the Marie Curie Initial Training Network, Power and Region in a Multipolar Order (PRIMO),[1] for my post-doctoral position at the Universität Hamburg. My colleagues at Hamburg—Stephan Hensell, Mónica Rodríguez de Luna, Jörg Meyer and Cord Jakobeit—have all helped me clarify my thoughts and gave me encouragement to complete this book. A special word of thanks to Ann-Katrin Braunmiller, who gave her time to help me with all manner of administration over many months.

To my friends and colleagues Owen Thomas and Sarah Bulmer, who set up a monthly 'troubleshooting' meeting where I could cry tears of frustration and receive invaluable feedback, I cannot thank you enough for your incisive interventions to almost every chapter of this book. Moral support in abundance also came from Andrew McInnes, James Worrall, Anne Flaspöler, Lev Ouzounian, Gordon Clubb, Aree Phothiyarom and Daniel Watson. A special thanks to Egle Cesnulyte and Stelios Moshonas for reading and giving comments on parts of the book, and to Hafiz Salae for his help in navigating the literature of Islam in Southeast Asia. Finally, I would like to thank my parents not only for their proofreading skills, but also for continuing to believe in me and giving me the best of foundations to move forward and find my way.

NOTE

1. This project has received funding from the European Union's Seventh Framework Programme for research, technological development and demonstration under grant agreement no. 607133.

List of Abbreviations

IR	International Relations
EU	European Union
FPA	Foreign Policy Analysis
IFI	International Financial Institution
MENA	Middle East and North Africa
NGO	Non-Governmental Organisation
OIC	Organisation of Islamic Cooperation
SAP	Structural Adjustment Programme
UN	United Nations

Glossary of Arabic Terminology

'Aqa'id	Profession of faith
Ahl al-Kitab	People of the Book
Al-Haqiqah	The Truth
Al-ihsan	Virtue
Al-iman	Faith
Al-islam	Submission
Al-Shari'ah	The Law
Al-Tariqah	The Path
Da'wah	Call to Islam
Dar al-ahd	Domain of treaty
Dar al-harb	Domain of war
Dar al-Islam	Domain of peace/Islam
Dhimmis	Protected minorities
Din wa dawla	Islam as religion and state
Falsafa	Islamic philosophy
Faqih	Islamic lawyers
Fiqh	Jurisprudence
Hadith (plural Ahadith)	Recorded saying or action of the Prophet Muhammed
Hekmet	Wisdom
Hijra	The Prophet's migration from Mecca to Medina in the seventh century
Ijma'	Consensus
Ijma' al-fi'l	Consensus of action

Ijtihad	Exercise of reason
Kalam	Theology
Madhab (plural Madhahib)	School of thought
Mahdi	12th, hidden, Shi'a Imam
Masjid	Mosque
Muhadithun	Specialist in *hadith*
Nas	Nation/peoples
Qiyas	Analogy
Rashid (plural Rashidun)	Rightly guided Caliph
Shari'a	Islamic holy law
Siyar	Classical Islamic theory on IR
Shahada	Declaration of faith
Sunna	'Way' of the Prophet Muhammed
Taqlid	Imitation
Ulema	Muslim religious scholars
Umma	Community (of believers)

Chapter One

Introduction

International Relations (IR) is a curious term which obscures a history which is less 'international', and more European. The *European* relations of the seventeenth century and afterwards is the genesis of what is now called *international* relations. But where is the African, Asian, Middle Eastern or South American heritage of 'international' relations? Indeed, what were European relations in the seventeenth century if not the relations of *Christian* nations? In this book I am responding to Amitav Acharya's call for Global IR, which he articulates as:

> commitment to pluralistic universalism, grounding in world history, redefining existing IR theories and methods and building new ones from societies hitherto ignored as sources of IR knowledge, integrating the study of regions and regionalisms into the central concerns of IR, avoiding ethnocentrism and exceptionalism irrespective of source and form, and recognizing a broader conception of agency with material and ideational elements that includes resistance, normative action, and local constructions of global order.[1]

Using Islam and the experience of Muslim statecraft as an 'ignored source of IR knowledge', I will reassess the relationship between IR and Islam, an undertaking all the more pressing given the increasingly manifold ways in which Islam is interacting with global politics. Such interactions can be seen with, for example, the Organisation of Islamic Cooperation (OIC), an international organisation of Muslim majority and minority states; continuing international migration and refugee flows from Muslim to non-Muslim states; the rise of popularly elected Islamist parties in North African states after the widespread Arab uprisings of 2011; the looming spectre of acts of terrorism and violence carried out in the name of Islam. In just this small list we can identify a diverse set of claims and actions, some entirely at odds with each other, yet all causing anxiety because of the 'unknown unknown' of what Islam means to IR, and vice versa. Taking my examples further, the OIC is a state-based international organisation which is committed to upholding the principles of the UN charter. Compare the OIC's commitment to the UN charter, to the explicit rejection of the international system by a group like Islamic State. Both groups justify their claims through 'Islam', but in comparing these claims, a few possibilities open up. First, if one group is 'correct' in its interpretation of Islam and IR, then they render the other group 'incorrect'. Secondly, neither group could be correct and there remains an elusive but 'true' interpretation of Islam and IR. Or, finally, the marker of 'Islam' in IR could be so inherently diffuse in meaning that it becomes meaningless—it becomes unusable as an object of analysis. In a world of continuing polarisation between 'Islam' and 'the West', I will engage constructively with Islamic traditions, consider what it is IR does well, and what it might ignore or marginalise. Exploring themes that are considered universal in IR such as state-based politics and the necessity for secularism, I show how the study of political Islam might help bring the 'international' back into international relations.

I have already invoked the idea that the origins of the international system lie with Western Europe. In such an understanding of IR, the non-West is considered passive, acted upon by a dominant European centre. It is not just that the contemporary international system begins with the European state system, but additionally that this system resulted from immaculate European conception. Interactions between West and non-West before the advent of the modern state system are not acknowledged, and the non-West enters the story as geography and peoples to be tamed and civilised (brought into the state system) through colonialism. John Hobson, in *The Eastern Origins of Western Civilisation*, has argued that the propensity to forward a world history in which the West pioneered a progressive and rational international system occurs because scholars 'begin by taking the present dominance of the modern West as a fact, but then extrapolate back in time to search for all the unique Western factors that made it so'.[2] While I am invoking this trope of European ascendancy in IR, I do so to further trouble that narrative, not advocate it.

In this book I wish to engage Islam, specifically political ideas that derive from the faith, in a discussion with theories of IR. Through this dialogue I explore Islamic religious traditions, showing that Islam contributes keen insights into how we 'do' IR, and how we might change that practise to be more inclusive. At the same time I highlight the limits of political Islam regarding IR, especially around notions of sovereignty and communal, faith-based solidarity, and I propose some constructive measures needed to address these limitations. Such a dialogue will necessarily bring me into contact with the foundational terms and narratives of the international system, such as 'West', 'East' and Westphalian sovereignty, but I do not intend to dwell on these. Instead, I will focus on one very specific incidence of Eurocentrism in IR: secularism and its relationship to the state. I will engage with secularism by developing an *embryonic* theory of Islamic IR. Rather than attempt to fully articulate an Islamic concept of IR, a task that I will argue to be unachievable in the abstract, I will instead use the case of Islamic IR, loosely defined, to challenge certain central concepts in IR that are seen as immutable. In this way, I am using the case of Islam as an example of a tradition on the margins of IR, to critique the 'centre'. I will therefore pursue dual themes: (1) exploring what an Islamic construction of IR looks like and (2) analysing the impediments that an Islamic IR faces when interacting with other, more dominant paradigms and concepts in the discipline.

I will explore the above goals by using a two-stage analysis. This two-stage analysis is necessarily multidisciplinary, using concepts and theories drawn from both IR and theology.

In the first stage, I examine the dominant concepts in IR which prevent the articulation of religious politics generally and Islamic politics specifically, in the international sphere. I will argue that these otherwise immutable IR concepts, which I will identify as secularism in the discipline and the continuing centrality of the state, to be unfounded given the specific cultural and religious setting of their genesis. After the first stage of this analysis I will have created a space in which alternative theories, which do not sit well with secularism or the state, can develop; in the Islamic example this is represented by the concept of the *umma* (community of Muslims). In the second stage of analysis I will construct, as much as is possible, a notion of IR derived from an Islamic heritage.

The two stages of analysis outlined above reflect my two broad contributions. The first contribution is to the literature on IR, wherein I question the nature and influence of religion in IR. Rather than examine Islam's place in IR, the originality of my argument is in how I examine IR's place in Islam, revealing how IR's dominant interpretations fall short of the schema of Islam, as I construct it. Specifically, I argue that the centrality of the state and liberal individualism in IR derive from specific socio-cultural backgrounds, and so do not satisfy the needs of an Islamic IR. Such an analysis is only made possible by articulating what in fact constitutes Islamic IR for the purpose of this book. To be clear, I do not define what Islamic IR is, but point out that whatever form it might take, it would be derived from communal sources, not abstract and universal reason, as is the case with dominant IR paradigms. This distinction between the abstract and the communally derived is one of the locations of friction between IR and Islam, and more broadly, religion in general. As such, I argue for a greater reflexivity on the part of IR scholars to not take for granted value-neutral and universal claims within the discipline, universal claims that Acharya points out had a dark side: 'the suppression of diversity and justification of European imperialism'.[3]

My second contribution is to the literature on political Islam. Here I argue that political Islam struggles to articulate a notion of IR because it aligns itself to theology in a prohibitive way. I suggest that theology and the Islamic source texts are too broad and abstract to provide guidance on the contemporary international sphere. This is not unexpected, however; as I argue that guidance on politics is distinct from guidance on how to develop a relationship with God. Moreover, I argue that Islamic source texts provide *guidance*, as opposed to canon, and always require interpretation with regards to temporal or mundane life. As such, I build on work that 'brings rationalism back in', supplementing theological guidance with other strands of Islamic thought, specifically philosophy. Pushing the inclusion of philosophy further, I attempt to balance a poststructural framework with that of a foundational faith such as Islam. This balance is distinct from a synthesis between the two positions; rather, I employ value pluralism to manage the incoherencies between the two positions (one foundational and the other anti-foundational), while these positions work together in a common critique of political modernity. Distinct from the commonly perceived threat that poststructuralism brings to Abrahamic (and other universal) faiths, undermining their belief in God, I attempt to demonstrate how these incommensurable positions affirm the nature of value pluralism, and need not (indeed cannot) be rationally resolved.

I will continue this introductory chapter by providing background and context to the broad themes presented above: Islam and politics; the state and the *umma*; and the relationship between liberalism, Islam and poststructuralism. Finally, I will outline the structure of the book and provide a summary of the remaining chapters of the book.

ISLAM AND POLITICS

Much of the literature on Islamic jurisprudence, or *fiqh*, and its relation to politics—loosely speaking, the literature on political Islam—has a very specific focus on the domestic rather than international sphere.[4] Much of this dialogue is reactionary, with influential Islamist writers such as Sayyid Qutb and Abdul A'ala Maududi developing their ideas as a response to the situations in their own countries.[5] For example, Qutb was writing in the shadow of an oppressive Nasserite regime and Maududi was clearly influenced by British rule in India and the subsequent partition into Pakistan.[6]

The Qur'an itself defines its function to the believer: 'And We have sent down to thee the Book explaining all things'.[7] However, there is debate over whether the explanation provided by the Qur'an pertains to every little detail of an individual's 'temporal life', or moral norms of behaviour which deal with an individual's relationship with the transcendental or 'divine life'. In Sunni orthodoxy[8] the overarching understanding is that the Qur'an is not a legal document, but a source of moral norms.[9] This is derived from chapter 2, verse 2 of the Qur'an: 'This is the Book in which there is no doubt, a guide for those who are God-conscious'.[10] The Qur'an defines its role here as a guide, distinct from law or doctrine. Joseph van Ess argues that the closest the Qur'an gets to being canon is chapter 2, verse 177:[11]

> Righteousness does not consist in whether you face the East or West. The righteous man is he who believes in God and the Last Day, in the angels and the Book and the prophets; who, though he loves it dearly, gives away his wealth to kinsfolk, to orphans, to the destitute, to the traveller in need and to beggars, and for the redemption of captives; who attends to his prayers and renders the alms levy.[12]

Again, the Qur'an is general about what it is that constitutes belief. Such general, normative advice lends itself to the argument that the Qur'an is a source of moral norms, rather than law. Another contributor to Islamic law is the sayings of the Prophet Muhammed, *ahadith* (singular: *hadith*). This catalogue of Prophetic actions and sayings help the jurisprudent extrapolate the sometimes abstract guidance in the Qur'an and 'fill the gaps' of Qur'anic content. *Ahadith* are considered the second most important source of Islamic knowledge, behind the Qur'an.[13]

For all that they do cover, neither the Qur'an nor *ahadith* contain explicit guidance on the state or IR. Nazih Ayubi notes that the very notion of an 'Islamic' state is a 'novel' idea, conceived in the early twentieth century by Rashid Ridda and later the Muslim brothers. The concept of the Islamic state developed as a 'response to the dissolution of the Turkish caliphate and in reaction to the pressures put on Muslim societies by the Western powers and by the Zionist movement',[14] not by Qur'anic imperative.

The lack of *explicit* guidance has not stopped Muslims in their quest for a government informed by religion rather than the secular nation-state model inherited from Europe after decolonisation. Such belief is articulated in the phrase *din wa dawla*, translated as 'religion and state'. However, the belief that Islamic guidance spans from the otherworldly concerns of worship to the temporal concerns of governance is hard to substantiate. As Qamaruddin Khan notes, 'if the first thirty years of Islam were excepted, the historical conduct of Muslim states could hardly be distinguished from that of other states in world history'.[15] Rather than explicit guidance or a separate body of law, IR in Islam is an extension of law regarding Muslim and non-Muslim interaction at a personal level. So strictly, 'there is no Muslim law of nations in the sense of the distinction between modern municipal (national) law and international law based on different sources and maintained by different sanctions'.[16]

Even if the *din wa dawla* slogan were true, one would still be hard pressed to find any information on *how* an Islamic state would participate in the international system. Indeed, political Islam is very much concerned with the domestic, defining what it *is not* and not how it would fit into or implement an international order.[17] In classical Islamic thought the world is simply demarcated into *dar al-Islam* and *dar al-harb*, the domain of peace (or Islam) and the domain of war, though a later addition by the Ottoman Empire saw the creation of *dar al-ahd*, the domain of treaty.

Majid Khadduri's exemplary work on war and peace in Islam posits the problem of a 'deficient' conceptualisation of IR in a different way. Khadduri states that '[s]imilar to the law of ancient Rome and the law of medieval Christendom, the Muslim law of nations was based on the theory of a universal state'.[18] Bassam Tibi highlights the resemblance that such a universal position has with political modernity: 'Islam resembles Western civilization, in the sense that it is universal in both its claims and its outlook'.[19] Failure to even recognise polities outside of its borders helps us to understand why discussion on the Islamic body politic is so embroiled in itself, its definition, capacities and functions toward its citizens, not the international system.

WARMING UP: THE STATE VERSUS THE *UMMA*

The leading political structure post World War II has undoubtedly been the liberal-democratic state that has dominated Western political philosophy.[20] This state was prescribed upon the rest of the world following decolonisation, and as Acharya argues, '[a]s a discipline, IR has neither fully accounted for, nor come to terms with, colonialism and its legacy'.[21] As Jeffrey Herbst notes of African states, '[i]t was immediately assumed that the new states would take on features that had previously characterized sovereignty [in Europe], most notably unquestioned physical control over a defined territory'.[22] Unquestioned control of territory here reads as adopting the state system. In Herbst's African example, those communities were only accepted into the international system because they accepted what Turan Kayaoglu refers to as the 'Westphalian narrative', a narrative, which 'maintains that Westphalia created an international society, consolidating a normative divergence between European international relations and the rest of the international system'.[23]

If the modern state creates a bias in IR whereby only those who accept this European normative heritage are to be accepted into 'international' society, to what extent is that society international? Kayaoglu argues that the society of states is a European society extended over the entire globe. Much in the same way the Islamic polity (or the Roman or medieval Christian polities) did not recognise those power structures beyond its borders, so too has the state system become universalised in such a way that no alternative is tenable.

Nicholas Onuf posits that the condition of anarchy is not a falsifiable assertion; one must be *told* that they live in a condition of anarchy—it cannot be proved. In constructing the conditions in which the state developed as a system of order, 'it is by no means clear that the Western state system is the only concrete instance of international relations available for study'.[24] With this as a point of departure, in analysing what it is about the *umma* construct that makes it incompatible with the state system, I will highlight some of the deficiencies in IR theory and/or the *umma* concept.

The historical Islamic polity (the pre–World War I caliphate) is described by Sami Zubaida as a 'political model'; he stops short of calling it a state.[25] Of primary importance in this distinction is the practice of rule over people, not territory. The modern state exercises control over territory, such unquestioned control being one of the cornerstones of state sovereignty.[26] In the *umma*, however, illustrated here however imperfectly in reference to the Ottoman Empire, 'law was still . . . personal rather than territorial'.[27] Despite this quite fundamental difference, some still think of the *umma* construct as an *equivalent* to the state[28] when rather, it is an *alternative*.

Turning to chapter 2, verse 143 of the Qur'an to substantiate the particularity of the *umma* construct: 'Thus have we made you an umma justly balanced, that you might be witnesses over the nations, and the Messenger a witness over yourselves'.[29] In the same verse both the words *umma* and 'nation' (*nas*) are used, indicating the distinction between the two in the Islamic tradition. Beyond this, as already mentioned, the *umma* is concerned with legislating over people, regardless of location, while the state legislates over territory.

As Islamic traditions of political organisation were dismantled during the colonial era to be replaced with modern state units,[30] IR, which uses the state as its unit of analysis, requires that contemporary political Islam define itself in a similar way in order to be accepted by the discipline. A return to what Michel Foucault describes as a 'pre-liberal' voice, that is, Islamic statecraft, may prove impossible given the 'totalizing discourse of Western, capitalist modernity'.[31] However, I will attempt to locate those 'genealogical fragments' of political Islam, and the *umma* in particular, which may challenge the 'best practice' of IR.

THE MAIN EVENT: LIBERALISM VERSUS ISLAMISM VERSUS POSTSTRUCTURALISM

For Michael Barnett, regional order in the Arab world is achieved not only by 'a stable correlation of military forces, but also because of stable expectations and shared norms'.[32] His emphasis on shared norms is peculiar, as normative theory is not generally considered a legitimate topic in IR; the discipline instead '[takes] for granted that the aim should be primarily descriptive and/or explanatory'.[33] In dealing with ideology and 'meta-narrative' I will explicitly challenge the overemphasis in IR towards objective explanation and against value judgements about its claims and practices; '[n]ormative questions are not answered by pointing to the way things are in the world'.[34]

There exists the popular notion that to the norms of the liberal state Islam is 'repellent and strange. . . . The notion commonly associated with it is the Sharia . . . which would seem to be incompatible with the rules of enlightened reason'.[35] Political Islam may overlap geographically with liberal 'spheres of influence', but it apparently operates 'relatively independently of the circuits and networks that define the structure of global liberalism'.[36] Indeed, Fiona Adamson calls political Islam and liberalism a competing set of ideologies.[37] This will not come as a surprise to some, like John Schwarzmantel, who contend that as a pervasive hegemony of ideology, liberalism is bound to conflict with any other belief system. He elucidates:

> While Liberal-democratic systems might in theory [have allowed] a wide range of political ideas to be departed and considered so that nothing was forbidden, in practice the span of effective political opinion was constrained by a dominant ideology which limited political debate to a set of questions concerned with managing the established system, and which blocked by various filter mechanisms any more systematic questioning or challenging of that system.[38]

While I do not seek to argue that liberalism is not as dominant as supposed by Schwarzmantel, I will analyse further the relationship between liberalism and political Islam. In an attempt to peel back the reasons for the antipathy between liberal and Islamist positions (acknowledging that there are substantial overlaps between these positions at times),[39] I will introduce a poststructural critique of liberalism specifically, and Enlightenment philosophy in general. While the poststructural critique breaks down the constitutive elements on both sides of the debate, allowing me to explore the foundations of this problematic dialogue, it creates an interesting question about poststructuralism and religion; religious adherents, specifically those of the Abrahamic faiths, believe in a foundational truth: God. Poststructuralism, however, is premised on a profound scepticism over any such foundational truths. I will return to this apparent conflict in later chapters.

Political Islam has, in a similar way with its dialogue with sovereignty, failed to make use of contemporary constructivist debates in IR. More traditional IR theory would contend, in accordance with realist or neo-realist theory, that ideologies are merely 'useful adjuncts to political power and are nurtured for that purpose'[40] by the actors of the neo-realist international system, states. The constructivist approach, however, contends that 'the role of shared ideas' is an 'ideational structure constraining and shaping behaviour'.[41] Rather than framing forms of realism and constructivism as competing paradigms, the latter can be used to emphasise the human aspect of existence; the state does not exist in a vacuum but is maintained and administered by the individuals within it. As individuals are given greater prominence in constructivism, so too can the Muslim achieve greater prominence in the society of states. It is this conclusion that violent proponents of political Islam fail to grasp, believing that they are unable to affect change without coming into a zero-sum conflict with the dominant liberal culture of international society.

STRUCTURE OF THE BOOK

The book is organised around three parts:

Part I: I will differentiate between Islam and political Islam or Islamism, defining this key term for the remainder of the book. With this definition in mind, Part I continues by forwarding a critique of IR on the basis of how religion is conceptualised in the IR of the Middle East and North Africa (MENA), sub-Saharan Africa and Southeast Asia. Finally, this critique of IR is located within a poststructural methodology which the book will use in Parts II and III.

Part II: I will begin to establish an alternative framework to comprehend the issues of religion, community and the state, and sovereignty in IR. This alternative framework is the nascent Islamic IR which I referred to earlier in the introduction, a form of political Islam which I call Normative Political Islam.

Part III: Having developed Normative Political Islam, at least in regards to sovereignty, community and secularism in IR, Part III untangles the conceptual difficulties which emerge when using a poststructural critique of IR theories which are capable of equally critiquing Normative Political Islam. In essence, Part III asks if it is possible to be a poststructural Muslim.

Part I consists of three chapters. In the next chapter, *Islam(ism) and International Relations*, I will embark upon answering the question: How extensive is the guidance offered in Islamic source texts with regards to international relations? Here I will make an important differentiation between Islam as it pertains to worship, Islam-as-faith, and Islam as it pertains to politics, Islam-as-politics. Here I will introduce the term Normative Political Islam, that is, the variant of political Islam that I will use to derive a notion of Islamic IR. Using the term Normative Political Islam highlights the fact that I am not speaking about a univocal tradition, or claiming to speak for how all Muslims are required to view the international sphere (a claim I would refute in any instance). Rather, I am differentiating my notion of Islamic politics from other variants. In doing so, I am not making any claims to 'greater legitimacy' for, as will be seen in later chapters, it is important to acknowledge how IR might mean different things to different communities.

In the third chapter of the book, *International Relations, Islam, and the Secular Bias*, I attempt to frame much of the debate that will develop when considering how the concept of *umma*, as an alternative to the state, challenges IR theories and concepts. Chapter 3 examines the major works that have applied IR to three regions of the world with prominent Muslim populations and Muslim majority, if not Islamic, states: the MENA; sub-Saharan Africa; and Southeast Asia. I examine these regions looking specifically for indication as to how these studies treat religion in those regions. I will argue that none of the IR approaches applied to these three regions deal with religion on its own terms, instead subsuming religion into pre-existing categories of analysis ('culture' being the prominent category). We will also glimpse in this chapter the beginnings of the debate between foundational and anti-foundational forces within IR, specifically with regards to the assumptions around liberal individualism, a theme that I will return to in later chapters of the book.

The final chapter of Part I, chapter 4, *Exploring the Interaction between Islam and IR: A Conceptual Framework*, will develop the tools needed to deal with the issues that the survey of IR literature in chapter 3 will highlight. In chapter 4 I will focus on explaining the methodology of the book in depth, expanding on the two-stage analysis I have begun to explain in this chapter, and placing the study in the broader context of the study of religion in IR. I will define my epistemological foundations as deriving from poststructuralism, that is, a scepticism towards meta-narrative and universalism. This chapter will purposefully leave my ontological position somewhat ambiguous, as resolving the ontological position of a believer in God and a poststructuralist informs the discussion of Part III of the book. However, chapter 4 does make some headway in regards to the synthesis between poststructuralism and Islamic critiques of IR, leaving discussion of the differences in these approaches to Part III.

The first chapter of Part II of the book, chapter 5, *Sovereignty and Political Islam*, takes on the task of the more constructive elements of the book, giving shape to Normative Political Islam. While earlier chapters will have arrived at a conclusion that Islamic source texts do not contain enough guidance to inform Islamic IR, in chapter 5 I will explore what *can* guide such a concept. I will here identify sovereignty as a key marker of difference between Islamic notions of IR and more dominant, secular variants. Trying to resolve the question of Islamic sovereignty will lead me to the revival of the exoteric, rational aspect of the Islamic message. I will show in this chapter how exotericism fell out of favour in Islamic history, and why bringing it back in helps deal with the constitutive elements of Islamic IR on which theological guidance (Islamic source texts) are silent or ambiguous. Using exotericism, I am able to be sensitive to the communal and societal origins of values that individuals hold. I conclude chapter 5 with a dual contract for deriving sovereignty which will illustrate the difference between Normative Political Islam and other notions of political Islam.

Having given some substance to a nascent Normative Political Islam, in chapter 6, *Accounting for Community*, I attempt to show how the principles that inform Normative Political Islam relate to IR. I identify the abstract universalism that liberalism is based upon; then, linking that universalism to the philosophy that resulted from the European Enlightenment, I argue that IR has also inherited that tradition of abstract universalism. The ramifications of this are discussed in the chapter, leading me to argue that communitarian sensitivity to the role individuals and society play in the construction of values is better placed than abstract universalism to give agency to Normative Political Islam in the international sphere. I show in this chapter that articulations of the *umma* in IR can range from thick to thin, giving more or less credence to the concept of the state. Lastly, I will demonstrate the shortfalls that these two positions, thick- and thin-*umma*, have with regards to the international system and the *umma* respectively.

Part III of the book begins with chapter 7, *Value Pluralism and the 'International' of International Relations*, in which I explore the ramifications of the communitarian IR elaborated in chapter 6. I examine here the way in which different communities might articulate different values in IR, and whether that will inexorably lead to conflict between competing value systems. Here I posit value pluralism as the solution to this question, arguing that managing conflict is a more just solution than attempting to eradicate conflict, the latter solution being one which I tie to the Enlightenment philosophy critiqued throughout the book. The final part of chapter 7 puts to rest the tension between poststructuralism and Islam which I have outlined briefly in the introduction. In answering this question I make the claim that bounding poststructuralism is the only way to prevent it becoming a metanarrative itself. At the same time, it is not inconsistent for a Muslim, believing in God, to utilise poststructural analysis in the construction of Normative Political Islam; poststructuralism helps to remind the Muslim of the limits of divine guidance in this temporal world.

The final, concluding chapter of the book forwards the final summary of the findings of the preceding chapters and outlines avenues for future research.

NOTES

1. Amitav Acharya, 'Global International Relations (IR) and Regional Worlds: A New Agenda for International Studies', *International Studies Quarterly* 58, no. 4 (2014): 647.
2. John Hobson, *The Eastern Origins of Western Civilisation* (Cambridge: Cambridge University Press, 2004), 295.
3. Acharya, 'Global International Relations (IR) and Regional Worlds', 649.
4. I take a loose view of what 'politics' means, so not to pre-empt what form Islamic IR might take. As a starting point, I adopt the perspective of Dale Eickelman and James Piscatori when they describe politics as the setting of boundaries. The setting of boundaries between secular/religious and obligatory/forbidden will be particular locations of interest as the book continues. For more, see Eickelman and Piscatori, *Muslim Politics* (Princeton: Princeton University Press, 1996), 18.
5. Nazih Ayubi, *Political Islam: Religion and Politics in the Arab World* (London: Routledge, 1991), 64.
6. Ibid., 128.
7. *The Holy Qur'an* (Dublin, OH: Ahmadiyya Anjuman Ishaat Islam), 16:89.
8. Defined as rulings from the four Sunni *madhahib* (Hanifi, Maliki, Shafi'i and Hanbali).
9. Fazlur Rahman, *Islam* (Chicago: University of Chicago Press, 1979), 37.
10. *Holy Qur'an*, 2:2.
11. Josef van Ess, *The Flowering of Muslim Theology* (London: Harvard University Press, 2006), 14–15.
12. *Holy Qur'an*, 2:177.
13. Albert Hourani, *A History of the Arab Peoples* (London: Faber and Faber, 1991), 69–71.
14. Ayubi, *Political Islam*, 64.
15. Qamaruddin Khan, *Political Concepts in the Qur'an* (Lahore: Islamic Book Foundation, 1982), 74.
16. Majid Khadduri, *War and Peace in the Law of Islam* (Baltimore: Johns Hopkins Press, 1955), 46.
17. Thomas Butko, 'Revelation or Revolution: A Gramscian Approach to the Rise of Political Islam', *British Journal of Middle Eastern Studies* 31, no. 1 (2004): 60.
18. Khadduri, *War and Peace in the Law of Islam*, 45.
19. Bassam Tibi, *The Challenge of Fundamentalism: Political Islam and the New World Disorder* (London: University of California Press, 1998), 15.
20. Will Kymlicka, *Contemporary Political Philosophy: An Introduction*, 2nd ed. (Oxford: Oxford University Press, 2002), 88.
21. Acharya, 'Global International Relations (IR) and Regional Worlds', 648.
22. Jeffrey Herbst, 'Responding to State Failure in Africa', *International Security* 21, no. 3 (1996): 121–22.
23. Turan Kayaoglu, 'Westphalian Eurocentrism in International Relations Theory', *International Studies Review* 12, no. 2 (2010): 193.
24. Nicholas Onuf, *World of Our Making: Rules and Rule in Social Theory and International Relations* (Columbia: University of South Carolina Press, 1989), 16.
25. Sami Zubaida, *Islam, the People & the State*, 2nd ed. (London: I.B. Tauris, 1989), 130–40.
26. Herbst, 'Responding to State Failure in Africa', 121–22.
27. Roderic Davidson, 'Turkish Attitudes Concerning Christian-Muslim Equality in the Nineteenth Century', in *The Modern Middle East: A Reader*, ed. Albert Hourani, Philip Khoury, and Mary Wilson (London: I.B. Tauris, 1993), 62.
28. Ayubi, *Political Islam*, 1–10.

29. *Holy Qur'an*, 2:143.
30. Fred Donner, 'The Sources of Islamic Conceptions of War', in *Just War and Jihad: Historical and Theoretical Perspectives on War and Peace in Western and Islamic Traditions*, ed. John Kelsay and James Johnson (London: Greenbridge, 1991), 58.
31. Giorgio Shani, 'De-colonizing Foucault', *International Political Sociology* 4, no. 2 (2010): 212.
32. Michael Barnett, *Dialogues in Arab Politics: Negotiations in Regional Order* (New York: Columbia University Press, 1998), 6.
33. Mervyn Frost, *Ethics in International Relations: A Constitutive Theory* (Cambridge: Cambridge University Press, 1996), 12.
34. Ibid., 2.
35. van Ess, *The Flowering of Muslim Theology*, 1.
36. Fiona Adamson, 'Global Liberalism versus Political Islam: Competing Ideological Frameworks in International Politics', *International Studies Review* 7, no. 4 (2005): 548.
37. Ibid.
38. John Schwarzmantel, *Ideology and Politics* (London: Sage, 2008), 11.
39. For a collection of Muslim writers talking about intersections between political liberalism and Islam see Charles Kurzman, ed., *Liberal Islam: A Sourcebook* (Oxford: Oxford University Press, 1998).
40. James A. Bill and Robert Springborg, *Politics in the Middle East*, 5th ed. (New York: Addison Wesley Longman, 1999), 25.
41. Dale Copeland, 'The Constructivist Challenge to Structural Realism: A Review Essay', *International Security* 25, no. 2 (2000): 189–90.

Part I

Critiquing International Relations

Chapter Two

Islam(ism) and International Relations

The Iranian revolution in 1979, which ushered in the clerical rule of Ayatollah Khomeini, also ushered in an interest in Islam and politics. After the Arab revolutions of 2011, and the elections of Islamist political parties, that is, parties that advocated *some kind* of Islamic order administered through the state, in Egypt and Tunisia, this interest is renewed. Such parties, however, are a world away from the Iranian Islamic state. As Asef Bayat explains, '[t]here is an unfortunate tendency to lump together quite different kinds of religiously inspired trends as "Islamist" while avoiding articulating any definition of the term'.[1] While there is controversy around the examples of both the En-Nahda party in Tunisia and the Freedom and Justice Party in Egypt (the latter removed from power by military coup within a year of election), these parties are perhaps more akin to Christian democratic parties in Europe than to the Islamic governments of Iran, Saudi Arabia or Pakistan. To cement this distinction, Bayat describes such parties as 'post-Islamist', that is, 'a different, more inclusive, kind of religious project in which Islam nevertheless continues to remain important both as faith and as a player in the public sphere'.[2] It goes without saying that it is of utmost importance to define these key terms 'Islam' and 'Islamism', which I will do, relating to IR, in this chapter.

I take Islam to be the broadest term. For some Muslims, separating 'political' Islam from 'Islam' is already an act of vandalism against the faith. For such Muslims, Islam is an inherently political religion, defining one's duties and obligations in all walks of life—recall the *din wa dawla* phrase from the introductory chapter.

If there is a separation to be made from an Islam that speaks to one's relationship with God and the care of one's soul, and social and political practices that *facilitate* the former, but are not in themselves a means to that end, then we can speak of political Islam or Islamism (I use the terms interchangeably).

What distinguishes Islamists from post-Islamists, for Bayat, is that the former focus on the fulfilment of duties, while the latter focus on the attainment of rights.[3] Post-Islamism would appear to be a clarification of the broader 'Islamist' label, a way to distinguish, conceptually, a different agenda within the broad umbrella of 'Islamism'.

Another prominent term in many discussions of Islam and politics is fundamentalism. Olivier Roy points out the difference between an Islamic fundamentalist and a political Islamist: The former wants 'a return to the old ways', while the latter wishes to develop their societies on the basis of modern technology and politics.[4] Arriving at Roy's definition of an Islamist or fundamentalist is not as easy as it would seem; John Voll states that '[t]he wide diversity of individuals and groups associated with Islamic fundamentalism indicates that it is not a monolithic movement and renders a simple definition difficult'.[5] For example, Henry Munson claims that the modern usage of the term fundamentalist refers 'to anyone who insists that all aspects of life, including the social and the political, should conform to a set of sacred scriptures believed to be inerrant and immutable'.[6] By Munson's understanding, the difference between Roy's Islamist and Islamic fundamentalist is trivial; both seek to establish God's rule on earth. For Sami Zubaida the term is even broader; any modern political movement seeking to establish an Islamic state is in fact fundamentalist,[7] and there are differences in opinion besides. For my purposes it is not necessary to see, as Roy does, a distinction between an Islamic fundamentalist and an Islamist, as Mansoor Moaddel and Kamran Talattof highlight that fundamentalism as a sub-category of Islamism. They distinguish between what they call modernist and fundamentalist Islamism. The former, modernism, 'covering a period between the late nineteenth and early twentieth century, consisted of a set of interrelated discourses that sought to bridge Islam with modernity'.[8] While the latter, fundamentalism, 'came in pari passu with the decline of liberal-nationalism between [the] 1930s and 1950s . . . this new discourse categorically rejected the Western model and outlook'.[9] Separating fundamentalism from the umbrella term Islamism writes fundamentalism out of the discussion. Rather than contribute to the idea that 'fundamentalists' do not read books in the darkness of their caves, I will not assume that political Islam is divorced from any fundamentalist interpretations and incorporate the term within what Islamism *might* be in global politics, in the method of Moaddel and Talattof.

Islamism is still a broad term then; it encompasses those groups that commit violence[10] against the state in the cause of 'enforcing good' in society, those who work within state systems via democratic means, those defined as fundamentalist *and* modernist. Additionally, in Moaddel and Talattof's modernist Islamism, Islamism may not refer to the capture of state power at all, but rather a social activism to increase the piety of ruling elites.[11] Those 'modernist Islamists' who do not seek state power or the replacement of the state with some other political assembly, those who are more concerned with religious piety in whatever political system, would not qualify, for me, as Islamist.

While I predominately focus on Sunni Islamic practice[12] (though we will see that this distinction means little given the multiplicity of competing narratives about 'real' Muslims), Shi'ism will be examined also, where relevant. Beyond defining these terms, I will look to Islam, a religion believed by some Muslims to provide the basis of their social order, for guidance on the international sphere. In doing so, I will articulate the nature of this guidance and begin to outline the extent to which Islamic scriptures and religious traditions can inform IR.

I am at great pains to point out that my discussion of Islamism, given its inclusion of the word 'Islam', does not point to a 'Muslim perspective on politics'; 'Islamists share the label *Muslim* with more traditional, liberal, modernist, mystical, and secular Muslims, with whom they may agree on many theological points but with whom they are often in vital disagreement on others'.[13]

NAVIGATING POLITICAL ISLAM

That Islam offers guidance on the political is a widespread but dubious assertion. Dietrich Jung points out how pervasive the link between Islam and politics can be:

> [T]he overwhelming majority of both Western scholars in oriental studies and followers of Islamist movements have defined Islamic culture first and foremost by its sacred moral and legal codes. Based on the almost axiomatic assumption that in Islam religion and politics are inseparably knitted together, they both view Islamic culture as intrinsically different from the modern democratic culture of the West.[14]

Like Jung, I find this assertion to be deeply problematic in how it posits an 'essential' and 'pure' Islam, independent of the people who constitute it. If this view of Islam holds true, then it implies that there is a 'pure' Islamic mode of governance. Historical precedence does not seem to support this essentialist position, as '[f]rom time to time theologians or *muhaddithun* (specialists in the traditions or saying of the Prophet, *hadith*) did write professions of faith (*'aqa'id*) that can be compared to Christian creed, but these texts entailed no obligation and remained valid only for a circumscribed time and place'.[15] Being valid in a specific time and place conflicts with the idea that there is a universal Islamic ideal valid for all Muslims, thought it does not deny smaller Islamic polities the potential to exist. In early or 'classical' Islam, Joseph van Ess maintains that the prevailing wisdom of the time derived from the Qur'anic verse 2:256, which states that there shall be 'no compulsion in religion'.[16]

Unlike Christianity, in Islam it is not the 'narrow path' that leads to salvation but simply the *shahada* (declaration of faith); it was considered that the wide path would save Muslims in the hereafter.[17] Such a relaxed posture is echoed by Khan, who, we will recall, points out that the argument of the *din wa dawla* adherents, that is, the inseparability of the faith of Islam from politics, is not one substantiated by the early history of Islam. He claims that 'if the first thirty years of Islam were excepted, the historical conduct of Muslim states could hardly be distinguished from that of other states in world history'.[18] Khan's statement is astute, if missing the point slightly. That the first thirty years of Islamic history were potentially unique *is* the call of many modern Islamists. For such Islamists (placed in the broad category of Salafism), the age-old practice of *taqlid*, imitation, has failed them and as such the many changes and accommodations made by Muslim jurists since the time of revelation are not worth imitating. As such, there is no use in pointing out, as Khan does, that Islamic polities have behaved in much the same way as non-Muslim polities thirty years *after* the revelation of Islam. This is something both sides of the debate agree upon. For the one side it is cause to point out how misguided Muslims have become following the passing of the *rashidun*, Rightly Guided Caliphs,[19] for the other side, it is cause to show how novel the idea of an Islamic state is. As such, both sides of the debate talk *past* each other, never addressing the points or grievances of the other. Engaging with such an ongoing debate is problematic; there is little chance to rest conclusively on one side or the other. However, while I may not conclusively settle the discussion, I must attempt to work through this issue regarding Islam's guidance on politics to arrive at a position that can then be used to examine IR—if this position is not satisfactory to some, I hope that my line of argument is at least clear enough to be followed.

Dale Eickelman and James Piscatori infer that the constant differentiation between the *rashidun* and their successors implies a cleavage between religion and state. Going further, perhaps this division happened at the Prophet Muhammed's death; he was the seal of the prophets, and thus no one could succeed his religious authority.[20] A similar yet different argument claims that the separation of religion and state happened during the reign of Abbasid Caliph Ma'mun (813–833). Ma'mun was sympathetic to Mu'tazilite theology and, to put it crudely, adopted it as a 'state' religion. This was rejected by the majority of Muslims, the Hanbali school in particular, effectively freeing religion from state. Going against the Caliphate in this way distinguished the limits of its authority, especially with regards to religion; '[h]enceforth, the

Caliphate was no longer the sole identifying symbol or the sole organizing institution, even for those Muslims who had been most closely identified with it'.[21]

These arguments do not claim that Islam and politics did not co-exist at one time; whether that ended with the death of the Prophet, the passing of the *rashidun* or the reign of Ma'mun does not matter. Rather, for one side of the argument, that of the unspectacular nature of Muslim politics, the separation of religion and state represents a precedent that means modern Muslims are able to live in and interact with political systems ostensibly 'foreign' to them. The opposing side of the debate, the *din wa dawla* advocates, see the cleavage between religion and state as a sign that modern Muslims have lost their way; emulation of the early Muslims is the key component of politics for these ideologues. Such emulation, for them, includes an Islamic state and distinctly Islamic political system. A third position, and the position which I will pursue, is an approach that allows some synthesis of Islam and politics, but challenges the all-encompassing and literal exhortations of *din wa dawla* advocates. In this way, my approach might be classified as post-Islamist.

But why is Islam the basis of this culturally specific normative foundation? Why not Arabism or some other ethnic affiliation? I claim that Islam is peculiar, though not unique, in its ability to incorporate many differing axes of identity into its ideology. One can be a student, male, female, a parent, elderly, nomadic, sedentary, upper-class, lower-class, Moroccan, Egyptian, Afghani, British, and still be Muslim.[22] In addition, Islam has been articulated as a project that strives for anything, from upholding the politics characterised by modernity, to mass emancipation within the boundaries of contemporary politics, all the way to a rejection of the system and complete revolution.

Khaled Abou El Fadl does not share the idea that revolution is the 'true' articulation of political Islam. Rather, it is a possible source of emancipation for Muslims from Orientalism, Westernisation and modernity, by taking control of power and its symbols.[23] However, what is specifically jarring to the Muslim world about the 'West' or political modernity is not defined by Abou El Fadl. Indeed, it often is not defined by authors trying to debunk essentialist accounts of Islam. This mistake is sometimes referred to as Orientalism in reverse, Occidentalism, whereby the author essentialises 'the West' for the purpose of their argument. Regardless, what El Fadl emphasises is that the pursuit of power by political Islam carries with it a *potential* emancipatory character, bringing power to Muslims where power currently rests in non-Muslim hands, though the nature of this power is entirely undefined beyond finger-pointing to 'the West'.

Bryan Turner deals with Islam's emancipatory nature in a much more articulate way. Here too is the assertion that political Islam, over ethnic affiliations or nationalistic projects, represents a potential global political system. Crucially, Turner articulates Abou El Fadl's 'West' as cultural baggage that accompanies modernisation, namely, 'a post-Enlightenment system of thought'.[24] Rather than using the language of emancipation, Turner prefers to use 'opposition' as his key word; '[Islam] can operate globally as an oppositional force'.[25] This 'opposition' introduces some much-needed nuance; for Turner political Islam is an ideology with the potential to contest the very Enlightenment rationality that current political structures are founded upon. The methods of this challenge are not so well defined; it is neither a revolution, nor, clearly, an ideology working within the boundaries of the contemporary political system. Beyond describing political Islam as filling an oppositional void left by the collapse of Communism, Turner, like many other writers on political Islam, does not attempt to explain what political Islam is *for*, but rather defines the concept by articulating what it is *against*.

Despite the problem of defining what political Islam stands for, my argument is that political Islam, over and above ethnic affiliation, nationally or regionally focused identity, presents a strong challenge to the discipline of IR. Briefly, that challenge is conceptualised as an Islamic politics based on a specific normative foundation derived from the Islamic faith. To get to this position, I must first deal with two competing visions for Islam in politics, that of the unspectacular nature of Islamic politics on one end of the spectrum, and the unique inseparability of religion and politics on the other end of it. The next section will begin by looking at the unspectacular nature of Islamic politics.

Unique Politics in Early Islam?

Fazlur Rahman argues that the Prophet Muhammed, through revelations and his religiously authoritative personal guidance, was the sole religious and political guide for Muslims during his lifetime. With his death this guidance was cut off, but the first four Caliphs, those who knew the Prophet best, 'met the ever-arising new situations by applying to these their judgements in the light of the Qur'an and what the Prophet had taught them'.[26] Only after the passing of the *rashidun* did the first theological sects emerge. While Rahman shows why many Muslims revere this period of Islam's history, a period before any infighting occurred between the Muslims, I argue that he inaccurately portrays the Prophet Muhammed as the sole political guide for Muslims in this era, a case put forward by Ali Abd al-Raziq.

Al-Raziq claims that there is a difference between 'kingly' and 'prophetic' rule.[27] Prophets, according to al-Raziq, have a special nature that cannot be emulated; '[the] Messenger may tackle the politics of his people as a king would, but the Prophet has a unique duty which he shares with no one',[28] that is, delivering the message of God to humankind. This is not a characteristic that can be replicated after the passing of the last of the Prophets, Muhammed; no one can hope to reproduce this prophetic authority and as such the period of Muhammed's rule is politically unique, and cannot be replicated. Now considering that al-Raziq says a prophet *may* tackle the politics of a king, it is necessary to clarify how a prophet exercising kingly authority is not as unique a situation as a prophet delivering a religious message. Carrying a religious call demands of a prophet leadership skills. These are skills which may also make a prophet a capable 'king', in al-Raziq's language. But were a prophet to exercise kingship, as Muhammed undoubtedly did in commanding the *hijra* to Medina, his negotiations with the various communities at Medina and his generalship at the battle of Badr and Uhud,[29] these actions may not be inspired by God. Such 'worldly' matters often fall beyond the purview of prophets. In exercising political authority, a prophet would draw upon his high status within a community, not his unique relationship to God (though the two are undoubtedly related). This, however, is not the only line of reasoning that al-Raziq takes. Rather, he seeks to further define Muhammed as a unique figure in history:

> [T]he authority of the Prophet, peace be upon him, was, because of his Message, a general authority; his orders to Muslims were obeyed; and his government was comprehensive. . . . This sacred power, special to those worshipers of God whom He had raised as messengers, does not hold within it the meaning of kingship, nor does it resemble the power of kings, nor can the [authority of the] sultan of all sultans approximate it.[30]

If one wants to call the community of Muhammed's followers a state, and Muhammed their king, then this is a matter of semantics to al-Raziq. The important point is that the politics practiced by the Prophet was grounded in his religious message, and as such is not a system of politics that can be replicated—nor should one try. The difference between prophets and kings is that the former governs over the heart while the latter over material things. 'The former is a religious leadership, the latter a political one—and there is much distance between politics and religion'.[31] Muhammed Khalaf-Allah defines the roles of prophets as 'explanation and analysis of Qur'anic texts—especially that which deals with beliefs, worship, and [social] interactions'.[32] This is a role that the *ulema*, Muslim religious scholars, have taken on with the passing of the last of the Prophets. That being the case, Khalaf-Allah states it is an error, in the contemporary world, to look to *ulema* for guidance on politics; as the practice of politics was not the primary role of the prophets, so 'religious scholars cannot do what the prophets, peace be upon them, could not do'.[33]

So, the politics practised by Muhammed was unique by virtue of his divine guidance in those matters, which no other can replicate. Also, the Prophet's politics was concerned only with delivering the message, and any governance he conducted 'was only a means that the Prophet, peace be upon him, would seek for the strengthening of his religion, in support of the call'.[34] Al-Raziq does not answer the question as to *why* the Prophet's successors could not pursue politics with a similar aim; what is particular of the call to Islam that is, for al-Raziq, incongruous with politics? Interestingly, this is the same question that is not answered by IR scholars: what is it that makes Islam incompatible with politics? As I will argue in the following chapter, a key reason why the IR of the MENA, sub-Saharan Africa and Southeast Asia is deficient is the Eurocentric assumption that the relationship between religion and politics that played out in Europe happened the same way the world over, or *should* play out in this mould.

However, there are some very real reasons that assuming a coherent and distinctive Islamic politics is not achievable, namely the fractious reality of the religion. As Piscatori observes, '[i]n practical terms, although not in theology, there are as many Islams as there are Muslims';[35] the lack of unity within the faith makes it unfeasible and unnecessary to unite politically. The aforementioned lack of unity is not something I posit as a negative thing, an issue that needs resolving. Rather, I take differences within the faith of Islam to be a divine mercy, as chapter 10, verse 99 of the Qur'an states: 'If your lord had willed it, all the people on the earth would have come to believe, one and all'.[36] As I demonstrated earlier in the chapter, there is *something* distinctive to Islamic politics, specifically the politics of the Prophet Muhammed, but what this is and whether it is applicable after the death of the Prophet Muhammed remains to be seen. Before proposing the content of this Islamic distinction, I will look at the most vehemently argued nature of this distinction, that of *din wa dawla*, the inseparability of religion and politics.

Taking Issue with *Din Wa Dawla*

Eickelman and Piscatori take great pains to highlight the problems regarding *din wa dawla*. For them,

> The presupposition of the union of religion and politics, *din wa-dawla*, is unhelpful for three reasons. . . . First, it exaggerates the uniqueness of Muslim politics. . . . Second, the emphasis on *din wa-dawla* inadvertently perpetuates 'orientalist' assumptions that Muslim politics, unlike other politics, are not guided by rational, interest based calculations. . . . Third, the *din wa-dawla* assumption contributes to the view that Muslim politics is a seamless web, indistinguishable in its parts because of the natural and mutual interpretation of religion and politics.[37]

That the *din wa dawla* assertion is unhelpful cannot be denied. As I have already noted, Muslim politics is not so unique that it fails or failed to interact and integrate with international systems now and through history.

But the other points raised by Eickelman and Piscatori are not so easily substantiated. The Orientalist problem is interesting as this is not a problem that cannot be overcome; 'inadvertent' ignorance is not a problem of the *din wa dawla* position, but of students of political Islam and as such is not a criticism that can be levied towards the position itself. In addition, it was noted earlier there is *something* distinct about Islamic politics, but whether that leads to difference and an Orientalist understanding remains to be seen. Indeed, Eickelman and Piscatori's criticism of the *din wa dawla* position radiates with assumptions about secular rationality, 'that Muslim politics, unlike other politics, are not guided by rational, interest based calculations',[38] suffers itself from a problematic assumption: why can a synthesis of religion and politics not be rational and interest based? The third part of Eickelman and Piscatori's criticism is the most interesting of all. That a combination of religion and politics that is indistinguishable from its separate parts is an issue at all highlights some of the limits of IR. *Din wa dawla* Islamists recognise little, if anything, which separates humanity other than faith. The state, that most fundamental of building blocks in IR, unacceptably divides the unity of believing Muslims and so is problematic to such Islamists. This is presumably one of the types of the inseparability of religion and politics that Eickelman and Piscatori allude to with their final criticism of *din wa dawla* adherents, and is one that previous work has tried to overcome by analysing how Islamism might be conceived in such a way as to 'fit' seamlessly with the discipline of IR, notably in Piscatori's work, *Islam in a World of Nation-States*. Rather than assume that secular rationality is inherently superior to a religious rationality, as Eickelman and Piscatori inadvertently do, I will instead proceed by critiquing the *din wa dawla* position as being theologically unsound, as defined by Islamic precedent itself rather than a comparison to dominant understandings of politics and religion in IR. I will save further discussion on the nature of secular rationality in IR for chapter 4, which will deal explicitly with the analytical framework employed.

If the call to Islam is not totally congruous with politics, it is because unlike more spiritual elements of the religion which are explicitly dealt with in the Qur'an and *sunna* (catalogued sayings and practices of the Prophet Muhammed), politics and other such 'worldly' matters are not. With regards to Qur'anic guidance, the Qur'an comments on the nature of political community; in chapter 49, verse 13, it says that God had 'made you as nations and tribes so that you may come to know each other'.[39] Another far more explicit excerpt states that 'if God had willed, He would have made them one community'.[40] This could be interpreted as either 'He would have made the Muslims one community' or 'He would have made humanity one community'. Either way, the meaning is explicit when applied to political unity. But of course the Qur'an, like historical precedent, can be interpreted to support both those who do and do not conform to the practices of the state. For example, a non-conformist, *din wa dawla* position which would argue that the state system is one that unacceptably divides the Muslim community can cite chapter 3, verse 103, which commands believers to 'hold fast all together the rope which Allah stretches out for you, and be not divided among yourselves'.[41]

Regarding the *sunna* and its relation to Islamic law, during the Prophet's time guidance on politics was not an issue; the Muslim community then could seek divine guidance on such matters. The need to codify law was moot when the Prophet held de facto authority (which de jure was vested in God) on religion. Religious law, *shari'a*, only coalesced approximately 100 years after the death of the Prophet Muhammed.[42] Islamic law, then, is developed through readings of the Qur'an, the *sunna*, *qiyas* (analogy) and *ijma'* (consensus). This is a system that was developed by Imam Shafi'i in the ninth century AD but later was adopted by all Sunni Muslims.

When the period of the *rashidun* passed, there was still 'no fully developed system of doctrine or law',[43] and only then did theological divisions in Islam begin to appear, the emergence of the Kharijite sect during the time of the last *rashid*, Ali, being a notable exception.[44] Piscatori argues that the presence of theological division marks the *practise* of Muslim polities acknowledging territorial pluralism, even if the dogma of some (*din wa dawla*) would reject it. Speaking of theological tradition, van Ess observes that for Muslims, 'orthopraxy is more important than orthodoxy',[45] a point that Piscatori forwards to highlight the validity of *ijma' al-fi'l*, consensus of action, understood here as an approximate term to historical precedent.

That there is the urge for Muslims to unite, either a unity amongst themselves or amongst all of humanity, does not diminish the fact, which Piscatori defends, of 'the actual *non*-universality of the Islamic community, and thus of ideological and political—and perhaps territorial—divisions'.[46] What is apparent with both historical precedent and Qur'anic guidance is how inconclusive such arguments are when relating to the state and IR. Evidence for both sides of the debate can be found, and the weight of evidence only begins to fall on the side of state conformists the further away from the Prophet's time examples are drawn. For this reason, I argue that history does not actually form any precedent as far as *din wa dawla* adherents are concerned; if examples of plurality and *realpolitik* cannot be found in the Prophet's time then for these ideologues the argument is already won. To cite Umayyad, Abbasid, and Ottoman examples of plurality, as, for example, Piscatori does, only strengthens the argument of non-conformists that after the time of the Prophet the Muslim community has gone astray. I would cautiously echo such a sentiment, though not to the extent that *din wa dawla* advocates do; calls for an Islamic polity united by the same call to faith as experienced during the Prophet Muhammed's time are doomed to fail; with no definitive dogma to guide Islamic politics one must ask, to *which* Islam should such a polity adhere?

There certainly exists a core concept of faith to which Muslims who identify as Sunni orthodox, Shi'a, Wahhabi and other creeds can adhere. This core would centre on the basic tenets of the faith, commonly referred to as the 'five pillars' of Islam: Belief in God and his Prophet Muhammed; prayer; fasting; charity; and pilgrimage. With this limited unity in mind Pakistani founder of the *jamaat-e-Islami*, Maulana Maududi, comments that the Sharia is not a method of governance but rather 'has always aimed at bringing together mankind into one moral and spiritual frame-work'.[47] Politics lies beyond the unifying spiritual framework that Maududi mentions, and so rather than asking to which *Islam* an Islamic polity should call, the correct question would be, to which *political* Islam the call should be made?

The Third Perspective: Normative Political Islam

Accepting that political Islam is distinct from Islam, then politics is not an articulation of the faith, as *din wa dawla* ideologues would have it. Rather, the type of political Islam I am invoking is the pursuit of politics that adheres to Islamic norms and values—but these are not static. I refer to this as Normative Political Islam. What Normative Political Islam signals for my argument is a distinction between 'Islam-as-faith' and 'Islam-as-politics'. The former references the link a believer might have to the transcendental, the articles of faith. The latter refers to the practice of politics, which I am arguing to fall outside of the explicit guidance of Islam-as-faith, but might still influence and be influenced by faith, depending on interpretation. This separation between Islam-as-faith and Islam-as-politics is similar to Tibi's distinction between 'Islam as a faith and a cultural system', and 'the politicization of Islam that results in a religionized politics'.[48] However, unlike Tibi, I do not wish to preclude the idea that political Islam can be *more* than secular politics with religious language. To insist on this separation would affirm the problematic belief in a pristine secular political order, a claim I will refute in later chapters by highlighting secularism's religious foundations and continuing relationships between religion and politics in 'secular' IR.

Accepting the differentiation between Islam-as-faith and Islam-as-politics, Normative Political Islam may well be wholly compatible with the international system if interpreted as such. Equally, Normative Political Islam could present an alternative to the international system as it stands, if it is possible to interpret it in that way. The reason such differing interpretations are possible is that depending on how one defines Islamic norms and values, one will derive a different interpretation of political Islam. What is important about Normative Political Islam is the *method* used, which relies on acknowledging human interpretation and fallibility, and the value pluralism that results. The distinction between Islam-as-faith and Islam-as-politics is one that I will return to and elaborate further in chapter 5. For now, I will continue by returning the discussion to IR, and discussing the unit of analysis in the discipline, and its relationship to the unit of analysis in Normative Political Islam's IR, that is, the relationship between the *umma* and the state.

Driven by their ideological world view of how the world *should* be, some political Islamists take issue with the structure of the international system, especially the centrality of the state. For them, Islam sees little that divides persons except faith. In this world view political association to a state which divides the unity of believing Muslims is problematic. Their solution: the *umma*, typical of medieval Islam, whereby one is affiliated to a political construct based on their faith. The *umma*, then, is distinct from an 'Islamic state', which articulates itself in the language of any secular state. Islamic states show no 'Islamic' character on the world stage, having, by and large, accepted the existing juridic and political state system.[49] So political Islam, in regards to the *umma*/state discussion, is 'an attempt to link religion by way of resisting it—political Islam is thus still on the whole a protest movement (with the partial exception of Iran)'.[50] In asking how the *umma* might interact on the international stage I posit that the *umma* as a different form of political affiliation than the Islamic state, and the two should not be confused in this exposition.

Nazih Ayubi describes the European state as having developed through individualism, law and justice while the Islamic equivalent, in contrast, developed on justice, group and leadership.[51] These are small differences to Ayubi, who proceeds to analyse the *umma* as an equivalent to the state. Rather, I argue that the *umma* is an *alternative* to the state. The form of affiliation in the *umma* is based on notions of community (rule over people), which is traditionally what the word *umma* denotes. The modern state, conversely, is based on territorial boundaries as formulated by Weber's definition of the state. Islamic tradition, however, makes little distinction over territory and instead focuses on individuals. Khadduri explains how the *shari'a* bound a community, not territory: '[T]he legal position of a territory would depend on the allegiance of its people to Islam, not a mere proclamation that it belongs to Islam'.[52]

Often used to justify the particularity of the *umma* is verse 143, chapter 2 of the Qur'an, in which God proclaims, 'Thus have we made you an umma justly balanced, that you might be witnesses over the nations, and the Messenger a witness over yourselves'.[53] In this verse the word *umma* is used in contrast to nations or peoples, *nas*, highlighting the difference between the two concepts. In reference to the contemporary world, we can note that the *umma* might be articulated in any number of ways: from non-governmental organisations (NGOs) resembling, perhaps, a global network of mosques, to global media activity, to state controlled articulation by way of 'Islamic states', to finally the re-emergence of a Caliphate.[54] The list offered here is in no way exhaustive, but represents different points on a spectrum wherein 'spiritual' articulations of the *umma* are placed at one extreme and 'political' articulations at the other. Such a spectrum is not ideal; it embraces a rather arbitrary separation of the spiritual from the political, again foreshadowing the discussion of secularism in IR to follow in chapter 4. What the spectrum does allow for is the discussion of the *umma* as a unit of political affiliation, and firmly places this discussion in the remit of IR. As a unit of political affiliation, the *umma* does not have a separate body of law but rather is an extension of law regarding Muslim—non-Muslim interaction, further emphasising the importance of rule over people not territory. Khadduri states that '[s]trictly speaking, there is no Muslim law of nations in the sense of the distinction between modern municipal (national) law and international law based on different sources and maintained by different sanctions'.[55]

In this way, I would designate an *umma* as a community of believers who are bound by the laws of that community irrespective of territorial boundaries. Conversely the state, as derived from the Peace of Westphalia, defines itself on the notion of territorial sovereignty[56] and in this very fundamental way differs from the *umma* which has, in theory, no such notion.

Presuming that the units which constitute Normative Political Islam's concept of the international sphere are *ummas*, not nation-states, then is it necessary for Normative Political Islam to develop a more substantive theory of IR, or find a way to 'fit' within the current discipline? This is a question that I will come back to in the next section of the chapter. For now, it is enough to have established that one of the centres of contention between Normative Political Islam and the current international system is the distinction between state and *umma*. However, this challenge to the international sphere also holds challenges for the dominant epistemology and ontology that IR is based upon.[57] For example, the *umma*, which does not respect territorial boundaries but rather communal affiliation over individual liberty, has to address the dominance of liberal individualism in IR. I will discuss the interplay between secularism and the discipline of IR in the following chapters; for now I will briefly explain the entry point of the discussion of liberalism and political Islam, and return to it in more depth later in the book.

A 'traditional' (Orientalist) view of Islam's incompatibility with liberalism is, unfortunately, still commonplace. This view sees Islam as inherently illiberal, due to some undefined yet all-powerful characteristic within the faith. Gregory Gause describes this uninformed yet prevalent position on the politics of the Middle East as the idea that

> [T]ribalism and Islam lead to a number of consequences for the political process: institutions are meaningless, as all politics are personal; the forms of rule

which exist now in these states have existed for hundreds of years, if not from time immemorial; political participation is not a serious issue; political loyalty is given and withdrawn on the basis of religious criteria.[58]

Bayat puts it more succinctly when he states that 'the anxiety over "religious rule" associated with the Arab revolts is partly to do with a long-standing habit of equating anything "Islamic" with intolerance, misogyny, and authoritarianism'.[59] To such assumptions Richard Bulliet replies that Islam has always been a mode of *resisting* despotic rule, a type of rule which existed in the Middle East long before the trauma of colonialism, though he admits, '[t]he merest glance at the history of the Islamic Middle East reveals that, in fact, Islam did *not* effectively prevent despotism'.[60] Islam was still a site for protest, however, and continues to be in the present day. The problem, as Bulliet sees it, is that Islam has not dealt with the realities of power; as a resistance movement it is defined by what it is not, but has not articulated sufficiently what it stands *for*.[61]

Islamism in command of the powers of the state is the unknown that is feared and assumed to be inherently despotic. For Sami Zubaida this comes as little surprise, for while religion has been stripped of much of its authority and social functions in 'modern' societies, it remains one of the most persistent markers of identity and difference.[62] It is little wonder to Zubaida that Islam is thus perceived as inherently problematic in the Western world, as it is religion, and the religious 'other' must be different to 'us', must be illiberal. The theme of difference in IR and how it is conceptualised and then managed is one that I will return to throughout the book.

CONCLUSIONS

Having highlighted the fact that political Islam has many competing variants, in this chapter I arrived at a working definition of the *type* of political Islam which will be used in this book, which I dubbed Normative Political Islam. This definition implied a separation between Islam as it is understood as a faith (Islam-as-faith) and Islam as it is understood in politics (Islam-as-politics). Such a separation derived from an understanding of the Prophet Muhammed's goal as being the spread of the faith, not the establishment of an Islamic empire. Furthermore, the acknowledgement of the separation between Islam-as-faith and Islam-as-politics does not necessarily deny a unique, transcendental element to the politics of that early Muslim polity. Rather, I accept the limitations of human capacity to replicate the polity overseen by the Prophet. The 'normative' aspect of Normative Political Islam refers to the way in which certain practices are overshadowed by a commitment to Islam-as-faith, though this is only true in the broadest sense, as will be examined in subsequent chapters. In beginning to give substance to

Normative Political Islam, I have shown that Islamic source texts offer limited guidance regarding IR. Importantly, however, the extent to which commitment to the transcendental elements of the faith (Islam-as-faith) influences the practice of politics has yet to be established, something that I will establish in chapter 5. For now, the next chapter will move on to an exploration of the IR literature of key Muslim majority areas of the world.

NOTES

1. Asef Bayat, 'Post-Islamism at Large', in *Post-Islamism: The Changing Faces of Political Islam*, ed. Asef Bayat (Oxford: Oxford University Press, 2013), 4.
2. Ibid., 25.
3. Ibid., 5.
4. Olivier Roy, *The Failure of Political Islam* (London: I.B. Tauris, 1994), 1–27.
5. John Voll, 'Fundamentalism in the Sunni Arab World: Egypt and the Sudan', in *Fundamentalisms Observed*, ed. Martin Marty and Scott Appleby. The Fundamentalism Project 1 (London: University of Chicago Press, 1991), 347.
6. Henry Munson, *Islam and Revolution in the Middle East* (New Haven: Yale University Press, 1988), 4.
7. Sami Zubaida, *Islam, the People & the State*, 2nd ed. (London: I.B. Tauris, 1989), 38.
8. Mansoor Moaddel and Kamran Talattof, 'Contemporary Debates in Islam', in *Modernist and Fundamentalist Debates in Islam*, ed. Mansoor Moaddel and Kamran Talattof (Basingstoke: Palgrave Macmillan, 2002), 1.
9. Ibid., 2.
10. For a (rather narrow) genealogy of violent Islamist groups and ideas, see Gilles Kepel, *Jihad: The Trail of Political Islam* (Harvard: Harvard University Press, 2002).
11. Moaddel and Talattof, 'Contemporary Debates in Islam', 2.
12. When referring to Sunni Muslims I am referring to the four schools (*madhahib*) of Sunni orthodoxy, the Hanifi, Maliki, Shafi'i and Hanbali schools, named after Abu Hanifa, Malik, al-Shafi'i, and Ibn Hanbal respectively. The first of these *madhahib*, that of Abu Hanifa, was formed in the eighth century AD and the last, that of Ibn Hanbal, near the end of the ninth century. For more, see Fazlur Rahman, *Islam* (Chicago: University of Chicago Press, 1979), 81–83.
13. Richard C. Martin and Abbas Barzegar, 'Introduction: The Debate About Islamism in the Public Sphere', in *Islamism: Contested Perspectives on Political Islam*, ed. Richard C. Martin and Abbas Barzegar (Stanford: Stanford University Press, 2010), 2.
14. Dietrich Jung, *Orientalists, Islamists and the Global Public Sphere: A Genealogy of the Modern Essentialist Image of Islam* (Sheffield: Equinox, 2011), 5.
15. Josef van Ess, *The Flowering of Muslim Theology* (London: Harvard University Press, 2006), 13.
16. *The Holy Qur'an* (Dublin, OH: Ahmadiyya Anjuman Ishaat Islam), 2:256.
17. van Ess, *Flowering of Muslim Theology*, 39–44.
18. Qamaruddin Khan, *Political Concepts in the Qur'an* (Lahore: Islamic Book Foundation, 1982), 74.
19. The first four successors to the Prophet Muhammed, according to Sunni Muslims.
20. Dale Eickelman and James Piscatori, *Muslim Politics* (Princeton: Princeton University Press, 1996), 47.
21. Ira Lapidus, 'The Separation of State and Religion in the Development of Early Islamic Society', *International Journal of Middle East Studies* 6, no. 4 (1975): 383.
22. Nazih Ayubi, *Over-stating the Arab State: Politics and Society in the Middle East* (London: I.B. Tauris, 1996), 28–29.
23. Khaled Abou El Fadl, 'Islam and the Theology of Power', *Middle East Report* no. 221 (2001): 33.

24. Bryan Turner, *Orientalism, Postmodernism and Globalism* (London: Routledge, 1994), 8.
25. Ibid., 12.
26. Rahman, *Islam*, 43.
27. 'Ali-'Abd Al-Raziq, 'Message Not Government, Religion Not State' in *Liberal Islam: A Sourcebook*, ed. Charles Kurzman (Oxford: Oxford University Press, 1998), 29–36.
28. Ibid., 30.
29. Albert Hourani, *A History of the Arab Peoples* (London: Faber and Faber, 1991), 17–18.
30. Al-Raziq, 'Message Not Government, Religion Not State', 31.
31. Ibid.
32. Muhammed Khalaf-Allah, 'Legislative Authority', in *Liberal Islam: A Sourcebook*, ed. Charles Kurzman (Oxford: Oxford University Press, 1998), 39.
33. Ibid.
34. Al-Raziq, 'Message Not Government, Religion Not State', 35.
35. James Piscatori, *Islam in a World of Nation-States* (Cambridge: Cambridge University Press, 1986), 10.
36. *Holy Qur'an*, 10:99.
37. Eickelman and Piscatori, *Muslim Politics*, 56.
38. Ibid., 56.
39. *Holy Qur'an*, 49:13.
40. Ibid., 48:48.
41. Ibid., 3:103.
42. Rahman, *Islam*, 43.
43. Hourani, *History of the Arab Peoples*, 24.
44. Bernard Lewis, *The Arabs in History*, 6th ed. (Oxford: Oxford University Press, 1993), 63.
45. van Ess, *Flowering of Muslim Theology*, 16.
46. Piscatori, *Islam in a World of Nation-States*, 46. Original emphasis.
47. Abu A'la Maududi, 'Nationalism and Islam', in *Islam in Transition: Muslim Perspectives*, ed. John Donohue and John Esposito (Oxford: Oxford University Press, 1982), 95.
48. Bassam Tibi, *Islam in Global Politics: Conflict and Cross-civilizational Bridging* (Abingdon: Routledge, 2012), 161–62.
49. Nazih Ayubi, *Political Islam: Religion and Politics in the Arab World* (London: Routledge, 1991), 122–23.
50. Ibid., 123.
51. Ibid., 1–10.
52. Majid Khadduri, *War and Peace in the Law of Islam* (Baltimore: Johns Hopkins Press, 1955), 155.
53. *Holy Qur'an*, 2:143.
54. Peter Mandaville, *Global Political Islam* (London: Routledge, 2007), 300–301.
55. Khadduri, *War and Peace in the Law of Islam*, 46.
56. Turan Kayaoglu, 'Westphalian Eurocentrism in International Relations Theory', *International Studies Review* 12, no. 2 (2010): 193.
57. Broadly understood, this challenge is referred to as the 'postsecular turn' in IR. The term has two meanings, both of which are relevant to this book. The first meaning is the attempt to explain the apparent resurgence of religion in modern life. The second is the idea that secularism, rather than being inclusive and value neutral, is in fact excluding and dependent on a particular socio-historical background. Such work, especially on the second definition, often does not carry the label 'postsecular'; indeed, I do not use the term postsecular as it commonly pertains to the work of Jurgen Habermas, which is incompatible with the Foucaultian poststructuralism I employ in the book. For more on the term postsecular, see Luca Mavelli and Fabio Petito, 'The postsecular in International Relations: An Overview', *Review of International Studies* 38, no. 5 (2012); Craig Calhoun, Mark Juergensmeyer, and Jonathan VanAntwerpen, eds., *Rethinking Secularism* (Oxford: Oxford University Press, 2011); Talal Asad, *Formations of the Secular: Christianity, Islam, Modernity* (Stanford: Stanford University Press, 2003); Jurgen Habermas and Joseph Ratzinger, *The Dialectics of Secularization: On Reason and*

Religion (San Francisco: Ignatius, 2007); Jurgen Habermas, *Between Naturalism and Religion: Philosophical Essays* (Cambridge: Polity, 2008).

58. Gregory Gause, *Oil Monarchies: Domestic and Security Challenges in the Arab Gulf States* (New York: Council on Foreign Relations, 1994), 3.

59. Bayat, 'Post-Islamism at Large', 4.

60. Richard Bulliet, 'Twenty Years of Islamic Politics', *Middle East Journal* 53, no. 2 (1999): 192. Original emphasis.

61. Ibid., 196.

62. Sami Zubaida, *Beyond Islam: A New Understanding of the Middle East* (London: I.B. Tauris, 2011), 3.

Chapter Three

International Relations, Islam, and the Secular Bias

Islam in international politics, following the attacks of September 11, 2001, is under constant review, both 'within' and 'without' Islam. What is considered 'within' is as contentious as the discussion gets, with every second Muslim group denouncing the other as un-Islamic or *kuffar* (apostates), not representative of the whole. Internal to the Muslim world, Tariq Ramadan speaks of a 'silent revolution in Muslim communities in the West', a revolution wherein these European and US Muslims slowly construct a 'Muslim personality' that speaks to both their religious beliefs and their cultural upbringing in countries like the United Kingdom, France and Germany.[1] While Ramadan speaks explicitly of Muslims living in Europe and the United States, the point applies across the Muslim world, especially regarding international politics. In the post-colonial period, a multitude of peoples continues to resolve the tensions, for better or worse, that have emerged as the state system has expanded across the globe. With relation to Muslim majority states, the least of these tensions is secularism.

Returning to post-9/11 Islam being constantly reviewed from without, Mahmood Mamdani identifies this discussion in international politics as a quest to identify 'good Muslims' from 'bad Muslims'. He states that '[w]hether in Afghanistan, Palestine, or Pakistan, Islam must be quarantined and the devil must be exorcized from it by a civil war between good Muslims and bad Muslims'.[2] In IR literature the notion of politics motivated by Islam is associated with violence, regressive communal politics and terrorism. Writing in 1986, in the midst of the Cold War and in the aftermath of the Iranian revolution, it is worth citing at length Piscatori's rationale for writing *Islam in a World of Nation-States*:

> There is no doubt that many people talk of Islam as posing a radical challenge to Western interests. This seems to be the case to them because they believe that Muslims have acquired a new political self-consciousness and activism. According to this view, this new activism will induce Muslims either to turn to the Soviet bloc in order to offset what they regard as Western economic and cultural neo-imperialism, or at the least to discriminate against Westerners in order to reaffirm an ancient hostility to Christians generally. Many people also draw the conclusion—from the media coverage of the harsh penalties of Islamic law and of the veiling of women—that Islam stands for a medieval legal and social order. This view in turn helps to suggest that, when it comes to international relations, Muslims are simply not at home in the modern state and in the modern politically and culturally diversified system of states, and therefore would like to see a revival of the early transnational community of believers as the primary political unit.[3]

Discounting the reference to the Soviet bloc, Piscatori's summary from 1986 is just as apt today as it was then: attacks by various Muslim terrorist groups all invoking Islam in different ways (from 9/11, to Bali, to Mumbai); regime change in Iraq, Afghanistan and Libya, sanctioned by the UN or otherwise; military intervention in Syria; continuing occupation of Palestinian territories and the election of Hamas in Gaza in 2008; the Arab Uprisings in 2011 which brought two Islamist governments to power through democratic elections—one in Tunisia becoming the first such government to hand over power peacefully at the end of its term, while the second in Egypt was deposed in a coup after a little over a year in power. All of the above serve to create a 'common sense' understanding of Islam as synonymous with insecurity, if not outright violence. In IR, with its secular bias (which I will elaborate on in the next chapter), Islam is either 'a formidable stumbling block to the rationalization and democratization of societies', or 'a potential threat to the cultural, moral, and religious foundations of Western civilization that must be successfully defused'.[4]

In many ways I locate myself as one of Ramadan's Muslims in flux, negotiating an identity that is coherent to both an Islamic and British upbringing. Moreover, as a student of IR it is striking to me that there is a corpus of non-European thinking on state-society relations and the governance of the international sphere that is not even slightly examined by the discipline: the historical examples of the Muslim world. The Muslim world is not unique here; other non-European regions of the world which possessed their own 'histories', before being written into the story of European colonialism, also highlight different ways of thinking and doing international politics. Nevertheless, it is the silhouette of a generic Islamic experience which I will hold up to the Eurocentrism of a generic IR theory, to establish the contours of synthesis and difference between 'IR' and 'Islam'.

I will problematise existing IR scholarship of three Muslim majority areas of the world: the Middle East and North Africa, sub-Saharan Africa, and Southeast Asia. While previously the object of our analysis has been political Islam itself, in this chapter it is the IR studies, and the theories they use, which are the object of analysis, while political Islam is the way in which I am critiquing those theories. Rather than ask how Islam might surface to find compatibility with a world view defined by the European Enlightenment, I will enter these two positions (Islam and IR) into a dialogue. The dialogue between Islam and IR will allow us to discover how the contemporary international system is deficient in reference to an Islamic world view, and importantly, it will highlight the points of contention which will form the basis of later chapters. I will conclude that the two predominant reasons for the deficiency of much current scholarship are:

1. The territoriality of the international system, briefly outlined here as an incongruence between 'state' and '*umma*' (community).
2. The incoherence in expecting liberal individualism to cater to the aspirations of the *umma*.

The two reasons outlined above fall into two distinct but interrelated areas of analysis—the international (state versus *umma*) and the theoretical (liberal individualism versus communitarianism)—which form the basis of the following chapters. As I will show, much of the literature discussed navigates the material-discursive divide in ways that oscillate between a material-heavy approach that interprets political Islam as a result of economic inequalities or means to power, or a discursive-heavy approach that interprets Islam as a 'mood', emotive and fickle. I do not claim that such interpretations are incorrect. For example, the rise of Siyyad Barre's military rule of Somalia from 1969 indeed used Islam as a means to power, delegitimising other subnational, clan-based challenges to his rule.[5] Rather, in navigating the material-discursive divide through this book, I hope to create another space wherein political Islam is not wholly instrumental or wholly ideational; rather, it might be constructively and genuinely animating the actions of agents. I will return presently to the claim that IR in fact struggles to incorporate religion into its analysis.

IR AND POLITICAL ISLAM IN THE MENA, SUB-SAHARAN AFRICA AND SOUTHEAST ASIA

The discipline of IR has traditionally treated religion as an adjunct to analysis. Religion played a role in the politics of different eras, but in the modern world the international sphere is ruled by different sensibilities. Painting IR theories in broad brushstrokes—and recognising that the theories I am talking about are not as coherent as made out—the lack of space afforded to religion in the study of the MENA, for example, is seen in the politics of realism, liberalism, Marxism and constructivism. For realism, material gain and a more abstract 'power' are the key influences on behaviour, over and above the power of norms or ideas, religiously founded or otherwise. In liberal thought vast structures of economic interconnectivity steady the hand of world leaders; if counter-ideologies (depicted religiously through Islam) exist, these are only contested within the ideational boundaries defined by liberalism. Classical Marxist analysis also places much weight on the material influences of behaviour; where ideology is accounted for, it is done so to reinforce its material analysis through 'false consciousness'. Constructivism begins to move away from such ideologically (and therefore religiously) dismissive analyses, looking to show how identity and discourse, religious or otherwise, play a powerful role in the international system. Such insights into identity help make foreign policy analysis (FPA) a strong explanatory force in the wider Middle East as it blurs the lines between domestic and international, showing how the internal dynamics of states affect their international relations. However, even in identity-based IR analysis, religion is placed on the back burner; it is deemed an ideology that does not play out at a regional or international level but at a domestic level only.[6]

The critique of IR theories which I will engage with here and throughout the book is dubbed meta-theory, which is distinct to IR theorising on the dynamics of the international system. As Alexander Wendt explains:

> The objective of this type of theorizing [meta-theoretical] is also to increase our understanding of world politics, but it does so indirectly by focusing on the ontological and epistemological issues of what constitute important or legitimate questions and answers for IR scholarship, rather than on the structure and dynamics of the international system *per se*.[7]

As such, I acknowledge that the ramifications for IR studies in not accounting for religion may not affect their analyses of the international system in any substantive way (though this depends on the nature of their enquiry, as will be demonstrated). The stronger assertion I lay claim to is that the way in which certain questions are formed about the nature and influence of religion in international politics is not even considered by the discipline. Therefore, structuralism may attempt to explain political Islam as a phenomenon deriving from unequal distribution of wealth and a response to low socio-economic status in a given situation. While plausible, such an explanation might be unable to account for the wealthy, educated Islamists who have come to characterise contemporary movements.[8] What can we infer from this brief example? First, while this hypothetical structuralist explanation will be unable to account for the rise of Islamism among the educated and wealthy, it does not mean that the rise of Islamism does not correlate with unequal distribution of wealth or low socio-economic status, so the conclusions may still be valid. However, the second inference from this example is that in relegating the articulation of religion in politics or politics in religion (Islamism) to a secondary consideration, the resulting picture of political Islam may be inaccurate and contributes to continuing confusion about the role of political Islam as a static set of ideas which influence actors on one end, and to a politicisation and thereby aberration of 'purely religious' Islam on the other extreme. While this confusion is evident in much political analysis, it is more pronounced in IR, as will now be explored.

Piscatori's *Islam in a World of Nation-States* is one of the few studies of Islam and its interface with the discipline of IR.[9] Piscatori's work is a study of Islam's place in the modern system of states, not an explanation of events (like the Iranian revolution). Piscatori's work then is narrative and historically based, rather than paradigm-based. This narrative/historical focus highlights a fault line between IR and study of the Middle East, what Louise Fawcett calls an 'International Relations–Area Studies divide';[10] as Piscatori's study is specific to the particular historical narrative of Islam, its use in IR scholarship is not to produce (indeed it does not attempt) a paradigm that is applicable outside of its specific narrative, that is, the Islamic Middle East. Rather, much like this book, Piscatori's work broadens the field of enquiry for IR scholars, using the example of Islam and Muslim history to reflect on how we conceive of IR and Islam.

Peter Mandaville's work is also noteworthy in its attempt to bring political Islam into the realm of IR. Mandaville's is more of a paradigm work than Piscatori's; however, the subject matter, global religious affiliation, moves Mandaville away from the centre of the IR discipline. Much like Piscatori, Mandaville must work hard at showing how political Islam can be relevant for study in the international sphere; in doing so, Mandaville in 2001 posited religion, as is often done, as a challenge to the dominant (secular) political experience. Specifically, he posits the *umma* as a challenge to the statist politics of the international system,[11] much as I did in the previous chapter. However, six years later his opinion relaxed and the idea that the *umma* was a spent concept permeated his work; religion was no longer a challenge to the status quo, but had learned and must continue to learn to operate 'within the system'.[12]

Building on Mandaville's reading of political Islam as having some role on the international stage, as challenger or otherwise, I will argue that the relegation of religion to the peripheries of IR is problematic for IR studies of the Islamic world, and is indicative of a wider problem in the discipline of IR regarding the place of norms, ideas and religion, which I will demonstrate by looking at IR studies of the MENA, sub-Saharan Africa, and Southeast Asia.

International Relations, Religion and the MENA

There are only a handful of IR treatments of the MENA, all of which broadly fall under five methodological categories: Marxist, realist, English School, constructivist and FPA, with cross-cutting approaches between these categories. The authors I have chosen here are not singled out for being particularly inaccurate or problematic; rather, they are paradigmatic of their particular theoretical approach and so make excellent examples. All of the studies considered are emblematic of dialogue between IR and area studies, and show the benefit of such an engagement, which has come to be called Global IR, as was discussed in chapter 1. Despite the value of these studies, I will argue that their treatment of religion is lacking for one of two main reasons. First, and easiest to address, is an Orientalist misunderstanding of Islam and its relationship to society which often leads to the idea that Islam is equivalent to despotism. Secondly, and demanding a more reflexive understanding of IR, is the problem of overly materialistic or statist accounts of Middle East politics. The studies of this latter category reinforce a post-colonial legacy of Westphalian politics, as outlined by Kayaoglu in his article 'Westphalian Eurocentrism in International Relations Theory'.[13] These are two criticisms that will recur numerous times as the chapter moves through the broad methodological and epistemological boundaries of IR scholarship of the Middle East.

Marxist-Inspired Study of the Middle East and North Africa

Marxist-inspired studies of the MENA show themselves to be problematic for two reasons:

1. The first study considered 'writes religion out' of the historical narrative of political change in the region, by claiming that Islam is too heterogeneous to influence other social and historical processes.
2. The second study highlights a materialist focus on what is 'real', and classifies religion as a sub-category to ideas and perceptions, questioning their capacity to influence the 'real' world.

Of the two studies mentioned above, broadly categorised as Marxist in epistemology if not methodology, Simon Bromley's *Rethinking Middle East Politics* will be considered first. Bromley is very aware and critical of theory that derives from analyses of Europe a set of categories, and then applies these categories to the rest of the world. In this way, he holds up Karl Marx's methodology as a means to avoid this problem: 'It [Marx's methodology] does not begin by privileging Western societies and then move on to explain non-Western development as a deviation. Rather, it applies a common methodology of explanation to all social orders'.[14] Bromley wholeheartedly endorses Edward Said's critique of Orientalism, but rather than try to take a more nuanced and specific definition of terms like Islam, he would emphasise the less abstract and historically precise 'social relations and material practices that constitute and transform societies'.[15] In essence, Bromley seeks to avoid the 'problem' of cultural explanations by tying them to material ones and making them one and the same; as a result, 'Islam remains rooted in broader sets of social and material practices, and thus its changing forms must also be related to the historically given organization of economy and polity'.[16] Such an account of religion over-emphasises material concerns[17] and denies the way in which ideas can affect the behaviour of agents in ways that might be in contrast to their material interests.

Furthermore, as Bromley takes on board Said's critique of Orientalism and emphasises the internal divisions of Islam, this becomes another reason for Islam to be neglected as a focus for analysis. Curiously, a lack of unifying nature means Islam cannot act as 'a cultural form operating to block other social and historical determinations',[18] the assumption being that if it were a unified concept, it might have more of an interaction with material interests. This is problematic for two reasons. First, I argue that while there is a plethora of Islamic sects or schools of thought, even between the largest schism, that of the Sunni and Shi'a divide, there is a certain continuity of the basic articles of faith (the *shahada*, declaration of faith). This continuity is largely abstract and theoretical, but important when we consider global forms of political Islam and Islamic solidarity.[19] Bromley is therefore incorrect in asserting that there is *no* unity in the faith, and is unspecific as to the *degree* of unity needed, and in what areas, before Islam can take a more constitutive place in his approach. Secondly, that Islam has geographical and theological differences does not mean that religion centred around different seats of learning, for example, could not have a more substantial effect on the material or social reality of people in the MENA. I can concur that 'Islam' may not be precise enough a term to chart such influence, but maybe the 'Islam of Baghdad' had considerable influence on the peoples and policies emanating from this historic seat of power. Likewise, the 'Islam of Damascus', 'Islam of Andalusia', 'Islam of Fatimid Egypt' and so on and so forth, surely had a more specific role on a specifically defined geographical area than Bromley gives credit for.

The second Marxist-inspired approach, broadly defined, is that of Fred Halliday's book *The Middle East in International Relations*. Like Bromley, Halliday emphasises the material interests of actors. However, Halliday takes a more nuanced position than Bromley with regards to Islam. Islam is rarely directly referenced; it falls under ideology and culture, as defined by Halliday. However, he goes to great pains to emphasise that timeless terms like Islam or an 'Arab mind' are not accurate descriptions of such culture or ideology; '[i]t is rather a matter of how, under modern political and social conditions, states, elites, whole political systems come to operate in broadly similar ways, in other words, how they are moulded by modernity and regional context alike'.[20] Here Halliday identifies the erroneous ways in which Islam has been invoked in other scholarship, and in his effort to avoid similar mistakes, like Bromley, he incorporates Islam into other material and social factors, effectively subsuming Islam into categories of analysis far more comfortable for his historical sociological approach, rather than deal with Islam on its own basis, that is, an ideology (but not a coherent or unitary one) that helps constitute the realities of its believers. Halliday argues: '[i]t is often mistaken to assume that a *difference of position within the international system* is necessarily equated with *difference of cultural perspective*'.[21] However, a difference of position in the international system is also not necessarily equated to a difference in material conditions—a balance needs to be struck between the material and the discursive.

Halliday leans towards material analysis; the impact of ideas and beliefs are, for him, related to understanding in terms of 'perception', and distinct from objective, 'real' criteria. While a balance must be struck between the two, as invariably the perceptions of actors affects their reality, Halliday is too cautious about approaches that emphasise ideology, namely constructivism; he explains: 'Constructivism and its outriders run the risk of ignoring state interests and material factors, let alone old-fashioned deception and self-delusion'.[22] With this criticism in mind, I will now move to two broadly constructivist analyses of international relations in the Middle East.

Constructivist-Inspired Study of the Middle East and North Africa

Constructivist-inspired studies of the MENA move away from the materially centred understanding of religion offered by Marxist-inspired approaches, but I will show how they run into their own troubles regarding the following:

1. The constructivist tendency to overlook structural explanations for international politics can create a blind spot regarding political Islam's challenge to the structure of the international system.
2. When constructivist studies incorporate structures and material interests in more of a synthesis, their reading of Islam is equivalent to culture, which I will argue can be problematic when making sense of political Islam.
3. When Islam is disaggregated from culture in constructivist studies, the pervasiveness of the state as the unit of analysis in IR rears its head, undermining some of the critique that political Islam offers to IR.

Each of points two and three attempt to address the preceding difficulties, and I will argue that constructivist-type analysis certainly provides an appropriate toolkit with which to analyse Islam in IR, a toolkit which will be elaborated on in the next chapter.

Two main constructivist studies of the MENA stand out: Barnett's *Dialogues in Arab Politics* and Shibley Telhami and Michael Barnett's edited volume *Identity and Foreign Policy in the Middle East*. A third work by Roger Owen, *State, Power and Politics in the Making of the Modern Middle East*, displays a synthesis of Marxist and constructivist assumptions. Barnett's solo work has more exposition on the constructivist method than that found in the other two works, so I will begin with *Dialogues in Arab Politics*. Barnett explains that

> Building on various strands of sociological theory, constructivism posits that the actions of states, like individuals, take on meaning and shape within a normative context, that their interactions construct and transform their normative arrangements, that these norms can in turn shape their identity and interests, and that the 'problem of order' is usually solved through social negotiations and a mixture of coercion and consent.[23]

A constructivist approach places much more emphasis on process than structure in explaining behaviour. The move away from structure distances constructivism from more Marxist-inspired theory, which classically focuses on a global structure which allows the continuity of a 'universal History'.[24]

The lack of focus on structure leads Barnett to completely relegate Islam out of his analysis of interstate behaviour in the Middle East. Indeed, the term 'Islam' appears only three times in the index of his book. Unlike the works of Halliday and Bromley, who subsume Islam into structural factors in their analyses, Barnett explicitly ignores political Islam; for him its primary challenge is to the domestic level, rather than the regional or international level.[25] I link this reading of political Islam to the lack of structural focus in constructivism; in arguing that political Islam is preoccupied with the domestic, as this is the sphere which it is able to influence, Barnett misses that it is in fact the *structure* of the international system and of IR scholarship that is working, through inertia, to ensure that political Islam cannot challenge the international sphere. Political Islam does compete in the international sphere through the concept of the *umma* (versus state), as argued in the previous chapter. However, the challenge is hard to articulate without reference to the structure of the international system and scholarship, namely the Westphalian narrative, which Barnett cannot attempt due to the inability, or unwillingness, to account for structure in his constructivist approach. This is redressed in Barnett's next work, in collaboration with Shibley Telhami.

In Telhami and Barnett's edited volume, *Identity and Foreign Policy in the Middle East*, the focus is still on constructivist methods, but more nuance is applied to the apparent rejection of systemic analysis. Telhami and Barnett state that the prevalence of identity politics in the Middle East region helped to make the region seem unique to scholars. Systemic IR theory removes the 'uniqueness' of the region, allowing IR to ostensibly explain it, and this is the reason Telhami and Barnett attribute to its popularity. What separates Telhami and Barnett from the dangers of cultural- and narrative-based explanations of the Middle East is the constitutive nature of culture that they constantly emphasise.[26] Rather than a monolithic Islam or a peculiar and standardised 'Arab mind', the authors emphasise the fact that terms such as Islam or Arabism do not have a causal standing in the behaviour of Arab states, but 'conditions the possible and the actual'.[27]

While constructivist theory affords much more space and power to the world of ideas, Telhami and Barnett struggle to separate and define clearly the difference between religion, culture and identity. In actuality very little attempt is made to understand religion except as related to culture, and then primarily only as a reaction to the forces of globalisation.[28] The lack of constructivist theorising on religion highlights where future research might go, and certainly an application of constructivist theory to political Islam will be central to my argument. However, space must be made for a political Islam (in the form of the *umma*) on the international level, which can only be done after recognising and deconstructing the structures in place that reinforce the narrative of states in IR. Acknowledgment of systems in this way can be dubbed as 'soft' constructivism. Such theory does not ignore the state or material interests, as Halliday feared, but rather 'the environment in which agents/states take action is social as well as material'.[29] Such a view acknowledges the material focus of systemic theory, but seeks to *supplement* it rather than displace it—a position I will try to emphasise throughout this book.

Roger Owen's *State, Power and Politics in the Making of the Modern Middle East* endeavours to analyse state-society relationships in the MENA, and this emphasis on the dynamics of state-society interaction is why I have located it loosely between a constructivist and Marxist tradition. While Middle Eastern states appear to function like European states, Owen argues that in most cases Middle Eastern states have quite different relationships with their citizens, which then affects their behaviour.[30] The constructivist influence is apparent with Owen's emphasis on identity. Like Telhami and Barnett, Owen ties up religion with identity, but distinguishes it from culture. Rather, religion has a prominent place in the building of the state; it is 'inextricably involved with central questions of identity and of communal values'.[31] He applies some depth to his understanding of religion, identifying that it is not religious experience, theology, or law that is relevant, only those aspects of the religion that provide 'motives and programmes for political action'.[32] This depth in the understanding of religion is important as I move forward; I will argue that the distinction between Islam-as-faith and political Islam is a distinction which holds the key to the applicability of a transnational Islamic *umma* to IR, while a transnational faith or theology remains impossible.

Returning to Owen, he additionally identifies the problem political Islam has in defining itself in oppositional terms; in doing so he reinforces Bulliet's notion that Islam *in power* is an unknown entity, with some notable exceptions like the *wilayat al-faqih* of Iran, Hamas in Gaza, the Taliban in Afghanistan, Omar al-Bashir and Hassan al-Turabi's implementation of *shari'a* in the north of Sudan, and most recently the Muslim Brotherhood in Egypt and *En-Nahda* government in Tunisia. As Owen states,

> [T]here is a general air of uncertainty about what a Muslim, or Jewish, polity would look like. And this in turn helps to explain some of the widespread opposition to religious movements which might conceivably seize state power without anyone being able to know in advance how exactly they would put it to use.[33]

Owen's approach is a positive step forward, acknowledging structural factors more than constructivist theory, yet taking heed of the power of ideas to shape reality more than classical Marxist-oriented theory. However, Owen still operates within a bounded reality whereby the state as a unit of analysis on the international stage is uncontested. He comments that for Islamists, 'the gap between religion and politics, religion and the state, impiously opened up by Western interference, had to be closed without delay'.[34] Here is the implicit assumption that the wish to close the gap between religion and politics *is* the quest to close the gap between religion and state. The question of the state's significance to religion, to Islam, is not even present. This is an understandable, if fundamental problem of IR scholarship which I will return to after completing my survey of the IR of the MENA.

Theoretical Pluralism: Foreign Policy Analysis and Realist-Inspired Study of the Middle East and North Africa

The remaining IR works applied to the MENA adopt (greater) theoretical pluralism, incorporating much of what I have already mentioned, alongside more FPA and realist theory. I will show that an FPA-style approach is very capable of rendering religion legible in IR; these approaches distinguish and link between domestic and international spheres, allowing for nuance in understanding the different claims that political Islam makes on IR. Conversely, I argue that the English School struggles to account for political Islam as a source of challenge to the international system as the global acceptance of states as units of political organisation is problematically accompanied by a normative acceptance about the desirability of the state. In such an understanding, some aspects of political Islam are necessarily seen as 'deviant', especially those that emphasise global religious solidarity over nationalisms. Finally, the more realist-inspired studies of the MENA return us to a materialist understanding of religion as a tool of the state, an instrumental thing to be used by the state for certain ends. While this certainly can be seen in many MENA states, which use Islam as a means to stave off popular discontent, or to compete with other states for prestige and influence, such an instrumental explanation does not capture the challenge and critique that political Islam can bring to IR. The theoretical pluralism and nuance shown by all these paradigms do begin to show a reflexive understanding about the place of knowledge production as problematically focused on the global North or the 'West', which are themes I will build on later in the chapter.

The first study is that of Gerd Nonneman's edited volume titled *Analyzing Middle East Foreign Policies and the Relationships with Europe*. Nonneman describes his approach as theoretically eclectic, though his emphasis remains on FPA which 'must be multi-level and multi-causal, as well as contextual'.[35] Nonneman's use of three levels of analysis, domestic, regional and international, allows him to incorporate the structural or systemic theories of Marxist-inspired theory at the international level, while giving credence to the constitutive power of ideologies and religion at the domestic and regional levels.[36] Islam is rendered as a transnational ideological issue, and thus only becomes a foreign policy determinant on the regional level. Its power has reduced as state identities have consolidated, but Nonneman argues that '[n]ever the less, [Islam] may become more problematic in times of crisis, not least because of popular pressure'.[37] Most interestingly, Nonneman begins to suggest a possible bias in IR and FPA scholarship regarding North-South politics. This bias sets the agenda for study as 'Euro-MENA' relations, for example, while the other perspective of 'MENA-Euro' relations remains neglected. The opportunity teased at here, which I will examine further in this book, is identifying the reason *why* political Islam does not play out at the international level of analysis. I will argue that the answer is a by-product of the North-South relationship which Nonneman is referring to, in this instance played out through a Westphalian narrative that perpetuates the state as the only form of social organisation on the international level.

Louise Fawcett's edited volume, *International Relations of the Middle East*, echoes the critique of Western-centric scholarship of the MENA made by Nonneman. Fawcett remarks, optimistically, that 'International Relations scholarship has increasingly freed itself from its Western origins: it has slowly become "globalised", with more and more critical voices getting heard'.[38] Unfortunately, this work unwittingly implies that a state-centric approach *is* a globalised IR approach. Undoubtedly the state in IR continues to find pride of place in many analyses, but as we will see in the English School treatment of IR, the prevalence of the state as the only form of political organisation in the international system does not imply the state is 'universal' principle, or that it is packaged with a 'universal' set of norms. Rather, the state is universally practiced, but behind it is a large body of conflicting norms about the value and purpose of the state, which cannot be taken for granted. Returning to Fawcett then, while she states that '[d]espite its contested, and at times fluid properties, the state system in the Middle East has proved remarkable for its survival and durability',[39] she is, like Owen earlier, very much sensitive to the demands of Global IR, but maintains an emphasis on the state. The emphasis on state is not, perhaps, a problem for many types of analyses, but related to questions of political Islam, as I have argued thus far, it very well might be.

Barry Buzan and Ana Gonzalez-Pelaez's edited book *International Society and the Middle East* also adopts a problematic take on the perceived 'neutrality' of the international system (of states), when applied to the Middle East. This work is an application of the English School of International Relations to a regional subsystem, in the tradition of Buzan's revival of the English School in recent years. Unlike Fawcett, however, the neutrality of the state system in Buzan and Gonzalez-Pelaez's work is not an unspoken assumption but is actively argued in Halliday's contribution, in the first chapter of *International Society and the Middle East*, which I will address below.

Initially it would seem that much of the nuance of Halliday's *The Middle East in International Relations* carries over to his contribution to this English School treatment of the Middle East. For example, he talks about the double challenge in applying any paradigm to a specific region, whereby the theory must attempt to explain 'a particular history, state or region', but also see 'how far this specific case . . . itself challenges the theory'.[40] Halliday's statement here, in a way, encapsulates the broad thrust of this book: an examination of the way political Islam challenges the IR theories used to explain it, and an exploration of what engaging these two traditions into a dialogue can yield. However, while Halliday acknowledges the way in which pan-Islam might challenge territorially based analyses, he does not seek to explore how that challenge plays out with the English School. Rather, he pushes pan-Islam into a conceptual box that 'fits' within the state-based analysis of the English School.[41] Too much, Halliday claims, is made of religious and cultural difference; '[i]n no supposedly different cultural or religious context are such universal principles as the right of nations to self-determination or the sovereignty of states formally or even implicitly rejected'.[42] It appears that Halliday himself struggles to believe this statement, as later he writes,

> The European 'state system' did indeed spread across the world, but in large measure by defeating, subjugating, forming and deforming the societies and polities with which it came into contact. The difficulties the modern world has

with the non-European world are, therefore, not the result of an incomplete spread of Westphalian values, or the resistance of undemocratic, or Islamic, or Asiatic societies and polities to democratic values, but to the very character, and violence, of that spread itself.[43]

The two positions shown here, between on the one hand an assertion that the spread of the state system rests on universally accepted principles of sovereignty and self-determination, and on the other hand an acknowledgement that the spread of these 'universal' principles involved in places considerable violence, are ones that I argue this English School treatment of the Middle East struggles to reconcile. Halliday attempts to circumvent this tension by emphasising the difference between the state system that spread from Europe (which for him is universally acceptable), and the nature of that spread, referring to, presumably, the violence associated with colonisation and decolonisation which gave birth to many of the states in the MENA. Without further study into the relationship between the use of violence and coercion involved in the spread of the state system, and the nature of the system itself, the assertion that there is a qualitative difference between the two is somewhat weak; it implies that violence in the spread of the system has no wider bearing on the normative grounding of that system. Put another way, Halliday's emphasis on the distinction between the spread of the system and the nature of the system reads as a belief that 'yes coercion was regrettable, but those Middle Eastern states would have adopted the same system on their own eventually. Now that they have adopted the state system, it affirms the universality of the system.' Regardless of the narrative Halliday uses to inform his history of the state system, he is accepting that Islam bears little relevance in the international system; it was 'acted on' during the spread of the international system, rather than having any agency in the creation of that system.

The next, a theoretically complex and eclectic approach, is an implicit synthesis of material factors, constructivist theory and explicit realism, apparent in Gregory Gause's work. In *Oil Monarchies: Domestic and Security Challenges in the Arab Gulf States*, Gause demonstrates a far more developed understanding of Islam as a factor, divorced from culture, which has bearing upon politics.

Briefly, Gause claims that the constitutive role of Islam (to which he ascribes what I would identify as a level of social and political constructivism) is reliant upon the state: 'the institutions of Islam are now much more dependent upon the state, and much more a subordinate part of the state apparatus, than was the case in the past'.[44] Gause describes Islam as 'tamed', and as such it becomes an important part of the state, 'providing institutional support and ideological legitimation'.[45] In this way Gause is emphasising that the role Islam plays in Muslim countries is by no means politically unimportant. Neither is Islam purely a contest on the domestic level; Gause points out that ideological competition between Saudi Arabia and Iran, involving the concept of political Islam, has regional implications in the Persian Gulf, for example.[46] The interplay between political Islam and the state is what is important; the fact that the state attempts to control the meaning of political Islam as a method of legitimising its rule does not mean that the concept is not contested. That this contestation is possible is testament to the interplay between the power of ideas and the power of material concerns. Before I move on to establishing some of the commonalities between all the surveyed applications of IR theories to the Middle East, I will analyse one final case, that of Hinnebusch and Ehteshami's edited work, *The Foreign Policies of Middle East States*.

Hinnebusch defines his approach as a modified realism: 'Realist solutions to the problem of order remain more relevant in the Middle East than elsewhere because . . . transnational norms restraining interstate conduct are the least institutionalized there'.[47] The reason a modified realism is used by Hinnebusch is an acknowledgement of the particular circumstances in which MENA states were established after World War I. Given the arbitrary nature of state boundaries, irredentism, 'dissatisfaction with the incongruity between territorial borders and "imagined communities"',[48] is especially prevalent in the Middle East, though it is by no means a phenomenon unique to the region. Hinnebusch observes that the 'state system was imposed on a preexisting cultural and linguistic unity that more or less persists';[49] more explicitly put, he is saying that the existence of a pre-existing trans-national identity, whether it be an Arab or Islamic one, combined with a legitimacy deficit for Middle Eastern states, requires realism to adapt; the peculiar dynamics of irredentism in the Middle East frustrates the national interest traditionally assumed by realism.

Unfortunately, Islam is not dealt with as a religion that helps constitute the reality of its believers. Instead it is treated as a surrogate for Arabism,[50] or is only mentioned as an oppositional force—opposing increased Western intervention in the Middle East. The problematic way in which Islam is perceived here is evident where the terms 'Middle Eastern' and 'Islamic' are used interchangeably; in doing so, Hinnebusch is not identifying, as Owen does, the ways in which Islam, even in the narrow confines of a transnational ideology in which Owen places it, operates in different ways to culture. The adoption of a realist epistemology and methodology, even modified ones, leads to an over-emphasis of the power of the state, for ideas are only entertained that play within the boundaries and use the vocabulary of 'the state'.

Having reviewed the ways in which Islam is sidelined or subsumed into material factors by existing IR scholarship of the MENA, it becomes apparent that further study of Islam in IR requires a different or at least modified analytical framework to adequately pay heed to the constitutive power of the faith. The development of this framework is the focus of the following chapter; for now, I will continue to analyse the ways in which IR literature studies Islam, this time moving to studies of sub-Saharan Africa.

International Relations, Religion and the African Continent

Previously I looked at the Middle East *and North Africa*, and now the chapter moves to 'the African continent'—a distinction needs to be made. In designating North Africa as part of the MENA, and therefore part of the region for many of the above studies, what remains of interest on the continent, to the student of political Islam, is sub-Saharan Africa. As René Otayek and Benjamin Soares explain about the prevalence of Islam in sub-Saharan Africa,

> Islam has been present in Africa for at least a millennium, and countries such as Somalia and Djibouti, along with Mauritania, have long been nearly entirely Muslim. . . . Today, Muslims constitute a clear majority in most of the countries in the Sahel in West Africa, including Senegal, Mauritania, Mali, and Niger. In Sudan, Chad, and Tanzania, Muslims are the largest religious group . . . approximately half of all Nigerians are Muslims. . . . Although Muslims are only a very small minority in South Africa, they make up sizeable minorities in Kenya and Uganda, as well as in such countries as Malawi and Mozambique.[51]

The Sahel region of Africa which Otayek and Soares refer to is the belt under the Sahara Desert. Sahel derives from the Arabic word for shore, being designated as the southern shore of the Sahara. From names of regions to the prevalence of Islam, the enduring influence of the Arab world of the MENA on sub-Saharan Africa is diverse and eclectic. Indeed, as surveyed in the previous chapter's definition of political Islam, when speaking of the Islamist goal of an Islamic state in sub-Saharan Africa, we can speak of Somalia, Sudan and Mauritania. Large Muslim minorities in Nigeria, for example, highlight the desire, at times, for the implementation of Islamic family law, but in countries where Muslims are a minority, Islamists have a hard time persuading the population, Muslim and otherwise, to implement an Islamic state.

In IR, the distinction between North Africa and sub-Saharan Africa fades away. William Brown argues that as problematic as it is to amalgamate the politics of an entire continent into 'African politics' or 'African IR', there are some ways to conceive of 'Africa' as a whole: 'as a collective international actor; as a collection of states with (in the "broadest of sweeps") a shared history; and as a discursive presence, used by both Africans and outsiders, in international politics and policy'.[52] My interests lie in political Islam and IR, and therefore not in Africa as a collective international actor. What remains, then, is an Africa with a (loosely) shared history, and Africa as a discursive presence. Of the former, while I am interested in sub-Saharan Africa, the further south of the Sahara one travels, the more diffuse the influence of a 'shared history' becomes, especially regarding the presence and influence of Islam in politics and society.[53] As a discursive category, perhaps there is more to work with regarding IR; despite the incredible diversity of the African continent, compounded by the diversity of Islamic theory and practice I have begun to reference, discursively both Africa and Islam share something in common, in that they both represent mythical 'others', for a Western 'self' to define itself.[54] Indeed, the self/other distinction is a keen debate in the IR of Africa, as is explored presently.

African Marginalisation in International Relations

William Brown writes that '[a]t best, we are told, "IR theory" misrepresents or misunderstands African reality, at worst it participates in an exercise of neo-colonial theoretical hegemony'.[55] John Anthony Pella Jr. claims that '[t]he neglect of Africa within international relations scholarship—and principally within the discipline's current trends—is remarkable'.[56] Whether through misrepresentation or neo-colonial hegemony, I will argue that this remarkable absence of Africa in IR is not only problematic, but also shares many parallels with the absence of religion as an explanatory factor in IR.

Kevin Dunn argues that '[t]he marginalization of Africa by Western policy makers has a correlation in the continent's marginalization by the dominant (Western-produced) IR theories'.[57] Here, emphasis is placed on knowledge creation in IR as problematic for Africa. As the 'architects' of the discipline, certainly realists of classical or neo varieties neglected Africa, Waltz emphasising great powers, while Morgenthau claiming Africa did not have a history before World War II.[58] Structuralists fare little better for Dunn; while Africa might be central in a critique of the exploitative nature of the international system, Africa lacks agency; it is always acted *upon*.[59] What Dunn refers to by 'Western-produced' IR theories is a cause of contention among IR scholars of Africa. The debates that occur reflect many of the themes that I will engage with as the book proceeds. Just because a theory is *produced* in Europe or the United States, does that mean that it does not *apply* outside of those historical and cultural contexts? If it does not apply, then why not? If it does apply, then how are such claims to be universality made? As Douglas Lemke explains, '[g]reat power bias and untested assumptions of the universality of patterns across the international system have resulted in a deep rift between standard international relations research and its critics'.[60] The claim that Africa is marginalised in IR is one such rift.

African marginalisation in IR is expertly surveyed by Sophie Harman and William Brown; their conclusion is that 'while Africa is the site of many issue-based studies and provides empirically detailed accounts of international relations, many such accounts remain at arm's length from core conceptual and theoretical debates in IR'.[61] In their survey of the reasons given for Africa's absence in IR, Harman and Brown note that it is either (1) a 'sin of omission' or (2) 'a lack of "fit" between the discipline's theoretical constructs and African realities'.[62] The sin of omission is possible to remedy. Harman and Brown claim that data on African states is hard to come by given the turbulent political atmosphere in which some African governments operate. However, I would argue that such data being hard to come by only reinforces the fact that research questions emphasise state-based scholarship. Where data is available, the focus of IR scholars on certain categories of organisation, like the state, can mean they are looking at the wrong actors. Where legal states exist, de facto governance is carried out by groups other than the 'official' government, but nevertheless, 'official' data is used. This focus on the wrong actors, Lemke argues, can explain why IR scholars use bad data when available, or ignore African examples altogether due to missing data.[63]

Addressing the notion that there is a lack of fit between IR and Africa is more problematic. Harman and Brown argue that this lack of fit could be explained by three reasons: (1) that IR maintains a Western bias; (2) that liberal theoretical underpinnings promote some sort of agenda for Africa; and (3) that the state in Africa does not coincide with the theory of state in IR.[64] All of these points relating to Africa and IR are of interest for our discussion of political Islam and IR. As outlined in the introduction, it is understandings of liberal individualism versus communitarian understandings of IR, and the state versus the *umma* which contribute to consistent oversight about the place of religion and specifically political Islam in IR theory. Regarding 'Western' bias, Harman and Brown also mention knowledge production as a factor. As the authors explain,

> Such Western bias is reinforced by profound inequalities in the production of IR knowledge itself . . . a wealth of commentary on Africa . . . is not from Africa. While geographical location and origin do not guarantee good scholarship, such undeniable bias remains an ongoing problem for a discipline that addresses the world as a whole.[65]

Such issues around knowledge production is echoed by Acharya in his call for Global IR,[66] and here again is another point of convergence between the IR of Africa and the study of political Islam. But the claims of Western bias are problematic in that they can be used to argue for essentialism for one or the other 'side' of this 'self/other' dichotomy. Either we can argue that the state system is European in its historical and cultural roots, and therefore Europe is unique in its position as instigator of the international system, or we can argue that Africa is unique in its experiences, which explains why the international system cannot apply on the continent. Either claim, as we will see in the next chapter, is highly problematic. As Brown warns, 'The double act of portrayal of Europe as essentially in accord with received theories, and of an African reality which is essentially different, cannot help but exoticise Africa and only widens the gulf between the IR mainstream and Africanist writings'.[67]

Other ways in which we might conceive of a marginal Africa in IR are endogenous to the continent. Ian Taylor speaks of structuralist studies which emphasise the inequality of the international system, especially the use of Structural Adjustment Programmes (SAPs) by International Financial Institutions (IFIs) in many African countries, to force changes in economic and political policies in exchange for monetary loans. Taylor argues that such studies forget why SAPs were introduced in the first place; structuralist studies which look to the 'evil' of the international system to explain Africa's marginalisation in IR, for Taylor, forget 'gross malgovernance and the imminent bankruptcy of many states on the continent'[68] as the precursor to SAPs. Rather, for Taylor, the governing elites in African states are responsible for the economic, political and social problems in many African states, 'the end result being Africa's continued subjugation in the global community'.[69] It is not that external factors do not have an influence in Africa's marginalisation in IR; in fact Taylor argues that '[p]romoting liberalization in Africa while keeping the West's doors closed to Africa's products is cynical and must come to an end'.[70]

On the other side of these discussions are those who reject or heavily qualify the claim that Africa is marginal in IR. Complete rejection seems difficult, as the neo-realist position of Stefan Andreasson demonstrates. Andreasson's focus on strong and weak states results in an argument in complete contrast to that of Dunn, wherein 'Africa's widespread problems of weak [states], by comparison to other regions . . . explains its historical experiences of colonial domination and neo-colonial subordination'.[71] This quite remarkable assertion is cyclical in the sense that 'Africa was colonised because it was weak, and it is now weak because it was colonised'. Either way, as weak international actors African states may be subjugated, but they are not marginalised; they have a prominent place as the play-thing of great powers. Suffice to say, such a view maintains its position based on a narrow definition of what it means to be marginal, namely, that the inability to act or shape an agenda is not an indication of being marginalised, rather marginalisation is manifest as being *acted upon*.

The qualified resistance to claims that Africa is marginalised in IR is more interesting. In the same year as publishing the journal article 'Blind Spots in Analyzing Africa's Place in World Politics', explored above, Taylor along with Paul Williams also argued that Africa *was not* marginal to IR; 'the continent has in fact been dialectically linked, both shaping and being shaped by international processes and structures'.[72] In this sense, it is much like the claims of Western bias discussed above, that rest upon notions of 'self' and 'other'. Such claims maintain that the position of disadvantaged 'other' (Africa) is a position on the margins, but in being part of the dialectic of 'self/ other' (Europe/Africa, United States/Africa, etc.), it is essential. In his book, *The International Relations of Sub-Saharan Africa*, Taylor argues that 'African elites have generally proved themselves excellent arch-manipulators of the international system'.[73] Much like Lemke's explanation of bad or missing data to explain Africa's absence in IR, Taylor and Williams are critical of the state-centrism of political analyses of Africa, claiming that 'many analyses of Africa's place in world politics suffer from an inability to conceptualize processes, events and structures that fall within the realm of what is usually considered private, illegal or—worse—mundane and apolitical'.[74] The notion that IR might too willingly designate objects of analysis as apolitical is one that I argue also applies to religion and political Islam.

Islam in Africa is not addressed in the literature I have covered above. Indeed, in debates where one must first argue for the relevance of an *entire continent* in IR scholarship, it is not surprising that anything less than the continent is not articulated. As the MENA is not seen as extremely peripheral in IR, which Africa is, we can analyse the ways in which Islam plays out in those IR studies, and discuss what might be overlooked in those studies given the secular bias in IR. Islam in Africa, however, is not addressed in the IR literature; this literature is struggling to make itself relevant to a discipline which largely uses the continent as an empirical example, or ignores it altogether. The point, however, is not to dismiss all IR theory as irrelevant to Africa, or dismiss all instances of Islamism in Africa as irrelevant to IR. As Brown points out regarding IR in Africa, '[w]e should not be surprised if neorealism fails to provide everything we need to know about West Africa, or Western Europe for that matter. The question is, does it provide some useful insights?'[75] Broadly sympathetic to Brown's position here, I will not insist that 'Islamic IR' is a different, unique and 'authentic' articulation of IR for Muslim peoples, but rather ask whether it provides any useful insights. Nor will I argue that IR 'doesn't work' when explaining political Islam (implicitly accepting that it does work in explaining politicised Christianity in Europe, for example). Rather, political Islam is only the tool used to unlock problematic elements of IR *that were there to begin with*, and which apply outside of the context of political Islam. Indeed, the convergence of some of the elements of the critique of African IR, and the critique of political Islam and IR, shows the extent to which I am engaging in a dialogue which is much larger than the specific 'case' of political Islam or Africa, a case that will be examined in more detail in later chapters. Currently, I will return to another potential source for Islamist politics, Southeast Asia, and examine the IR literature of the region in the hopes of discovering further synergies with the critique of the IR of the MENA and Africa.

International Relations, Religion and Southeast Asia

As a geographic region, South and Southeast Asia are remarkable regarding the diverse interactions between Islam and formal state politics. Malaysia and Indonesia both blend democratic politics and Islamic rhetoric in innovative ways—Malaysia boasts impressive economic development and tries to 'export' to other Muslim countries its mixture of economic liberalism and conservative modernity, 'comprising a form of virtuous syncretism between universal modernity and Islam'.[76] In Indonesia, the Muslim population is greater than the total population of the entire Middle East, yet Indonesian thinkers are not part of the 'canonical' Islamist thinkers. The only other Muslim majority state in the region is Brunei, but it is 'Indonesian and Malaysian discourses [which] dominate the Southeast Asian Islamic scholarly scene'.[77] Moving to South Asia, to include the Indian subcontinent, the impact of Pakistani thought on political Islam, specifically that of Maulana Maududi, is extensive. Pakistan itself has endured military coups and a state-led Islamisation process. I have already touched upon the work of Maududi, and will return to his ideas and their relation to IR later in the book. This leaves us with the key states of Malaysia and Indonesia to discuss.

Southeast Asia, Religion and International Relations

In IR, the region of Southeast Asia, like sub-Saharan Africa, provides somewhat of a conundrum for the discipline. On the one hand, the states of Southeast Asia seem to embrace the institution building that characterises a liberal world order. In particular, the Association of Southeast Asian Nations (ASEAN), reports in article one of its charter that its purpose is 'To maintain and enhance peace, security and stability and further strengthen peace-oriented values in the region'.[78] ASEAN appears to typify the liberal peace-building model that relies on institutional rulemaking to bind states into pacific actions, if not embedding the notion of peace as a norm. On the other hand, this same liberal ideology is often challenged domestically as a 'foreign' element, casting 'modernity' as a Western condition, and indigenous modes of production or social relations as more 'authentic'.[79] In Indonesia, for example, this challenge to liberal ideology is encapsulated by political Islam, 'as a major articulator of social justice issues in relation the social contradictions associated with rapid capitalist development in the late twentieth century'.[80] Adding to the forces of liberal economy versus social justice, 'the region has been subjected to two centrifugal forces of globalization: one nationalistic and the other *ummatic*'.[81]

Political Islam in the region functions much as it does in sub-Saharan Africa and many MENA states, that is, as a protest movement. However, Southeast Asia does offer some examples of a more proactive, though I use the term loosely, use of Islamic solidarity. '[O]ne could argue that Indonesian and Malaysian discourses dominate the Southeast Asian Islamic scholarly scene',[82] and Malaysia represents the case of political Islam in IR par excellence. Malaysia agitates for greater cooperation amongst Muslim states. During the premiership of Mahathir Mohamad (1981–2003) Malaysian policy showed frustration with the stagnation of the OIC, and became a founding member of the D-8 Organization of Economic Cooperation in 1997.[83] The D-8, a collaboration of Turkey, Egypt, Iran, Indonesia, Pakistan, Bangladesh and Nigeria, is an interstate organisation that is an implicit critique of the OIC, though it 'remains highly inefficient relative to its initial aims'.[84] As with any discussion of political Islam in IR, Malaysia's rhetoric in favour of the *umma* is mitigated by its actions. As Delfolie notes, '[in] 2012, with the exception of Indonesia, no Muslim-majority country was among the top-ten most important trading partners of Malaysia'.[85] Malaysia encapsulates the analytical problem in accounting for political Islam in IR: is political Islam a tool for maximising state interests, or is it a 'genuine' phenomenon that represents an alternative way of 'doing' IR? Indeed, so-called state Islamisation, including Malaysia's foreign policy preference towards the *umma*, is entangled with domestic competition to manipulate Islamic language and symbols to garner votes in general elections.[86] Joseph Chinyong Low characterises the dynamics of democratic politics in Malaysia as an 'Islamization race' between ruling and opposition parties.[87] Such a race has 'caused democratic processes to give rise to patently undemocratic outcomes',[88] the eventual outcome of this race will have a lasting impact on Islamism's historical record with democracy. Bringing the discussion back to IR, the fact that such issues are discussed in the scholarly literature goes some way to showing how the discipline does engage with the themes pertinent to political Islam in the region. I will continue by exploring the specifics of IR engagement with political Islam in Southeast Asia.

Linda Quayle's English School approach to Southeast Asia is particularly promising as a reflexive piece of work. In her book, *Southeast Asia and the English School of International Relations: A Region-Theory Dialogue*, she takes as a starting point the notion that the English School is critiqued for its state-centrism and its inability to develop into a 'grand theory'. Quayle takes Southeast Asia as an opportunity to deal with these unexplored issues. At once she is using the English School as a lens to view the region but also, and importantly, she is using the region to inform the theory. In this reading, Southeast Asia represents two narratives: One, power, is more familiar to the student of IR; the second is community, as seen by ASEAN, for example.[89] While the English School solidarist-pluralist divide helps to conceptualise both the notions of power (pluralist) and community (solidarist), Quayle points out that solidarism is not especially useful, as it is too concerned with human rights and offers little in regards to how deeper cooperation can be achieved in other areas. She goes on to write that 'the ES [English School] can already envisage non-liberal bases for solidarism, such as identity, economics and functional cooperation, but needs more input on the extent to which such bases can support a level of consensus strong enough to bear the beginnings of an enforcement process'.[90] It is here that Southeast Asia can enrich the English School, providing a means to conceive of solidarism which is not based in a human rights discourse.

Pointing out that the English School is sensitive to issues of culture and identity, Quayle argues that the attempt by ASEAN leaders to develop a top-down regional identity is rather weak. Such top-down regional identity building must make little use of Islam as a marker of identity, given the diverse range of faiths present in Southeast Asia. However, as I pointed out earlier with regards to Malaysia, top-down Islamisation is a domestic practice tied to nation-building.[91] When dealing with religion, Quayle's study somewhat problematically combines ethnicity and religion as '[t]hese two markers . . . are often extraordinarily difficult to pull apart on the ground, especially in conflict situations, and partly because the discourses that seek to explain them are very similar'.[92] While I am broadly sympathetic to such treatment of these identity markers, especially regarding their interaction with nationalism and nation-building in post-colonial states, conflating ethnicity and religion proves difficult at the intra- and super-state levels. Beyond the domestic, political Islam can be a potent transnational phenomenon which engenders, for good or ill, a sense of commonality and 'we feeling' separate from (and sometimes in direct opposition to) ethnic identities. Following my critique of the English School's approach to the MENA, it is not that the English School lacks the tools to deal with such a 'non-Western' world as political Islam, but lacks, perhaps, exposure to the ideas and practices which constitute Islam at the international level. In Southeast Asia, the conflation of ethnicity and religion necessarily relegates political Islam to a domestic factor, only 'overtly internationalized when it involves terrorism or destabilizing refugee flows'.[93] Reducing political Islam to outbreaks of violence, especially in social analysis, risks moving Islam as a motivating factor into the category of barbaric 'other'.[94] The record in Southeast Asia is somewhat different, as I will continue with exploring with reference to Indonesia and Malaysia.

Both Indonesia and Malaysia have displayed parts embrace, rejection and innovation regarding secularism. As colonial states they were subjected to a policy of secularisation by their masters, partially as a bulwark against insurrections based on pan-Islamic loyalties.[95] In gaining independence, Islam was both a marker of 'traditional' (read backwards) civic life, and a marker of indigenous resistance to colonial powers. In Indonesia, neither of the above poles were realised, though the organisation Darul Islam fought for an Islamic state from 1948.[96] That Indonesia was fertile ground for secular/ Islamic innovation is partially explained by the Cold War. In an environment where being an unbeliever was one step removed from being a Communist (a capital offence during the Cold War), critique of authoritarian capitalism came through Islam.[97] Harun Nasution (1919–1998) and Nurcholish Madjid (1939–2005) were two of Indonesia's most prominent religious thinkers, both of whom navigated the secular/religious divide in inventive ways, which still bear their mark on political Islam in Southeast Asia.[98]

Of the first, Nasution's position bears more than a passing resemblance to my own, as Ahmed Fauzi describes, 'Nasution became an apologist for religious pluralism, Greek philosophy, and secularism à la Kemal Ataturk and Ali Abd al-Raziq'.[99] For Nasution, Islam is not a truth contained within scripture, but is conditional upon time and place. Such a contextual position echoes that of the second Indonesian thinker, Nurcholish, who advocated secularism 'as a religiously purifying process', but rejected secularism 'as a belief system carrying atheistic and humanistic implications'.[100] What has resulted in Southeast Asia is the interaction of Islam and state which is neither secular as understood in 'the West', nor is it an Islamic state as pursued by fundamentalist Islamists. Indeed, those Islamists who did not engage in democracy have remained on the fringes.[101] Malaysia's first prime minister, Tunku Abdul Rahman, claimed that Malaysia was not an Islamic state as traditionally understood. However, in 2001 Prime Minister Mahathir Mohamad announced that Malaysia was unapologetically an Islamic state, a claim justified by Malaysian religious scholars under considerable and ongoing controversy.[102] While some Islamists use political Islam as a means to reject what they understand as political and economic modernity, Southeast Asia highlights that 'Islam might be better placed as offering a more encompassing vision of modernity itself'.[103]

Now I will bring together the various critiques offered to the underlying problem that Islam faces when articulated on the international level: the legacy and power of the state system.

The Westphalian Narrative in International Relations Scholarship

One of the claims I can derive from the study of the MENA, sub-Saharan Africa and Southeast Asia in IR is that in using the nation-state as its unit of analysis, IR demands that political Islam define itself in similar terms to be accepted or be considered a legitimate subject by the discipline. Put crudely, political Islam must 'play the game', at least a little, to be considered a 'legitimate' theory.

Piscatori notes that Muslim elites were keen to accept and adopt the nation-state system; it granted them supposed immunity from external powers and *legitimacy* externally.[104] Such a position of necessity is one echoed by Maududi, who while scornful of the nation-state, saw it as necessary for his native India to be able to gain independence from the British Empire. The nation-state, however, was not to be an end point in and of itself. Instead, having achieved independence the Muslim states could begin to unify again without interference from colonial powers.[105] While the first part of his vision was realised, and independence was gained, the second phase never really materialised. Muslim states, as Ayubi notes, give no special treatment to fellow Muslim states, territorial sovereignty is adhered to and there is no preferential treatment between Muslim states in economic terms.[106] Given the advent of supra-national organisations, especially, for example, the European Union (EU), it may be possible to talk of a European *umma* already existing.[107] A group of nation-states in this instance united on common normative grounds (which would be the unity easiest achieved in a Muslim *umma*) as well as, substantially and originally, economic and some judicial grounds. This being the case, is may be possible for a Muslim *umma* to coalesce from the state-centric foundations in IR that have been evidenced in the preceding review of IR studies of Muslim majority areas of the world, an assertion I will explore in later chapters.

In the discipline of IR the dominance of power, self-interest and material factors (otherwise put, the dominance of neo-realism) often closes the doors to other, less well articulated themes in the relations of states. Globalisation here represents a contemporary challenge whereby 'sovereignty and nation-states are undergoing severe delimitation and mutation'.[108] Former UN Secretary-General Boutros Boutros-Ghali wrote his now infamous *Agenda for Peace* over two decades ago in 1992, within which he highlights the predicament for the 'old' Westphalian ideal. He stated that

> The foundation-stone of this work [maintenance of international peace and security] is and must remain the State. Respect for its fundamental sovereignty and integrity are crucial to any common international progress. The time of absolute and exclusive sovereignty, however, has passed.[109]

Rather than claim, as Boutros-Ghali did, that the time of absolute sovereignty has passed (if indeed it ever existed in practice), my starting point is to recognise that at the least, the world exists in a period of flux. As notions of sovereignty are changing, the opportunities for alternative theories of IR proliferate. The chance to bend conceptual boundaries and reshape the discipline, if only slightly, is far more achievable than was so when Maududi envisioned a Muslim *umma* sprouting from the various nationalistic projects at the end of Empire. Indeed, Mandaville's assertion that 'the authority of statist politics is currently under threat from a variety of . . . transformations which serve to disembed political identities from national contexts and also stretch social relations across time and space',[110] reads almost exactly as the challenge the *umma* construct brings to IR.

The Legacy of Westphalia

While the Western state system appears to be the dominant mould to conduct international relations, it is not the only instance of IR available for study. As such, it is worth analysing briefly, how the state system became the prevailing instance of IR. Political modernity was achieved, so the story goes, with the advent of the modern state system, which coalesced in the seventeenth century with the Treaty of Westphalia. This development came with far more than the idea of territorial sovereignty; the fifteenth, sixteenth and seventeenth centuries saw 'the birth of modern capitalism, modern science and technology and [Christian Protestantism]'.[111] In this narrative of development, political modernity is seen as a progression, 'from the mythical to the scientific, from the barbaric to the rational/democratic, from the constrained, ordered subject to the utilitarian individual "free to choose"'.[112] Taking these binary distinctions as staple in IR, a community is looked down on that does not develop or articulate its politics in the mould that Europe did in the seventeenth century. Jim George speaks of the 'post-Kantian sovereign man'[113] who represents the rationale for states in Hobbes's anarchical world. For him, this is the moment where the absolute pursuit of rationalism, 'logocentrism', became embedded in Western thought.[114] This logocentrism is apparent in IR especially, which Assis Malaquias describes as 'fundamentally a scientific attempt to explain—and, if possible, predict—the behavior of states in the complex relationships with each other'.[115] Here the logocentrism is twofold: first is the emphasis on scientific explanation, and secondly is the emphasis on states, a far more subversive example which typifies the state-centrism in IR theory in broad terms, and realism and its variants more specifically. As such, 'the Kantian moment represents not just Enlightenment progress, potential, and openness but also devastating closure, the closure of critical, historical, and social reflection upon critiques, histories and societies'.[116]

Kayaoglu argues that if the peace of Westphalia created an international society, it did so by creating a normative divergence between these 'civilised' states and the rest of the world; '[n]on European states, lacking this European culture and social contract, remained in anarchy until the European states allowed them to join the international society'.[117] In this way, 'international relations', with its suppositions about sovereignty and secularism, is not truly 'international'. The legacy of Westphalia, perhaps, is the legacy of a lack of global pluralism in the discipline. IR, according to Kayaoglu, should abandon the Westphalian narrative for four reasons:

1. It misrepresents the emergence of the modern international system.
2. Its state-centrism can lead to misdiagnoses of many aspects of IR.
3. It prevents the theorising of cross civilisational interdependencies as many 'international' norms are posited as transcendental.
4. It prevents the development of global pluralism in the discipline.[118]

Points three and four are the most relevant to this book; if articulating an Islamic IR is to be attempted, a key component will be the 'cross civilisational' dialogue between, in this example, the state and *umma*. The term 'cross civilisational' is problematic however, as it can easily be misunderstood to resonate with an essentialist character. Mandaville summarises a similar point to Kayaoglu in such a way to avoid misunderstanding; he claims that

> As the sovereign nation-state system began to reproduce itself in parts of the world culturally and historically distinct from Europe—settings possessing their own understandings of how religion and politics do or do not fit together—it was inevitable that tensions would flare around the question of secularism.[119]

Reconciling a place for religion in IR will be one of the main challenges of this book, but rather than a broad statement about reconciling 'Islam' with 'the West', I will attempt to specifically engage the *umma* and the state in dialogue. Reconciliation is only one result of that dialogue, and we should not pre-empt the analysis by assuming it is possible or even desirable. Beyond this, a second challenge the *umma* poses, if indirectly, to the international system is the notion of the community over the individual, which has been teased at in some of the IR approaches to Muslim regions, above.

LIBERAL INDIVIDUALISM, THE UMMA AND COMMUNITARIANISM

Liberalism is a term that is not well defined in IR, though it is a term that permeates the discipline. Michael Doyle wrote in the late 1980s that '[t]here is no canonical description of liberalism'.[120] Yet, the entire Western political system is founded on its principles, that is, the principles of the European Enlightenment.[121] The fundamental pillar of liberalism is the respect for individual autonomy.[122] This respect leads to a collection of rights that differentiate liberal states from other, non-liberal states; these include, but are not limited to, 'equality before the law, free speech and other civil liberties, private property, and elected representation'.[123] As noted in the previous chapter, there exists the notion that to the values of the liberal state Islam is 'repellent and strange';[124] political Islam and liberalism are perceived to provide competing discursive opportunities.[125]

The lowest common denominator in a liberal world view is the individual (citizen).[126] When free, these individuals can come together and form society later. For Islam the modus operandi is reversed: Society is assumed to exist already, an Islamic society that is, and its aim on the social level is to bring individual Muslims into that society.[127] Returning to the liberal foundation of the individual, the idea of individuals as 'sole generators of their wants and preferences'[128] is misleading; individuals are, at the very least, influenced by their surroundings as much as they constitute them. This leads to a distinction between autonomy and freedom.

Autonomy, or negative liberty, is perhaps best exemplified by John Mill, who states 'that there ought to exist the fullest liberty of professing and discussing, as a matter of ethical conviction, any doctrine, however immoral it may be considered'.[129] Freedom, or positive liberty, on the other hand, would see the highest goal of society to prevent any external factor impinging on an individual's decisions. As such, a transcendental authority is required to coerce society towards some goal 'which they [society] would, if they were more enlightened, themselves pursue, but do not, because they are blind or ignorant or corrupt'.[130] What is important for my discussion here is that liberalism is not *just* about autonomy. Liberalism does not provide Islamists with a way to achieve agency (in IR or otherwise); it provides them a *particular way* to achieve agency; it is an exercise in power. In this liberal exercise in power, secularism reigns supreme, for if liberal individuals need to be sole generators of their wants and needs, that individual needs to be divorced from religion.

Removing secularism from liberalism helps to reconcile it with Islam. As liberalism is concerned with 'tolerance, individual liberty, and rights' and secularism with 'separating life or politics from religious concerns', a less secular liberalism may well lead to an Islamic liberalism.[131] The dominance of liberal ideals in IR scholarship means that the debate is almost always one of either 'how best to raise Islam to a level whereby it is compatible with liberalism', or a zero-sum conceptualisation whereby *only* liberalism *or* Islam can exist in contemporary international politics. I will attempt the reverse; much in the same way as the state versus *umma* debate, I will endeavour to develop a form of political Islam and then assess the ways in which *liberalism* falls short of its schema. In doing so, the hope is to enter the two positions into a dialogue where it might be seen how and why liberalism in IR (and as we will see, also political Islam) can be an impediment to 'global' thinking.

It might be that political Islam is capable of offering its own conception of humanity as an alternative to the conception of humanity monopolised by liberalism, a concept of humanity that rests on a different understanding of the individual than liberalism, as alluded to earlier in this section. This being the case, then to engage political Islam with liberalism in the contemporary political environment may give Islam a greater degree of agency in IR, moving it away from the category of 'other' to IR's 'self', and through dialogue incorporate both libraries of ideas into a 'Global IR'. Such a dialogue would form the 'glue' to mesh an Islamic union and secular, liberal union together, less problematically, perhaps, than the current glue of liberalism in the international system.

CONCLUSIONS

In this chapter I surveyed how IR conceptualises political Islam in three Muslim majority regions of the world: the MENA, sub-Saharan Africa and Southeast Asia (Malaysia and Indonesia specifically). It appears, however, that political Islam is not considered in the IR of sub-Saharan Africa; the continent as a whole 'remain[s] at arm's length from core conceptual and theoretical debates in IR'.[132] That is, African states are present as case studies, especially regarding the effect of neo-liberal economics, state formation and state reform, but conceptually the continent does not inform 'international' politics. This perception is changing. Even in my survey, those arguing for Africa's relevance highlight a number of ways in which the experience of African states and peoples might be cause for reassessment of the category of state as the unit of analysis in IR. Moreover, these African experiences might trouble some of the 'universal' aspects of IR theory, asking us to reassess our understanding of the international system, its origins, and its benefits. These are not trivial conceptual tasks, and as such we might be able to point to some ways in which the African continent is engaged with conceptual debates in IR. This is perhaps an optimistic reading of the situation; such scholarship remains on the periphery, coalescing around the Critical IR subfield. Regardless, being so marginal means that while my goal was to assess how IR conceptualises and interacts with political Islam in sub-Saharan Africa, political Islam was nowhere to be seen in these discussions, taking as they were the entirety of Africa to argue for relevance in IR.[133] Africanist studies of course disaggregate the continent and deal extensively with the position of Islam vis-à-vis politics, and these studies were drawn upon in the previous chapter's definition of political Islam.

The IR studies of the MENA were more fruitful regarding political Islam. Here I argued that despite the variety of theoretical approaches applied, political Islam as a factor in IR was limited. Reasons varied from treating political Islam as epiphenomenal to limiting its scope to the domestic to arguing its irrelevance as a non-material factor.

Regarding Southeast Asia, the analysis of two key Muslim majority states, Malaysia and Indonesia, reveal some very interesting and innovative ways in which Islam and the *umma* are used to push an international agenda which counters 'Western' dominance. Part of this agenda is the notion that modernities are different, and that an 'Islamic' modernity is possible *within* the current state system, rather than in opposition or rejection of it (is the latter being common in the fundamentalist strand of Islamism). Importantly, religion was considered as a factor in the IR of the region, though at times it is conflated with ethnicity in a way which helps analysis of the domestic, but hinders consideration of the international.

What united the approaches of all the regions covered was a subtle (or not so subtle) 'othering' of the geography/people/religion. This aspect of IR is fundamental in claims of Eurocentrism and secular bias, which I will unpack and address in the following chapter, as I try to develop a way out of 'self/other' dichotomies when studying IR.

It is important to remember that while I argued that the studies/theories/approaches discussed may have been deficient in their conceptualisation of religion in IR, political Islam is not an all-encompassing phenomenon that colours the politics of all Muslim peoples. Rather, the omission/distortion of political Islam is problematic for students of globalised political Islam who find IR unable to effectively analyse the object of their enquiry. That is not to say that the IR of the regions in question is therefore unproblematic. Rather, the IR studies of the MENA, sub-Saharan Africa and to some extent Southeast Asia begin to paint a picture of an IR which is Eurocentric in its assumptions of liberalism, secularism, and the state. The implication of this Eurocentrism is an inability to accept different categories of analysis which, as in the example of political Islam (though this is by no means the only example of a different category of analysis), animate the behaviour of a great many people. Bringing these differences into dialogue with IR in the hope of embracing a 'Global IR' will be my goal for the remainder of the book.

NOTES

1. Tariq Ramadan, *Western Muslims and the Future of Islam* (Oxford: Oxford University Press, 2004), 4.

2. Mahmood Mamdani, 'Good Muslim, Bad Muslim: A Political Perspective on Culture and Terrorism', *American Anthropologist* 104, no. 3 (2002): 766.

3. James Piscatori, *Islam in a World of Nation-States* (Cambridge: Cambridge University Press, 1986).

4. Elizabeth Hurd, *The Politics of Secularism in International Relations* (Princeton: Princeton University Press, 2008), 47.

5. Marleen Renders, 'Global Concerns, Local Realities: Islam and Islamism in a Somali State under Construction', in *Islam and Muslim Politics in Africa*, ed. Benjamin F. Soares and René Otayek (Basingstoke: Palgrave Macmillan, 2007), 49.

6. Michael Barnett, *Dialogues in Arab Politics: Negotiations in Regional Order* (New York: Columbia University Press, 1998), 23.

7. Alexander Wendt, 'Bridging the Theory/Meta-Theory Gap in International Relations', *Review of International Studies* 17, no. 4 (1991): 383.

8. For example, in Sudan, see R. S. O'Fahey, 'Islamic Hegemonies in the Sudan: Sufism, Mahdism and Islamism', in *Muslim Identity and Social Change in Sub-Saharan Africa*, ed. Louis Brenner (London: Hurst & Company, 1993), 31–33.

9. There are many studies carried out, primarily by Muslim authors, on the historical narrative of Islamic international relations, *siyar* in Arabic, but these rarely provide insight on how Islam might play out in the modern world. See for example Ahmed Bsoul Labeeb, 'Theory of International Relations in Islam', *Digest of Middle East Studies* 16, no. 2 (2007) and 'Abdul-Hamid AbuSulayman, *Towards an Islamic Theory of International Relations: New Directions for Methodology and Thought* (Herndon, VA: International Institute of Islamic Thought, 1993). Bassam Tibi is notable for his discussions of Islam's place in international politics. His work is more attuned to the critique of Islamism (especially the position of *din wa dawla* advocates), than to a critique of political modernity. While I am broadly sympathetic to his positions, it will become evident in my discussion of poststructuralism that I am navigating a different divide (poststructuralism/religion) than Tibi (modernity/religion). See for example Bassam Tibi, *Islam's Predicament with Modernity: Religious Reform and Cultural Change* (London: Routledge, 2009); Bassam Tibi, *The Challenge of Fundamentalism: Political Islam and the New World Disorder* (London: University of California Press, 1998); Bassam Tibi, *Islam in Global Politics: Conflict and Cross-civilizational Bridging* (Abingdon: Routledge, 2012).

10. Louise Fawcett, 'Introduction: The Middle East and International Relations', in *International Relations of the Middle East*, ed. Louise Fawcett, 2nd ed. (Oxford: Oxford University Press, 2009), 2.

11. Peter Mandaville, *Transnational Muslim Politics: Reimagining the Umma* (London: Routledge, 2001), 2.

12. Peter Mandaville, *Global Political Islam* (London: Routledge, 2007), 342–43.

13. Turan Kayaoglu, 'Westphalian Eurocentrism in International Relations Theory', *International Studies Review* 12, no. 2 (2010).

14. Simon Bromley, *Rethinking Middle East Politics* (Oxford: Blackwell, 1994), 9.

15. Ibid., 13.

16. Ibid., 43.

17. That Bromley and later, Halliday, place such emphasis on material interests is not to deny the way in which much contemporary Marxist scholarship attempts to move into a postmaterial reality; for example see Michael Hardt and Antonio Negri, *Empire* (Cambridge, MA: Harvard University Press, 2000).

18. Bromley, *Rethinking Middle East Politics*, 43.

19. Mandaville, *Global Political Islam*, 280–98.

20. Fred Halliday, *The Middle East in International Relations: Power, Politics and Ideology* (Cambridge: Cambridge University Press, 2005), 39.

21. Ibid., 34. Original emphasis.

22. Ibid., 32–33.

23. Barnett, *Dialogues in Arab Politics*, 5.

24. Laclam Ernesto and Chantal Mouffe, *Hegemony and Socialist Strategy: Towards a Radical Democratic Politics*, 2nd ed. (London: Verso, 2001), 2. This work is an example of neo-Marxism that surrenders the universality of the tradition and detatches itself from material interests. However, by and large such a perspective has not had bearing on Marxist study of the Middle East.

25. Barnett, *Dialogues in Arab Politics*, 22–23.

26. Shibley Telhami and Michael Barnett, 'Introduction: Identity and Foreign Policy in the Middle East', in *Identity and Foreign Policy in the Middle East*, ed. Shibley Telhami and Michael Barnett (Ithaca: Cornell University Press, 2002), 18.

27. Ibid., 7.

28. Ibid., 1–13.

29. Jeffery Checkel, 'The Constructivist Turn in International Relations Theory', *World Politics* 50, no. 2 (1998): 325.

30. Roger Owen, *State, Power and Politics in the Making of the Modern Middle East*, 3rd ed. (New York: Routledge, 2004), 3.

31. Ibid., 154.

32. Ibid.
33. Ibid., 155.
34. Ibid., 157.
35. Gerd Nonneman, 'Introduction', in *Analyzing Middle East Foreign Policies and the Relationships with Europe*, ed. Gerd Nonneman (London: Routledge, 2005), 2.
36. Gerd Nonneman, 'Analyzing the Foreign Policies of the Middle East and North Africa: A Conceptual Framework', *Analyzing Middle East Foreign Policies and the Relationships with Europe*, ed. Gerd Nonneman (London: Routledge, 2005), 12–15.
37. Ibid., 12.
38. Fawcett, 'Introduction', 7.
39. Ibid., 5.
40. Fred Halliday, 'The Middle East and Conceptions of "International Society"', in *International Society and the Middle East*, ed. Barry Buzan and Ana Gonzalez-Pelaez (New York: Palgrave Macmillan, 2009), 2.
41. Ibid., 10.
42. Ibid., 11.
43. Ibid., 18.
44. Gregory Gause, *Oil Monarchies: Domestic and Security Challenges in the Arab Gulf States* (New York: Council on Foreign Relations, 1994), 11.
45. Ibid., 14.
46. Ibid., 32.
47. Raymond Hinnebusch, 'Introduction: The Analytical Framework', in *The Foreign Policies of Middle East States*, ed. Raymond Hinnebusch and Anoushiravan Ehteshami (Boulder: Lynne Rienner, 2002), 21.
48. Ibid., 7.
49. Ibid., 8.
50. Ibid., 10.
51. René Otayek and Benjamin F. Soares, 'Introduction: Islam and Muslim Politics in Africa', in *Islam and Muslim Politics in Africa*, ed. René Otayek and Benjamin F. Soares (Basingstoke: Palgrave Macmillan, 2007), 2.
52. William Brown, 'A Question of Agency: Africa in International Politics', *Third World Quarterly* 33, no. 10 (2012): 1890.
53. J. Spencer Trimingham, *The Influence of Islam upon Africa* (London: Longmans, Green, 1968), 114.
54. For Africa's place in this discourse see for example Kevin Dunn, 'Introduction: Africa and International Relations Theory', in *Africa's Challenge to International Relations Theory*, ed. Kevin Dunn and Timothy Shaw (Basingstoke: Palgrave Macmillan, 2001), 2–4. For Islam's place in this discourse see for example Luca Mavelli, *Europe's Encounter with Islam: The Secular and the Postsecular* (New York: Routledge, 2012), 57–61.
55. William Brown, 'Africa and International Relations: A Comment on IR Theory, Anarchy and Statehood', *Review of International Studies* 32, no. 1 (2006): 119.
56. John Anthony Pella, *Africa and the Expansion of International Society: Surrendering the Savanah* (London: Routledge, 2015), 32.
57. Dunn, 'Introduction: Africa and International Relations Theory', 2.
58. Ibid., 2.
59. Ibid., 2.
60. Douglas Lemke, 'African Lessons for International Relations Research', *Review of International Studies* 56, no. 1 (2011): 115.
61. Sophie Harman and William Brown, 'In from the Margins? The Changing Place of Africa in International Relations', *International Affairs* 89, no. 1 (2013): 70.
62. Ibid., 71.
63. Lemke, 'African Lessons for International Relations Research', 133.
64. Harman and Brown, 'In from the Margins?', 71–74.
65. Ibid., 71.
66. Amitav Acharya, 'Global International Relations (IR) and Regional Worlds: A New Agenda for International Studies', *International Studies Quarterly* 58, no. 4 (2014): 654–55.

67. Brown, 'Africa and International Relations', 129.
68. Ian Taylor, 'Blind Spots in Analyzing Africa's Place in World Politics', *Global Governance* 10, no. 4 (2004): 411.
69. Ibid., 414.
70. Ibid., 416.
71. Stefan Andreasson, 'Elusive Agency: Africa's Persistently Peripheral Role in International Relations', in *African Agency in International Politics*, ed. William Brown and Sophie Harman (London: Routledge, 2013), 150.
72. Ian Taylor and Paul Williams, 'Introduction: Understanding Africa's Place in World Politics', in *Africa in International Politics: External Involvement on the Continent*, ed. Ian Taylor and Paul Williams (London: Routledge, 2004), 1.
73. Ian Taylor, *The International Relations of Sub-Saharan Africa* (London: Continuum, 2010), 6.
74. Taylor and Williams, 'Introduction: Understanding Africa's Place in World Politics', 1.
75. Brown, 'Africa and International Relations', 124.
76. David Delfolie, 'Malaysian Extroversion towards the Muslim World: Ideological Positioning for a "Mirror Effect"', *Journal of Current Southeast Asian Affairs* 31, no. 4 (2012): 24.
77. Abdul Hamid Ahmed Fauzi, 'Religion, Secularism and the State in Southeast Asia', in *Thinking International Relations Differently*, ed. Arlene B. Tickner and David L. Blaney (Abingdon: Routledge, 2012), 255.
78. ASEAN, 'The ASEAN Charter', 2007, accessed 13.12.2015, http://www.asean.org/images/2015/October/Charter-of-the-ASEAN-Singapore-20-November-2007/7%20ASEAN%20CHARTER%20rev.2%20update%20on%2002%20Oct15%20IJP.pdf.
79. Vernon Hewitt, *The New International Politics of South Asia* (Manchester: Manchester University Press, 1997), 3.
80. Vedi Hadiz, 'Indonesian Political Islam: Capitalist Development and the Legacies of the Cold War', *Journal of Current Southeast Asian Affairs* 30, no. 1 (2011): 4.
81. Ahmed Fauzi, 'Religion, Secularism and the State in Southeast Asia', 266.
82. Ibid., 255.
83. Delfolie, 'Malaysian Extroversion towards the Muslim World', 5.
84. Ibid., 7.
85. Ibid., 17.
86. Farish Noor, 'The Malaysian General Elections of 2013: The Last Attempt at Secular-inclusive Nation-building', *Journal of Current Southeast Asian Affairs* 32, no. 2 (2013): 93.
87. Joseph Chinyong Liow, *Piety and Politics: Islamism in Contemporary Malaysia* (Oxford: Oxford University Press, 2009), 15.
88. Ibid., 16.
89. Linda Quayle, *Southeast Asia and the English School of International Relations: A Region-Theory Dialogue* (Basingstoke: Palgrave Macmillan, 2013), 27.
90. Ibid., 82.
91. Noor, 'The Malaysian General Elections of 2013', 91.
92. Quayle, *Southeast Asia and the English School of International Relations*, 118.
93. Ibid., 119.
94. Hadiz, 'Indonesian Political Islam', 5.
95. Sulastri Osman, 'Jemaah Islamiyah: Of Kin and Kind', *Journal of Current Southeast Asian Affairs* 29, no. 2 (2010): 159.
96. Ibid., 160.
97. Hadiz, 'Indonesian Political Islam', 9–11.
98. Ahmed Fauzi, 'Religion, Secularism and the State in Southeast Asia', 258–59.
99. Ibid., 260.
100. Ibid., 260.
101. Hadiz, 'Indonesian Political Islam', 27.
102. Liow, *Piety and Politics*, ix.
103. Ahmed Fauzi, 'Religion, Secularism and the State in Southeast Asia', 269.
104. Piscatori, *Islam in a World of Nation-States*, 69–71.
105. Ibid., 101

106. Nazih Ayubi, *Political Islam: Religion and Politics in the Arab World* (London: Routledge, 1991), 122–33.

107. Faiz Sheikh, 'Two Sides of the Same Coin? The Muslim Umma and the European Union', *Politics, Religion and Ideology* 14, no. 3 (2014): 455.

108. Mitchell Dean, *Governing Societies: Political Perspectives on Domestic and International Rule* (Berkshire: Open University Press, 2007), 5.

109. Boutros Boutros-Ghali, 'An Agenda for Peace: Preventive Diplomacy, Peacemaking and Peace-keeping', 1992, accessed 7.5.13, http://www.unrol.org/files/A_47_277.pdf.

110. Mandaville, *Transnational Muslim Politics*, 2.

111. Assis Malaquias, 'Reformulating International Relations Theory: African Insights and Challenges', in *Africa's Challenge to International Relations Theory*, ed. Kevin Dunn and Timothy Shaw (Basingstoke: Palgrave Macmillan, 2001), 12.

112. Jim George, *Discourses of Global Politics: A Critical (Re) Introduction to International Relations* (Boulder: Lynne Rienner, 1994), 42.

113. Ibid., 201.

114. Ibid., 191–216.

115. Malaquias, 'Reformulating International Relations Theory', 12.

116. George, *Discourses of Global Politics*, 201.

117. Kayaoglu, 'Westphalian Eurocentrism in International Relations Theory', 193.

118. Ibid., 195.

119. Mandaville, *Global Political Islam*, 7.

120. Michael Doyle, 'Liberalism and World Politics', *American Political Science Review* 80, no. 4 (1986): 1152.

121. Maureen Ramsay, *What's Wrong with Liberalism? A Radical Critique of Liberal Political Philosophy* (London: Continuum, 2004), 1.

122. Hamid Hadji Haidar, *Liberalism and Islam: Practical Reconciliation Between the Liberal State and Shiite Muslims* (New York: Palgrave Macmillan, 2008), 7; Ramsay, *What's Wrong with Liberalism?*, 1.

123. Doyle, 'Liberalism and World Politics', 1151.

124. Josef van Ess, *The Flowering of Muslim Theology* (London: Harvard University Press, 2006), 1.

125. Fiona Adamson, 'Global Liberalism versus Political Islam: Competing Ideological Frameworks in International Politics', *International Studies Review* 7, no. 4 (2005): 548.

126. David Chandler, 'Critiquing Liberal Cosmopolitanism? The Limits of the Biopolitical Approach', *International Political Sociology* 3, no. 1 (2009): 62.

127. Labeeb, 'Theory of International Relations in Islam', 72.

128. Ramsay, *What's Wrong with Liberalism?*

129. John Stuart Mill, 'On Liberty', in *Modern Political Thought: Readings From Machiavelli to Nietzsche*, ed. David Wootton (Cambridge: Hackett, 1996), 614.

130. Isaiah Berlin, *Four Essays on Liberty* (Oxford: Oxford University Press, 1969), 132–33.

131. Haidar, *Liberalism and Islam*, 21.

132. Harman and Brown, 'In from the Margins?', 70.

133. Political Islam is heavily analysed in security studies, particularly on the Horn of Africa. See for example James Gow, Funmi Olonisakin, and Ernst Dijxhoorn, eds., *Militancy and Violence in West Africa: Religion, Politics and Radicalisation* (London: Routledge, 2013).

Chapter Four

A Framework for Studying Religion in International Relations

Turner tells us that it is contemporary living, rather than theories, that pose a threat to religion. It is Tina Turner and Coca-Cola that will bring about the corruption of faith, rather than 'rational arguments and rational inspection of presuppositions and the understanding of Western secularism'.[1] But my father is a big fan of Tina Turner and is very much still a Muslim (with a beard and everything). The contemporary world with its shortening of time and space has not, as per theories of secularism, reduced the importance of religion in the modern world.[2] The binaries that we rely on to distinguish between the '(post)modern' world, represented here by Tina Turner and Coca-Cola, and the 'old world' of religion, which in reference to Islam means headscarves, violence (as if 'modern' peoples did not commit violence) and beards (unless you are not my dad and are in fact a fashionable young man in thick-rimmed spectacles and a flannel shirt). Talal Asad challenges us to discard such binaries:

> What politics are promoted by the notion that the world is *not* divided into modern and nonmodern, into West and non-West? What practical options are opened up or closed by the notion that the world has *no* significant binary features, that it is, on the contrary, divided into overlapping, fragmented cultures, hybrid selves, continuously dissolving and emerging social states?[3]

Asad's challenge is what I try to address in this chapter, developing a conceptual framework which will be employed to study political Islam and IR. This framework takes two positions which are otherwise binary opposites, Islam with its claims to universalism, and poststructuralism with its rejection of such universalism, and shows the *similarities* between these positions. The similarities, as we will see, rest in their shared critique of IR and its foundations of political modernity. The exploration of Islamic/poststructuralist synthesis will also lead me to address the place of religion in the study of IR, presenting a way in which to study political Islam specifically, and religion more generally, in the discipline.

Briefly, by way of summary, I have outlined the position of this study as second-order IR theorising. To make conceptual space for my endeavour I will be engaging with poststructuralism, influenced by the work of Foucault.[4] I will argue that Islam and poststructuralism converge in the critique of IR, but diverge in the construction of alternatives, before moving on to arguing the reasons for studying religion in IR, opening another necessary space with regards to the secularism of the discipline. After creating this conceptual space, I will expand on the method used to unpack concepts into this newly created space, specifically, the use of constructivism to distinguish Islam-as-politics from Islam-as-faith. Finally, I will outline some methodological concerns deriving from the problems in defining 'Islam', and Edward Said's warning against Orientalism. In this final section I will explain and define the limitations of the concepts used throughout the book.

Previously I have outlined the overarching aim of this book as an analysis of IR theory and the problems that this theory presents in the face of Islam's conception of politics in the international sphere, and vice versa. I am using theory as my object of study, rather than using theory as a tool to make empirical data its object of study.

My method roots the book firmly in second-order meta-theorising;[5] as such, I will be problematising the epistemological groundings of various IR theories. Second-order theorising requires a certain level of abstraction. With regards to the term 'Islam', I do not use the term in an *entirely* abstract sense; rather, 'Islam' refers to Sunni orthodoxy, which has most predominately interacted with contemporary political structures in the MENA (Iran withstanding), sub-Saharan Africa and Southeast Asia.

The analysis of epistemology, the nature of knowledge, might also be categorised as critical theory, in the way Robert Cox defined it in 1981. For Cox, critical theory 'is critical in the sense that it stands apart from the prevailing order of the world and asks how that order came about'.[6] In Cox's mould of critical theory I attempt to challenge and broaden the research agenda of IR, allowing us to pose new questions and thus pave the way to new and different first-order work. As Wendt summarises, the most important contribution of second-order questions is the way in which, 'making explicit and critiquing the foundational assumptions that structure research agendas they [second-order questions] may free up first order theorists to ask more questions than they have previously'.[7]

If a conceptual framework defines and outlines the ontological and epistemological positions of a study, and the methodology explains how a study relates to and interacts with its object of inquiry, then the two are analogous in this study. The ways in which this research might place itself in disciplinary terms is a continuing question for me. My study is not exclusively IR theory; I draw as much on political philosophy and theology as I do on IR scholarship. It is not an area study; there is no interest in incorporating non-Western social constructs into pre-established frames of reference.[8] Once more turning to Wendt, we can note what he describes as the 'insider/outsider dichotomy'. Diagnosing this dichotomy is a holdover of a positivist legacy; it is the idea that outsiders explain while insiders understand, and the purpose of science, and the purpose of social science, is to explain. IR may be a social science, but does that mean that studies which hope to *understand* are not important in IR? Wendt argues that there is a place for both in the discipline; insider/outsider explanations often deal with different questions, but it is not the case that there are *always* two stories to tell. Depending on the question being asked, one account will make more sense than the other. In the case of Islam in IR scholarship, I have argued that the existing treatments do not understand Islam, and religion in general, and therefore their accounts do not always hold up to scrutiny on these terms. I will explicitly explain why that is so, by attempting to *understand* the faith as it relates to believers, and thus explain more rigorously Islam's place in the discipline of IR.

EPISTEMOLOGICAL FOUNDATIONS

To allow Islam, and other religions, to be accounted for in IR, some conceptual space needs to be opened up for such alternative ideas to be fully articulated and so scrutinised. Addressing the concern that currently political Islam is too often defined by what does not, rather than what it may stand for,[9] I will argue here that the dominant epistemology of the Enlightenment, as transmitted to the present day through concepts of political modernity, is one of the impediments to the failure of political Islam to articulate a theory of IR. Of equal concern in this regard is the failure of Islam to come to terms with the realities of power in the modern world, with some Islamists looking to emulate a system of international politics last operationalized from the medieval period to the early nineteenth century.[10] Such reverence to a 'golden age of Islam' leaves Muslims in positions of power confused as to how that 'ideal' can in any way come to be in the world of nation-states. Even after the successful elections of two (three) Islamist governments in Tunisia and Egypt (and the Gaza Strip), the efficacy of Islamism is hotly debated. From the success story of an exiled and persecuted En-Nahda being voted into government, to the failure of the Muslim Brotherhood in Egypt to carry out even a quarter of its term in office before its overthrow, to Hamas abandoning the establishment of an Islamic state after coming to power, the potential for political Islam to be the next 'spent ideology', following Communism before it, is a question that looms over Islamism long after Olivier Roy's proclaimed *Failure of Political Islam*.[11]

I will focus on IR theory and opening the conceptual space for narratives not tied to the Enlightenment to be expanded upon, an Islamic narrative of IR being just one of such alternate voices. This is not to say that these alternative voices are any more valid or authentic than current theory. Indeed, 'we must be extremely wary of sliding from references to new possibilities of thinking, acting, and being to a *positive* evaluation of such possibilities'.[12] But unless these voices have the space to develop, their worth can never truly be evaluated, leading to arguments defined by what they are opposed to, rather than by what they support.

The point of departure regarding the epistemology of this study then, will be Foucault. Foucault's work, as I will show later in the chapter, has informed an already very successful analytical framework which is heavily related to the topics of this book, namely, Said's Orientalism. Referring to 'truth' as a goal, perhaps *the* goal of knowledge, Foucault elucidates his perspective:

> In societies like ours, the 'political economy' of truth is characterised by five important traits. 'Truth' is centred on the form of scientific discourse and the institutions which produce it; it is subject to constant economic and political incitement (the demand for truth, as much for economic production as for political power); it is the object, under diverse forms, of immense diffusion and consumption (circulating through apparatuses of education and information whose extent is relatively broad in the social body, not withstanding certain strict limitations); it is produced and transmitted under the control, dominant if not exclusive, of a few great political and economic apparatuses (university, army, writing, media); lastly, it is the issue of a whole political debate and social confrontation ('ideological' struggles).[13]

What Foucault is getting at here is the fact that much of what is considered 'truth' is knowledge that has particular motives behind it; his examples are the quest for political power, truth as a commodity, truth produced or legitimised through certain institutions, and finally truth as ideologically contested. Essentially, Foucault rejects, in the broadly poststructuralist tradition, the idea of some totalising or universal narrative of knowledge.[14] There are, following from this, culturally specific truths, not *a* truth. For Friedrich Nietzsche, whose ideas Foucault used extensively, the nature of human experience is always changing and evolving, and relying on truth as a fixed quantity is fallacious.[15] Where Nietzsche's insight reminds us of the temporal relativity of truth and knowledge, 'Foucault emphasized the local character of critique'.[16] All of this is not to claim emphatically on Foucault's behalf that an objective truth is not possible. It is the ambiguity here between objective truth and anti-foundationalism that is one of the reasons some might resist classifying Foucault as a poststructuralist. For my purposes however, Foucault is the route taken into the debates over the status of knowledge production; it is his focus on anti-foundationalism and his emphasis on excavating 'subjugated knowledges', that is, 'historical contents that have been buried or masked in functional coherences or formal systemizations',[17] which aligns Foucault with poststructuralism for my purposes. Different aspects of Foucault's ideas, taken in different contexts, may well conflict with the poststructural label used here, and such ambiguity betrays the limitations of labels and categorisations and indeed, can be attributed to the opaque nature of Foucault's body of work. As Foucault leads me to poststructuralism, which itself is an ambiguous term, I will next spend some time defining that concept.

A Note on Terminology

Nicholas Rengger jests that '[p]ostmodernism is one of those words that has a tendency to reduce sensible people to a mad scramble for the nearest and deadliest instrument of destruction that they can find'.[18] The same, presumably, can be said for the term poststructuralism, which is employed in this research. There is some ambiguity between the terms postmodernism, poststructuralism and more besides. I will here briefly try to clear up some of the confusion with these terms; I proceed to use those terms in this and following chapters.

Turner makes the distinction between postmodern political theory and the 'postmodern condition' or 'postmodernity'. He writes that '[b]y . . . [postmodernism], we should mean the philosophical critique of grand narratives, and by . . . [postmodernity], we should mean the postmodern social condition'.[19] This social condition is defined as the effects of 'information technologies, globalization, fragmentation of lifestyles, hyper-consumerism, deregulation of financial markets and public utilities, the obsolescence of the nation-state and social experimentation with the traditional life-course'.[20] The intellectual resistance to postmodernism can often derive from the misunderstanding that postmodern political theory is somehow linked to, or accentuates, the postmodern condition. Even when the distinction between postmodern political theory and the postmodern condition is acknowledged, scepticism about postmodernism might also derive from the belief that 'the claim that the collapse of representation . . . [has] left us only with the realization that our categories are merely infinitely different and more or less preferable, never better or worse'.[21] Unlike this misconception, postmodern political theories do not necessitate a rejection of 'rational' thinking or Enlightenment values, but rather attempts to remove any universal grounding to that reason.

Rengger speaks of Richard Rorty's position in exemplifying the above assertion: 'For Rorty, therefore, there is nothing wrong with believing in the hopes of the Enlightenment since our [European] societies are largely built on these hopes; we simply do not need a transcendental grounding for them'.[22]

In Turner's analysis, poststructuralism would appear to be a synonym for postmodernism, and both are distinct from the postmodern condition. Distinct from Turner's usage, I use the term poststructuralism in the way Jim George and David Campbell use the term, as challenging 'the foundationalism and essentialism of post-Enlightenment scientific philosophy, [and] its universalist presuppositions about modern rational man [and woman]'.[23] In this way, I am differentiating poststructuralism and postmodernism in that the former is an ontological statement about the indeterminacy of knowledge (resembling Foucault's position outlined earlier), while the latter refers to the particular set of circumstances in the late twentieth century that gave rise to the current scepticism of meta-narratives (resembling the tradition of Jean-Francois Lyotard's use of the term postmodern).[24] Simplified another way, poststructuralism would maintain that humanity *has not and will not* find a universal and objective standpoint from which to judge actions, while postmodernism would say that humanity is currently unable to lean on such a universal and objective standpoint *because of late-twentieth-century changes in society*. While both terms may come to the same 'end point', the former is an ontological and meta-theoretical statement, while the latter is linked to a specific historical narrative. I arrive at that same end point through the former position, poststructuralism, which in turn is arrived at, however imperfectly, through the ideas of Foucault, and poststructuralism and postmodernism will continue to be differentiated throughout the remainder of this book.

It needs noting here that in making an ontological statement about the indeterminacy of knowledge, poststructuralism does not embrace an alternative ontology; to do so would represent a truth claim the likes of with it is inherently uncomfortable with. Rather, it leaves its ontological position ambiguous, maximising the scope for geographical and temporal specific truth claims. As such, I will use the term 'poststructural perspective on ontology' in place of where one might expect the phrase 'poststructural ontology', to highlight this ambiguity.

Connecting a poststructuralist epistemology to IR is related to the Enlightenment and political modernity, as I alluded to earlier. In one understanding, political modernity 'is understood in developmental terms, as a progression—from the mythical to the scientific, from the barbaric to the rational/democratic, from the constrained, ordered subject to the utilitarian individual "free to choose"'.[25] Here, the idea that there is but one end point of knowledge and understanding of politics, represented on a scale with mystics and barbarians on the one hand and democratic scientists on the other, proves problematic. My argument is not 'why can there not be mystics and barbarians in the contemporary age', but rather 'why must modernity be defined by *only* democratic scientists?' The connection between political modernity and the Enlightenment is explained by John Gray, who comments that 'Western societies are governed by the belief that modernity is a single condition, everywhere the same and always benign . . . Being modern means realising *our* values—the values of the Enlightenment, as we like to think of them'.[26] While unfairly brushing all IR paradigms with a systemic brush, François Debrix argues that IR is governed by 'the idea and belief that there is or must be one discourse, one modality of knowledge, and one practice of the global and the political to which "we" all participate'.[27] This line of reason is shown in practice when one looks at the legacy of Westphalia as it relates to the non-European world, as I outlined in the previous chapter. Poststructuralist epistemology helps to resolve the dilemma regarding mystic barbarians and scientific democrats; the emphasis on challenging hitherto truths creates exactly the space needed to be able to take Islam on its own terms in IR, where it is currently constrained by these 'truths', to try to articulate itself in the mould of scientific democrats or not at all.

ISLAM, POSTCOLONIALISM AND MODERNITY

The discourse of political Islam is also preoccupied with the Enlightenment and modernity. The quintessential Islamic reformer, Jamal al-Din al-Afghani, talks of science and civilisational progress as tied to achieving modernity. Unlike Enlightenment rationality, however, this modernity is not a recreation of some European model. For him, science is not bound to nations, so the idea of 'Muslim' or 'European' science is a fallacy.[28] This position is reflected in al-Afghani's student Muhammed Abduh, who believed the European history of Enlightenment is an Islamic destiny.[29] Such a perspective, even if implicitly critical of the Enlightenment, sees the solution to Islam's place in the world as *more* Enlightenment.[30] I will now turn to consider two more Muslim perspectives on modernity which closer adhere to poststructuralist epistemology as has been defined in the previous section.

Founder of the Muslim Brotherhood, Hasan al-Banna, claimed that the first and foremost reason for the creation of the brotherhood was the failure of the Western way of life. He explains that

> The Western way of life—bounded in effect on practical and technical knowledge, discovery, invention, and the flooding of world markets with mechanical products—has remained incapable of offering to men's minds a flicker of light, a ray of hope, a grain of faith, or of providing anxious persons the smallest path towards rest and tranquillity.[31]

Al-Banna here emphasises the technical and scientific nature of this 'Western way of life'. The relation these elements have with day-to-day life is not my focus, as it was for al-Banna. Instead, what I would call attention to in al-Banna's critique is the presence of the same methods with which poststructuralism critiques the Enlightenment sciences as having bounded notions of rationality. A final voice to consider in this brief appraisal of Muslim positions regarding the Enlightenment is Aziz al-Azmeh.

Al-Azmeh explains that Islamic political thought should not be thought of as analogous to modern political thought. Islamic political theory, according to al-Azmeh, 'is not so much a coherent, deliberate and disciplined body of investigation and enquiry concerning a well defined and delimited topic, but is rather an assemble of statements on topics political, statements dispersed in various discursive locations'.[32] Here again the suitability and power in using a poststructural epistemology becomes apparent, as this epistemology proceeds from a view that the Enlightenment provided an 'oppressive straitjacket'[33] to social science—that which could not be counted, measured or in essence 'reduced to numbers' becomes at best suspect but at worst an illusion. Islamic political theory, as outlined by al-Azmeh, falls outside of the 'straitjacket' of the Enlightenment, and it is little wonder that Islamic ideas have such a difficult time unpacking their concepts in IR. Adopting a poststructural epistemology helps legitimise use of theological arguments, for example, in a discussion of IR theory. However, there is more than one way to engage with the themes of modernity and marginalism. Postcolonialism represents an existing body of literature upon which to draw which is distinct yet related to poststructuralism, as I will now explore.

Postcolonial Critiques of Modernity

Gurminder Bhambra attempts to summarise postcolonial approaches as '[working] to challenge dominant narratives and to reconfigure them to provide more adequate categories of analysis, where adequacy is measured in terms of increasing inclusivity'.[34] The similarity with my broad approach as outlined thus far is more than a passing one, as Dipesh Chakrabarty comments:

> [I]t would be wrong to think of postcolonial critiques of historicism (or of the political) as simply deriving from critiques already elaborated by postmodern and poststructuralist thinkers of the West. In fact, to think this way would itself be to practice historicism, for such a thought would merely repeat the temporal structure of the statement, 'first in the West, and then elsewhere'.[35]

Historicism here stands in for the Enlightenment rationalism and developmentalism defined previously. Postcolonial studies also attempt to engage with dominant political forms linked to political modernity and, like poststructuralism, recognise many aspects of that modernity as being rooted in a European heritage, thereby opening the door to questions of universalism. Turning once more to Chakrabarty for a summary of the overlap between postcolonial and poststructural engagements with modernity:

> European thought is at once both indispensable and inadequate in helping us to think through the experiences of political modernity in non-Western nations, and provincializing Europe becomes the task of exploring how this thought—which is not everybody's heritage and which affect us all—may be renewed from and for the margins.[36]

Furthermore, while I am focused on Islam's place in IR, certainly an endeavour on the 'margins', as Chakrabarty explains it, I am concerned more broadly with religion's place in IR. The exploration of religion's place in IR shares much of the critique of postcolonialism, as seen briefly here, but does not share the postcolonial context that the study of Islam might do. Put another way, the (meta-theoretical) study of religion in IR is on the margin of the discipline, but not the same margin that Chakrabarty's postcolonialism is coming from, even while both might engage with the same concept of secularism, for example. As such, I have come to the critique of Enlightenment rationalism in IR via poststructuralism, and it is poststructuralism that supplies the specific meanings to the terms used, and commits me to a certain ontological perspective. Acknowledging the above, however, does not mean that I cannot utilise postcolonial studies at all. Rather, the lines between postcolonial studies and poststructuralism can be blurred further by turning to the work of Said.

Said developed an analytical framework which pertains to the subjects I have been grappling with. That framework was an analysis of various representational practices which he dubbed 'Orientalism', and the remainder of this section will assess the contribution Said's work will make to the framework of this book. Said's work sits at the boundary of postcolonial and poststructural studies, and indeed Said also arrived at poststructuralism via Foucault, and uses those concepts in his work. Said's concept of Orientalism critiqued knowledge production on the 'Orient' as being tied to the needs and presuppositions of those who studied it in the West. One of his responses to this was to highlight how categories like 'East' and 'West' are deficient analytically; they draw upon essentialist, racist stereotypes to give them meaning. However, Said drew significant criticism about how, when trying to remove the ontological categories of 'East' and 'West', he unwittingly relied on and reinforced these categories.[37] Aijaz Ahmed summarises this criticism when he states that 'Said quite justifiably accuses the Orientalist for essentialising the Orient, but his own processes of essentialising "the West" are equally remarkable'.[38] Ahmed identifies different and irreconcilable uses of the term Orientalism in Said's work. In one reading, Orientalism is synonymous with colonialism. In a second reading, Orientalism is perhaps only a by-product of colonialism. In a third reading, Orientalism is a trans-historical process that is apparent even in ancient Greek stories.[39] Hobson puts the problems with Said's use of Orientalism down to the reductivist way in which Said uses the term: 'the widely-used Saidian conception of Orientalism has to perform a great deal of leg-movement beneath the waterline in order to keep it afloat'.[40]

In an attempt to address these criticisms of Said's Orientalism, Hobson presents a framework for understanding Orientalism which separates various *types* of the phenomenon. To avoid the reductivism in Said's usage, I will employ the adapted framework of Hobson, outlined below.

Whereas Orientalism bundled together various concepts, Hobson separates these into (1) racism; (2) the standard of civilisation; (3) agency; (4) imperialism; and (5) Western triumphalism. For Hobson, racism is a contingent feature of Orientalism, which interacts with the other factors to influence the pro- or anti-imperialist sentiments of the West. Hobson's conception of Orientalism, like Said's, places the 'standard of civilisation' as a central measure and justification of the Western self, on the Eastern other. On the question of agency, unlike Said who conceptualised the West as monopolising all agency, Hobson sees agency as a contingent part of Orientalism; the West is always the pioneer, but the East can imitate with low to high levels of agency. Whereas Said saw Orientalism as synonymous with imperialism, Hobson differentiates a type of Eurocentrism that sees non-Western societies emulating the path that the West pioneered but *that path only*. The West simply got there first. Finally, regarding Western triumphalism, again Hobson distinguishes between triumphalism in the service of imperialism and against it.[41]

What Hobson achieves is a differentiation of the constitutive elements of Orientalism, addressing all of the weaknesses of Said's original. Hobson's non-reductive Orientalism need not always imply racism; Eurocentric institutionalism would claim that all humans, from any race or society, can 'progress' into civilisation given the right institutions (modelled after European institutions).[42] Likewise, non-reductive Orientalism does not always imply that the East has no agency as when combined with racism; ideas of the 'yellow peril' imply high levels of agency, but racism allows for the distinction between progressive and regressive or barbaric agency.[43] Eurocentrism and triumphalism, combined with another type of racism, would see non-reductive Orientalism not necessarily synonymous with imperialism; a fear of racial-contamination might lead to a fear of any interaction between 'East' and 'West'.[44]

While Hobson continues at length to outline and define the nuances of his non-reductive Orientalism,[45] it is sufficient to point out here that in the remainder of this book I will use 'Orientalism' as a catch-all term for all the different but overlapping concepts of *agency, imperialism, Western triumphalism*, and *the standard of civilisation*. Where appropriate I will differentiate what *type* of Orientalism is being employed in reference to the brief summary presented here. One final note on Orientalism is to clarify the usage of the terms 'East' and 'West'. Given the fact that I am engaged in a critique of the distinction between East and West, it may seem objectionable to continue to use these terms. I will turn to Hobson one last time to clarify the usage of these terms:

> I deploy these terms because they are fundamental to the lexicon of Eurocentrism/racism and that, as such, what matters is not the geographical dimension but the ideational. That is, within Eurocentrism and scientific racism, East and West are constructs that are differentiated not by geography but either by a rationality/civilizational divide or a rationality/racial divide.[46]

That being so, in the remainder of the book I will make use of inverted commas to talk of 'East' and 'West', where possible, to remind us that these terms are contingent on how we choose to construct them. For example, one can see the shores of Spain from Morocco, yet one is in the 'West' and the other the 'East'.

Poststructuralism and Islam: A Shared Agenda?

The use of poststructuralism is not without its limitations. Turner is overtly critical of the capacity of such an epistemology to help study the Middle East. He states that '[poststructural] epistemologies do not promise an alternative orthodoxy and reject the possibility of 'true' descriptions of the 'real' world. This epistemological scepticism does not lead itself either to political action or to the development of alternative frameworks'.[47] It is true that being critical of the concept of truth can lead one to question whether a reformulated notion of Islam in IR is any more a representation of the 'truth' as the current take on Islam and religion in IR. Moreover, Turner here is foreshadowing the discussion in Part III, *Pluralism or Polarisation,* about the compatibility of Islam's call to truth (the *shahada* being an exemplar of this truth), and the scepticism inherent in poststructural analysis.

I will first address the point concerning the perceived inability for poststructural analysis to provide alternative understandings. While Turner sees such a paradox as epistemological scepticism, he is perhaps too involved in meta-theoretical pursuits; there is ample cause to attempt a reformulation of Islam in IR as first-order IR theorists try to analyse and account for increasingly Islamised politics in North Africa and the continuing Islamic politics of the Persian Gulf region, for example. Turner is correct to highlight the problem here, but it cannot become an insurmountable one due to scepticism alone; as Wendt explains, '[h]aving once explicated and reformulated such assumptions, however, the trick is then to move the discussion off of the level of meta-theory and onto the task of constructing substantive arguments about world politics'.[48] To Turner's second point concerning the compatibility of a religious truth and poststructural analysis, that is not a question I will address in this chapter. Rather, taking a cue from the incongruity presented by the two approaches, I will utilise a two-stage analysis. The first stage, which is embarked on in this chapter, exploits the symbiosis in the critique of IR offered by both Islamic and poststructural sources. The second stage will explore the divergence between Islam and poststructuralism, attempting to reconcile them. Having outlined the epistemological foundations of the book, and shown how Islamic perspectives on modernity can represent different aspects of, and are congruous with certain poststructural (and postcolonial) debates on what constitutes modernity, I will move on to demonstrate the first stage of my analysis with a brief scrutiny of the place of religion in IR.

THE STUDY OF RELIGION IN IR

Religion, whether articulated as fundamentalism or purely as a marker of difference, is re-emerging as a prominent factor in international conflict. In interpreting the apparent 'return' of religion to IR, 'it was Huntington's clash thesis that carried the day in the 1990s by offering a way of making sense of the apparent return of religion albeit within an all-too-familiar Cold War "us vs. them" framework'.[49] As seen in the literature on IR in the MENA in the previous chapter, Islam is a factor that can animate some actors in the region in ways not accounted for by subsuming religion into socio-economic factors, or some generic 'cultural' phenomenon. To analyse the place of religion in IR I will be availing myself of the insights of postsecularism. Postsecularism has both a descriptive and innovative definition. As a descriptive term, postsecularism 'has been used to explain the return or resilience of religious traditions in modern life'.[50] As an innovative term, postsecularism is 'a form of radical theorising and critique prompted by the idea that values such as democracy, freedom, equality, inclusion and justice may not necessarily be best pursued within an exclusively immanent secular framework'.[51] For me, then, it is not democracy, freedom, equality and inclusion which I am exploring outside of secular frames of reference. Rather, it is political modernity which might have a distinctly 'Islamic' IR, which I will explore in this book. Postsecularism is not a prominent theme in IR due to the myths of its beginnings, that is, the idea spawned by Westphalia that 'cultural and religious pluralism cannot have a public dimension, as this would clash with the very possibility of international order'.[52]

To summarise the preceding chapter's assessment of the IR of various Muslim majority regions, Elizabeth Hurd points out that

> [T]he power of this religious resurgence in world politics does not fit into existing categories of thought in academic international relations. Conventional understandings of international relations, focused on material capabilities and strategic interaction, exclude from the start the possibility that religion could be a fundamental organizing force in the international system.[53]

Hurd's study is fascinating, revealing two distinct stands of secularism that contribute to IR's presumed 'neutrality': The first is laicism, '[presenting] itself as having risen above the messy debate over religion and politics, standing over and outside the melee in a neutral space of its own creation'.[54] The second is referred to as Judeo-Christian secularism, through which secularism becomes an extension of religious tradition, exclusively the Jewish and Christian religions.[55] Both of these varieties of secularism are, for Hurd, present in IR; they are 'part of the cultural and normative basis of international relations theory . . . [they] are part of the ontological and epistemological foundation of the discipline'.[56] Both versions of secularism problematise the place of Islam in IR while at the same time ignoring the way that the Judeo-Christian norms underlay that very notion of secularism or neutrality. She states that '[i]n this [Judeo-Christian] evaluative stance, political Islam is the manifestation of a unique, culturally rooted and irrational commingling of religion and politics that is distinct from the Judeo-Christian separationist approach to religion and state'.[57] Erin Wilson's study of Christianity in the United States also supports the argument that in the Judeo-Christian tradition certain aspects of religion are rendered unproblematic for 'secular' society. Wilson's example is a conception of history that is eschatological, that is, 'that singular events are significant and suggest a gradual progression towards a penultimate historical endpoint, an approach associated with various strands of the Christian tradition'.[58] Working in synthesis with the obfuscation of religion's enduring influence in secular society and politics, is the notion that religion is irrational. For some it can be religion in general that is irrational, as Wilson points out,[59] while for others it is Islam specifically which is uniquely irrational, arguments which Mavelli critiques Weber for making: 'Weber thus replaces the seemingly irredeemable lost dualism God/ man with that between "Western/European subject" and "non-Western subject", with the latter crucially epitomized by the Muslim other'.[60]

Here Hobson's non-reductive Orientalism can label Judeo-Christian secularism as the pioneering agency of the West, and while political Islam possesses agency enough to refuse that particular mould, its agency is regressive and less enlightened than the aforementioned 'Western' position. In engaging with postsecularism I am complementing my previous scepticism of political modernity. As Joseph Camilleri points out of postsecularism, 'it is not simply secularism that is in question but the larger intellectual framework of "modernity" itself, of which secularism is a part'.[61] In attempting to renegotiate the place of religion in IR it is necessary to be reflexive and recognise that an unquestioned acceptance of a secular separation between politics and religion is a source of much of the difficulty in accounting for Islam on its own terms in IR.

Islam as it relates to politics, that is, political Islam, is for Hurd 'a modern language of politics that challenges, sometimes works outside of, and (occasionally) overturns fundamental assumptions about religion and politics that are embedded in the forms of Western secularism that emerged out of Latin Christendom'.[62] Mohammed Arkoun pre-empted Hurd's assessment of the modern secular space as a reformulation of medieval Christian ideas, and goes so far as to refer to modern day ideologies 'secular religions'.[63] Arkoun concludes that the relationship between Christianity and secularism means that the latter has common features with all religions (though that relationship cannot be asserted outside of the Abrahamic faiths). Specifically, both secular and religious society are built on order, it is therefore the nature of this order, the nature of power, which needs to be understood vis-à-vis Islam.[64] Beyond finding space in secularism, political Islam is poised to find space in IR; in a post-Communist era the implication of political Islam (and other 'alternative' frameworks such as feminism or humanism, for example) becoming part of how the international is conceived, is not impossible. That a space has presented itself for alternative theories to develop,[65] may go some way to explaining the resurgence of religion in IR, as Hurd sees it.

Beyond space for religion and Islam in IR, I will also briefly discuss the space for IR in Islamic studies. Tibi problematises the space Islamic studies affords to IR, and it is worth recounting his concerns here as they relate to the dearth of Muslim literature on this issue and add impetus to this study. Tibi highlights that 'Islamic studies are mostly dominated by disciplines other than the social sciences, not to mention international relations . . . which is almost absent from Islamic studies'.[66] Having made the space for Islam in IR, and before moving to the specific methods I will use to begin to coalesce an Islamic theory of IR, I will end by briefly dealing with Zubaida's assertion that Islam *should not* be a substantial factor in the study of the politics of the Muslim world.[67]

Zubaida problematises the place of Islam next to modernity much in the same way that Tibi does, and finds issue with many of the issues I have already discussed: Islamic history perceived as utopian by Muslims; the perception of a unitary Islamic politics; the trouble with speaking through religion to a secular 'Western' world.[68] It is frustrating for Zubaida to see analysis of the MENA so skewed by the above issues, and his solution is to trouble the very notion that Islam is a term with any meaning, considering the vast spatial and temporal differences in concepts that are lumped together as 'Islamic'. Instead, Zubaida identifies two main styles of politics in the Middle East, 'the modern politics of ideology and organization, and the universal politics of faction, kinship and patronage'.[69] Islam is not constitutive of either form of politics, but its language is used as a mask for both. Troubling the unitary nature of Islamic politics to such an extent as to remove it from the political realm is, perhaps, a way to escape the frustrating accounts of the MENA so prevalent in IR. However, Zubaida's move obfuscates the constitutive nature of religion on peoples. Zubaida's desire to remove religion from analysis is in fact *overcorrecting* when it comes to Islam and politics. It is possible to deny unitary treatments of Islam and politics and yet still recognise the constitutive role the many *Islams* of believers can have upon their behaviour.[70] What to take from Zubaida is the knowledge that attempting to grasp at fundamentals or universals applicable to all Muslims, everywhere, for all time, is always problematic. That is not to say that analytical endeavours in local or otherwise specific terms are invalid, and presents a methodological imperative for me to avoid invoking a 'universal' Islamic politics. As I have begun to talk of a more specific methodology, I will continue now with more on how Islam might unpack its concepts with regards to IR, followed by further methodological concerns and limitations.

UNPACKING POLITICAL ISLAM USING CONSTRUCTIVISM

Regarding the two-stage analysis of this book, I have outlined the critical tools necessary for the first stage, to make space for Islam in IR, but those same poststructural tools are complemented by constructivism in the second stage of the analysis. As has been noted briefly, and will be explored in later chapters, the synthesis between Islam and poststructuralism is problematic in the formation of 'alternative orthodoxies', and it is here that constructivism helps us. IR constructivism is a perspective that focuses on 'the content and sources of state interests and the social fabric of world politics'.[71] With an emphasis on social fabric, constructivism is a theory that seeks to give a greater place to ideas in IR. The theory, first articulated[72] in IR by Alexander Wendt, claims that rather than the structure of IR presumed by neo-realism, a structure beyond our control, vested in the nature of man or the security dilemma, IR is a social reality we make for ourselves. To presume that individuals can shape their surroundings with impunity leans too heavily towards the agency side of the agency/structure debate. A more nuanced understanding is offered in Wendt's *Social Theory of International Politics*, wherein it is explained that while individuals are capable of changing their social reality, that reality has already shaped the individual to some extent, and so the relationship is more cyclic than would first appear[73] (see point three, below). The basics of Wendt's theory make it distinct from other IR theorising for three reasons:

1. Constructivism emphasises the social aspect of existence; 'the role of shared ideas as an ideational structure constraining and shaping behaviour'.[74]
2. The theory gives ideas a role in constituting actors, not just regulating their behaviour.
3. Ideas and actors 'co-constitute and co-determine each other'. As alluded to earlier, '[s]tructures constitute actors in terms of their interests and identities, but structures are also produced, reproduced, and altered by the discursive practices of agents'.[75]

Accepting these points, nothing need be taken for granted in IR. Relating this to political Islam and the *umma*, for example, constructivism allows scholars of IR to not take the concept of the state as their unit of analysis, if political reality is constructed to that end.

Nickolas Onuf, another constructivist theorist, makes the claim that IR represents a bounded social reality:[76] that neo-realism, for example, holds *universal* explanatory power, falsely limiting the behaviour of actors; they become bounded by this universalism. That a universal and therefore ahistorical view of IR sees a bipolar world as 'the best of all possible worlds',[77] betrays the fact that the theory was heavily influenced by the time of its dominance during the Cold War.

In comparison to Onuf's constructivism, Jeffery Checkel sees constructivism not as a theory but as an approach to bridge the divide between 'mainstream' and poststructural IR theorists; thus, the constructivist's point of contention with mainstream theory is ontological, not epistemological.[78] The social aspect of life which Wendt emphasises has indeed broadened the contours of the discipline of IR. However, Checkel warns that it lacks as a theory of agency, often over-relying on structures and norms. As such, Checkel is less blunt in his appraisal of the place of ideas in IR. For him, 'the environment in which agents/states take action is social as well as material'.[79] Such a view acknowledges the material focus of realism but seeks to *supplement* it, rather than displace it. Checkel's approach, which builds upon Wendt's own desire to 'find a *via media* between positivism and interpretivism',[80] highlights a dualism which on the one hand refuses to accept that ideas are explained solely by material interest, but on the other hand asserts that one can know about the world through scientific enquiry.[81]

Whether one defines constructivism as an approach or a theory, Onuf would reject the dualism of Wendt and Checkel, and would like IR to move away from the idea of scientific endeavour; for him there can be no paradigm theories in the discipline. Base assumptions are something you have to be told in IR (in the case of realism, anarchy); they cannot be proven, as in the natural sciences. Onuf's hard-line constructivism sees 'no one world more real than others. None is ontologically privileged as the unique real world'.[82] Such an ontological position shares much with the poststructural position outlined above, and indeed Onuf relates his constructivism to the ends pursued in this book when he states that 'while it was claimed that anarchy is the distinctive condition to which the discipline responds, it is by no means clear that the Western state system is the only concrete instance of international relations available for study'.[83]

Onuf's position, representative of a 'harder' constructivism, which shares much with the poststructural position outlined earlier, also shares poststructuralism's weakness. Recalling Turner's critique of poststructuralism (which equally applies to hard constructivism), 'epistemological scepticism [of the real world] does not lead itself either to political action or to the development of alternative frameworks'.[84] As I explained earlier in the chapter, this tension will manifest itself as an incoherence between the assertion of faith by the Muslim and the scepticism of such assertions by poststructuralists, and will be dealt with later in the book. That being so, it is the dualism[85] of Wendt and Checkel which the I will use to give meaning to the term constructivism; in this way, constructivism is poised to act as a bridge between the ideational and the material. As Ronald Bleiker and Mark Chou put it, albeit when discussing Nietzsche and IR: 'Acknowledging an inevitable link between form and content is not to deny that facts exist in the real world. But it is to acknowledge that these facts only make sense through our practices of interpretation'.[86]

Constructivism has 'succeeded in broadening the theoretical contours of [international relations]',[87] allowing ideology and the realm of ideas to play more of a role in how one constructs and implements a world view. I argue that political Islam fails to keep up in this regard, and for this reason constructivism is uniquely placed to help me construct a concept of Islamic IR. Constructivism helps to blur the lines between different disciplines, sociology and IR in particular, helping also to penetrate the barriers between 'domestic' and 'international' levels of analysis. Here constructivism's role in ameliorating the divide between poststructuralism and 'mainstream' IR becomes apparent. Political Islam's rudimentary conception of the international sphere could thus capitalise on a constructivist approach to IR, helping it 'construct' a more comprehensive world view from its existing religiopolitical foundations. Having outlined how I will use constructivism in the framework of this book, as a bridge between the ideational aspects of poststructuralism and the more material aspects of dominant IR paradigms, the final part of the chapter will deal explicitly with some methodological problems and limitations.

Chapter 4
PROBLEMS AND LIMITATIONS

As I stressed earlier, I cannot claim to represent the views of the entire global Muslim population. The 'Islam' I refer to, unless stated otherwise, is derived from Sunni orthodoxy. Limiting this key term gives me a certain focus; my aim is to comment on IR theory, not make comments on theological positions. To talk about how the entirety of 'Islam' perceives the practise of IR would be a separate project; comparing Islamic notions of IR to 'Western' notions requires that I limit the use of these terms to make the project feasible. Other denominations of Islam will be used to illustrate points where appropriate; specifically, I will turn to Shi'a thought on politics and the state in particular in chapter 5.

Even within Sunni orthodoxy, I do not claim that there is a univocal body of opinion to draw upon; there is no single *shari'a* code, even in the four schools of Sunni orthodoxy, which constitutes some sort of 'canon' with regards to Sunni thought on politics. One of the fundamental differences between Sunni Islam and Roman Catholicism, for example, is that Sunni Islam has no 'church' structure or hierarchy of clergy. While papal decree might be observed to be the 'definitive' Catholic view on matters, no such authority exists in the Sunni Muslim world. Therefore, I will look at the jurisprudence of all four schools, where necessary, in an attempt to glean information about state conduct. One school of thought offering more on this subject than the others will not lessen the applicability of my findings; the four schools *together* are considered theologically orthodox; that some schools may not offer as much guidance on the criteria I am assessing does not diminish any credibility from these sources. Specifying Sunni orthodoxy as the definition of 'Islam' helps it be precise with religious sources. How these sources are interpreted by me immediately removes it from the Sunni orthodox position by a measure of some degree. In a sense my position becomes just one more Islam amongst many, and so boxing it into a denominational, or similar definitional category, would be counterproductive.

Similarly, when talking about 'IR' or indeed 'Western IR', I cannot hope to grapple with the disparate strands of theory that make up the discipline. Rather I am engaging with two dominant concepts in IR: that of the state, and liberal individualism.

A quick word on the method of deriving law in Sunni orthodoxy and its relation to the book: In Sunni orthodoxy, Islamic law derives from four sources, including the Qur'an, the word of God, and the *ahadith*, example of the Prophet Muhammed, *ijma'* (consensus) and *qiyas* (analogy).[88] *Qiyas*, the use of analogy, or applying reason is how jurisprudents, *faqih*, expanded on the specific matters covered in the Qur'an and *sunna*, to all aspects of life. This 'disciplined exercise of reason'[89] is known as *ijtihad*. However disciplined, this exercise of reason is very subjective, so, 'alongside this free, individual legislative activity [qiyas/ijtihad], which . . . produced an uncoordinated body of opinion, went another balancing and complementary movement of coordination and unification [ijma']'.[90] *Ijma'*, consensus, was formalised by ninth-century jurist al-Shafi'i as tool to balance the individualistic tendencies of *ijtihad*. Theorising on an Islamic state only crystallised in the early twentieth century with Rashid Rida and later the Muslim Brothers of Egypt, effectively modern-day attempts of *ijtihad* and reinterpretation of Islamic source texts. In this way, I am engaging not only with the Islamic source texts but also with the more contemporary interpretative scholarship on Islam and politics.

At this point I come up against a Saidian criticism which specifically relates to the methods outlined above. This criticism centres round the idea that reading into secondary sources temporally distinct from modern events always deals with ideals and abstractions, never more pertinent and historically relevant factors.[91] Said summarises this critique, claiming that 'abstractions about the Orient, particularly those based on texts representing a 'classical' Oriental civilization, are always preferable to direct evidence drawn from modern Oriental realities'.[92] While I am using classical texts to abstract on ideas ostensibly Islamic, as second-order theorising I am not making any substantial claim as to the applicability of these abstractions to the realities of Muslims. As stated earlier in the chapter, any such abstractions derived from these sources will be applicable at a philosophical and theoretical level. Only after such a position is shown to be tenable theoretically can those abstractions be compared to and integrated with the lives of Muslims and 'Oriental realities', though the desirability of doing so is far from certain. Going further, in a diverse range of countries from Tunisia to Egypt, to Saudi Arabia and Pakistan, the realities of many Muslim peoples is a call to an 'Islamic state' or 'Islamic politics', a concept of IR being part and parcel of any such politics; at the level of 'reality' people are reaching for a concept that is either missing or insufficiently articulated at that second, 'theoretical' level, which is where I hope to contribute.

Related to Said's criticism about timeless source texts is the problem of essentialism. Essentialism posits that there is an essential element to entities that 'determine[s] or limit[s] the possibilities of their social and political developments'.[93] Olivier Roy critically summarises the essentialist view of Islam as a closed, specific and timeless system that is 'the major obstacle prohibiting access to political modernity'.[94] However, Islam is an unsatisfactory term. It does not explain, for example, Saddam Hussein's decision to invade Kuwait, so there is more than an 'Islamic character' at work in the Middle East.[95] Equally, there is no 'West' with which to grapple; 'Western' normative authority can emanate from Australia just as easily as it can from Europe or the American continent. The plurality of theorising *within* this Western normative block is also underplayed in Islamist literature. Bobby

Sayyid's account of the War on Terror is a prime example of this. Sayyid states that '[t]he crusade on Islam(ism) demonstrates the failure of legitimacy, and the difficulties Western cultural practices and values have in trying to pass themselves off as universal and natural'.[96] Here Sayyid's use of the word crusade incorrectly lumps the entirety of 'Western' culture with the actions of Roman Catholics in the Middle Ages, giving that 'timeless quality' to the term that Roy criticises. Also, in claiming that Western cultural practices find no currency in Muslim countries, Sayyid also incorrectly depicts the two positions as zero-sum, all or nothing. While it is true that the struggle against the cultural dominance of the 'West' has found currency with the populations of many Muslim countries, this animosity is tempered by the fact that the governments in these countries still buy weapons and medicine from, and develop significant economic ties with 'Western' states.[97] Often things are far more complex than scholars of IR or Islamism may profess. One need not balk at the notion of 'Western' cultural notions when there is nothing intrinsic to many of these notions that prevent the practice of the religion of Islam.

CONCLUSIONS

In summary, I have explained in this chapter the framework of the book as consisting of a two-stage analysis. In the first stage, I will 'make space' in IR for the articulation of alternative, in this case religious, specifically Islamic, conceptions of IR. This space will be made by exploiting the synthesis between poststructural and Islamic critiques of the European/'Western' rootedness of the discipline. This rootedness has been argued to lie in the foundational ideas that spawned from the European Enlightenment.

Poststructuralism was defined broadly as a scepticism towards universalising narratives. There is considerable divergence on what the term poststructuralism means. However, I arrive at poststructuralism through Foucault, however imperfect that label is for him. For my purposes, then, poststructuralism is defined as distinct to postmodernism, the latter being tied to a historical moment of scepticism, the former an ontological statement about the nature of knowledge. The great limitation of poststructuralism for this book is that while there might be considerable similarity in the criticisms made of IR by poststructuralism and Islamic sources, they diverge considerably in the construction of alternative theories; Islam involves a call to truth (the *shahada*), and poststructuralism is sceptical towards such a position. I will explore in chapter 7 the way in which these two positions, sometimes diverging and sometimes converging, interact with each other.

If the first stage of analysis is concerned with the synthesis between Islam and poststructuralism, the second stage of the analysis concerns their divergence. In this second stage I will employ constructivism as a means to give agency to new notions of Islam-as-politics that might be created to fill the conceptual gap, which the first stage of analysis will open up in the discipline of IR. Again, the term constructivism is broad, and I overviewed briefly the advent of this mode of thought in IR, starting with Wendt. Given that this book is operating in the second-order or meta-theoretical level of analysis, it is appropriate to use constructivism; this approach also gives a prominent place to the world of ideas. Indeed, the review of constructivist study of the MENA identified those studies as coming closest to being able to account for Islam on its own terms, and so presents us the best opportunity moving forward. In addition, I highlighted the *way* which constructivism will be used; resonating with Checkel's usage of constructivism, I will use the theory as a bridge between the ideational world of poststructuralism and the more material world of the dominant IR paradigms.

I discussed briefly the ramifications of the Enlightenment and the way in which its ideas find their way into modern IR especially with regards to the concept of secularism. Here, I explored the way in which secularism represents a development of a specifically Christian tradition, now remade as a value-free institution. The implications for Islam-as-politics when faced with this 'secular bias' in IR is that political Islam always appears as an aberration. In challenging this secular bias, I argued that it is incorrect to speak for Islam as a belief system binding all Muslims of the world together. Rather, Islam-as-faith represents a diverse archive of tools, symbols and norms for (many forms of) Islam-as-politics to draw upon.

When discussing Islam I narrowed its definition to refer to only Sunni Islam; this provides a clear and concise example to interact with IR; similar analyses could be made with other 'non-Western' traditions, and in my previous survey of Islam and politics in the MENA, sub-Saharan Africa and Southeast Asia, it was Sunni Islam that most often manifested as 'political Islam'.

In the next chapter I will intersect with all the main themes of the book, placing Islamic notions of sovereignty, such as they are, into dialogue with how the term is used in IR.

NOTES

1. Bryan Turner, *Orientalism, Postmodernism and Globalism* (London: Routledge, 1994), 10.
2. Talal Asad, *Formations of the Secular: Christianity, Islam, Modernity* (Stanford: Stanford University Press, 2003) 1.
3. Ibid., 15.
4. While I acknowledge that Foucault worked hard to avoid the labelling, seeing his ideas as 'instruments'. In *Society Must Be Defended* he states that 'Ultimately, what you do with them [Foucault's ideas as instruments] both concerns me and is none of my business'. See

Michel Foucault, *Society Must Be Defended* (London: Penguin, 2004), 2. As the chapter unfolds I will clarify the use of Foucault and poststructuralism.

5. Alexander Wendt, 'Bridging the Theory/Meta-Theory Gap in International Relations', *Review of International Studies* 17, no. 4 (1991): 383.

6. Robert Cox, 'Social Forces, States and World Orders: Beyond International Relations Theory', *Millennium: A Journal of International Studies* 10, no. 2, 1981): 129.

7. Wendt, 'Bridging the Theory/Meta-Theory Gap', 392.

8. Fred Dallmayr, 'Exit from Orientalism', in *Orientalism: A Reader*, ed. Alexander Lyon Macfie (New York: New York University Press, 2000), 365.

9. See the previous chapter for the various ways Islam is conceptualised in IR.

10. Piscatori contests the homogeneity of the behaviour of Muslim polities in this period, undermining the claims of some idealised Islamic past from which to draw lessons about the IR of modern Muslim states. See James Piscatori, *Islam in a World of Nation-States* (Cambridge: Cambridge University Press, 1986).

11. Olivier Roy, *The Failure of Political Islam* (London: I.B. Tauris, 1994).

12. Richard Bernstein, 'Foucault: Critique as a Philosophical Ethos', in *Critique and Power: Recasting the Foucault/Habermas Debate*, ed. Kelly Michael (London: The MIT Press, 1994), 231. Original emphasis.

13. Michel Foucault, *Power/Knowledge: Selected Interviews and Other Writings 1972–1977* (Harlow: Longman, 1980), 131–32.

14. Gerald Gaus and Chandran Kukathas (eds): *Handbook of Political Theory,* (London: Sage Publications Ltd, 2004), pg. 46-47

15. Friedrich Nietzsche, *Human, All Too Human* (London: University of Nebraska Press, 1984), 23–24.

16. Giorgio Shani, 'De-colonizing Foucault', *International Political Sociology* 4, no. 2 (2010): 210.

17. Foucault, *Society Must Be Defended*, 7.

18. Nicholas Rengger, 'No Time like the Present? Postmodernism and Political Theory', *Political Studies* 40, no. 3 (1992): 561.

19. Turner, *Orientalism, Postmodernism and Globalism*, 14–15.

20. Ibid., 14–15.

21. Rengger, 'No Time like the Present', 563.

22. Ibid., 565.

23. Jim George and David Campbell, 'Patterns of Dissent and the Celebration of Difference: Critical Social Theory and International Relations', *International Studies Quarterly* 34, no. 3 (1990): 280.

24. Jean-Francois Lyotard, *The Postmodern Condition: A Report on Knowledge* (Manchester: Manchester University Press, 1984), 3–6.

25. Jim George, *Discourses of Global Politics: A Critical (Re) Introduction to International Relations* (Boulder: Lynne Rienner, 1994), 42.

26. John Gray, *Al Qaeda and What It Means to be Modern* (London: Faber and Faber, 2003), 1. Original emphasis.

27. François Debrix, 'We Other IR Foucaultians', *International Political Sociology* 4, no. 2 (2010): 198.

28. Jamal al-Din al-Afghani, 'An Islamic Response to Imperialism', in *Islam in Transition: Muslim Perspectives*, ed. John Donohue and John Esposito (Oxford: Oxford University Press, 1982), 16–19.

29. Muhammed 'Abduh, 'Islam, Reason, and Civilisation', in *Islam in Transition: Muslim Perspectives*, ed. John Donohue and John Esposito (Oxford: Oxford University Press, 1980), 26–27.

30. Such a position is typical of Jurgen Habermas, who while critical of the Enlightenment, sees postmodernism, and Foucault specifically, as throwing the baby out with the bathwater. See Jurgen Habermas, *The Philosophical Discourse of Modernity: Twelve Lectures* (Cambridge, MA: MIT Press, 1991).

31. Hasan Al-Banna, 'The New Renaissance', in *Islam in Transition: Muslim Perspectives*, ed. John Donohue and John Esposito (Oxford: Oxford University Press, 1982), 79.

32. Aziz Al-Azmeh, *Islam and Modernities*, 2nd ed. (London: Verso, 1996), 128.

33. Torbjorn Knutsen, *A History of International Relations Theory* (Manchester: Manchester University Press, 1997), 274.

34. Gurminder Bhambra, *Rethinking Modernity: Postcolonialism and the Sociological Imagination* (Basingstoke: Palgrave, 2007), 15.

35. Dipesh Chakrabarty, *Provincializing Europe: Postcolonial Thought and Historical Difference* (Princeton: Princeton University Press, 2000), 6.

36. Ibid., 16.

37. Sadik Jalal al-'Azm, 'Orientalism and Orientalism in Reverse', in *Orientalism: A Reader*, ed. Alexander Lyon Macfie (New York: New York University Press, 2000), 219.

38. Aijaz Ahmed, 'Between Orientalism and Historicism', in *Orientalism: A Reader*, ed. Alexander Lyon Macfie (New York: New York University Press, 2000), 289.

39. Ibid., 288.

40. John Hobson, *The Eurocentric Conception of World Politics: Western International Theory, 1760–2010* (Cambridge: Cambridge University Press, 2012), 13.

41. Ibid., 4–9.

42. Ibid., 4–5.

43. Ibid., 9.

44. Ibid., 8.

45. See especially ibid., 5–9 for discussion of paternalistic and anti-paternalistic Eurocentrism.

46. Ibid., 22–23.

47. Turner, *Orientalism, Postmodernism and Globalism*, 101.

48. Wendt, 'Bridging the Theory/Meta-Theory Gap', 392.

49. Pinar Bilgin, 'Civilisation, Dialogue, Security: The Challenge of Post-secularism and the Limits of Civilisational Dialogue', *Review of International Studies* 38 (2012): 1103.

50. Luca Mavelli and Fabio Petito, 'The Postsecular in International Relations: An Overview', *Review of International Studies* 38, no. 5 (2012): 931.

51. Ibid., 931.

52. Ibid., 933.

53. Elizabeth Hurd, *The Politics of Secularism in International Relations* (Princeton: Princeton University Press, 2008), 1.

54. Ibid., 5.

55. Ibid., 6.

56. Ibid., 10.

57. Ibid., 126.

58. Erin Wilson, *After Secularism: Rethinking Religion in Global Politics* (Basingstoke: Palgrave Macmillan, 2012), 152.

59. Ibid., 168.

60. Luca Mavelli, *Europe's Encounter with Islam: The Secular and the Postsecular* (New York: Routledge, 2012), 61.

61. Joseph Camilleri, 'Postsecularist Discourse in an "Age of Transition"', *Review of International Studies* 38, no. 5 (2012): 1020.

62. Hurd, *Politics of Secularism in International Relations*, 19.

63. Mohammed Arkoun, 'Rethinking Islam Today', in *Liberal Islam: A Sourcebook*, ed. Charles Kurzman (Oxford: Oxford University Press, 1998), 218.

64. Ibid.

65. Turner, *Orientalism, Postmodernism and Globalism*, 6.

66. Bassam Tibi, *Islam's Predicament with Modernity: Religious Reform and Cultural Change* (London: Routledge, 2009), 4.

67. Such a position coincidentally lines up with much IR theorising of the region that chooses to relegate Islam as a factor out of its analysis. However, unlike those IR treatments of the Middle East, Zubaida's account of Islam is far more deliberately argued and nuanced.

68. Sami Zubaida, *Beyond Islam: A New Understanding of the Middle East* (London: I.B. Tauris, 2011), 3.

69. Ibid., 104.

70. See Piscatori, *Islam in a World of Nation-States* for a similar, nuanced and far less problematic approach to Islam(s) and politics.

71. Jeffery Checkel, 'The Constructivist Turn in International Relations Theory', *World Politics* 50, no. 2 (1998): 324.

72. These ideas have a passing resemblance to Marx's statement that '[m]en make their own history, but they do not make it as they please; they do not make it under self-selected circumstances, but under circumstances existing already, given and transmitted from the past'. See Karl Marx, 'The Eighteenth Brumaire of Louis Bonaparte', 1852, accessed on 31.05.2013, https://www.marxists.org/archive/marx/works/1852/18th-brumaire/ch01.htm.

73. Alexander Wendt, *Social Theory of International Politics* (Cambridge: Cambridge University Press, 1999), 371–72.

74. Dale Copeland, 'The Constructivist Challenge to Structural Realism: A Review Essay', *International Security* 25, no. 2 (2000): 189.

75. Ibid., 190.

76. Nicholas Onuf, *World of Our Making: Rules and Rule in Social Theory and International Relations* (Columbia: University of South Carolina Press, 1989), 6.

77. Robert Cox, 'Social Forces, States and World Orders: Beyond International Relations Theory' in *Neorealism and Its Critics*, ed. Robert Keohane (New York: Columbia University Press, 1986), 248.

78. Checkel, 'Constructivist Turn in International Relations Theory', 327.

79. Ibid., 325.

80. Alexander Wendt, 'Social Theory as Cartesian Science: An Auto-critique from a Quantum Perspective', in *Constructivism and International Relations: Alexander Wendt and His Critics*, ed. Stefano Guzzini and Anna Leander (London: Routledge, 2006), 182.

81. Ibid., 183.

82. Onuf, *World of Our Making*, 37.

83. Ibid., 16.

84. Turner, *Orientalism, Postmodernism and Globalism*, 101.

85. The dualism referenced here is not unproblematic in its usage, but is embroiled in much the same dilemma as I am attempting to deal with; where I seek a position tenable to both poststructuralist *and* Muslim, so too does Wendt's constructivism seek a position tenable by both materialism *and* interpretivism. For more on this debate on constructivism see Hidemi Suganami, 'Wendt, IR, and Philosophy: A Critique', in *Constructivism and International Relations: Alexander Wendt and His Critics*, ed. Stefano Guzzini and Anna Leander (London: Routledge, 2006) and more broadly, Fredrich Kratochwil and John Ruggie, 'International Organization: A State of the Art on an Art of the State', *International Organization* 40, no. 4 (1986).

86. Ronald Bleiker and Mark Chou, 'Nietzsche's Style: On Language, Knowledge and Power in International Relations', in *International Relations Theory and Philosophy: Interpretive Dialogues*, ed. Cerwyn Moore and Chris Farrands (London: Routledge, 2010), 17.

87. Checkel, 'Constructivist Turn in International Relations Theory', 325.

88. Joseph Schacht, *The Origins of Muhammadan Jurisprudence* (Oxford: Oxford University Press, 1950), 1–5.

89. Albert Hourani, *A History of the Arab Peoples* (London: Faber and Faber, 1991), 68.

90. Fazlur Rahman, *Islam* (Chicago: University of Chicago Press, 1979), 72.

91. See Edward Said, 'Shattered Myths', in *Middle East Crucible*, ed. Aruri Naseer (Wilmette: Medina University Press, 1975).

92. Edward Said, 'Arabs, Islam and the Dogmas of the West', in *Orientalism: A Reader*, ed. Alexander Lyon Macfie (New York: New York University Press, 2000), 104.

93. Zubaida, *Islam, the People & the State*, 122.

94. Roy, *The Failure of Political Islam*, 7.

95. Fred Halliday, *Islam and the Myth of Confrontation* (London: I.B. Tauris, 1996), 207–10.

96. Bobby Sayyid, *A Fundamental Fear: Eurocentrism and The Emergence of Islamism* (London: Zed, 2003), xvii.

97. Fred Halliday, *The Middle East in International Relations: Power, Politics and Ideology* (Cambridge: Cambridge University Press, 2005), 155.

Part II

Developing an Alternative

Chapter Five

Sovereignty and Political Islam

Political Islam presents itself in a wide variety of guises. Generally the use of the adjective 'political' implies a distinct object of analysis from simply 'Islam'. That may be true for, broadly speaking, 'Western' analysts, but making that very distinction, or not, is something that can define what it means to be an Islamist. As I outlined in chapter 1, much of what gives Islamism its vitality and appeal is related to the simplicity of *salafi*-inspired thought over the inseparability of faith and politics of the temporal world, of *din wa dawla*. To paraphrase Eickelman and Piscatori, *din wa dawla* proponents exaggerate the unique nature of Muslim politics, which inadvertently propagates the view that Muslim politics is irrational. Such a position presents Muslim politics as a mesh of various world views, due to the 'natural' fact of the inseparability of faith and politics.[1] In contrast to the *din wa dawla* approach, Carl Brown eloquently writes about how:

> No one suggests a timeless and unchanging Christian approach to politics. The same should not hold for Islam. The possible difference in its worldly manifestations between the Christianity of Paul, Augustine, Aquinas, or Luther is readily accepted. Christianity has a history. So does Islam.[2]

Put another way by Talal Asad, the Qur'an is said to have some power to bring about particular beliefs, while the Bible is a passive thing to be interpreted by Christians.[3] These differing perspectives on Christianity and Islam are contradictory and smack of othering. It is a particular and contextual Islamic history which I will now explore in more depth, continuing to evaluate the extent to which Islamic source texts offer guidance on IR.

In chapter 2 I reached a workable definition of political Islam that was neither reliant on religious source texts to provide a 'unique' slant on Muslim politics nor incumbent on a 'Muslim reformation' that would separate the temporal and otherworldly, as happened in Christendom. The latter is a result that is highly unsatisfactory doctrinally, as, for example, chapter 5, verse 40 of the Qur'an demonstrates regarding sovereignty, where it says: 'Knowest thou not that to Allah alone belongeth the dominion of the Heavens and the Earth'.[4] Rather, I defined political Islam as the pursuit of politics that adheres to Islamic norms and values and facilitates the practice of the faith. This definition necessarily distinguishes between the faith, as derived from religious source texts, and Islamic norms and values. I labelled this political Islam 'Normative Political Islam', and that is the term used as I continue the argument of this chapter. On top of the fact that Normative Political Islam is exceptionally broad and relatively permissive, deriving a political model is difficult; norms and values are far more nebulous and harder to define than the tenets of the faith. While norms and values may well be attributed to and derive from religious source texts, source texts are not the *only* source of their content, unlike the tenets of faith.

With a definition in hand I will move to explore the implications of Normative Political Islam in the international sphere, leading to a discussion on the prime articulation of political Islam, normative or otherwise, on IR: transnational Islam and the *umma*. I will argue that the essence of the challenge transnational Islam poses to IR centres on sovereignty, and resolving the issue of sovereignty is my primary focus here.

I find two specific reasons for the focus on sovereignty: First is the doctrinal imperative to ensure that God remains sovereign over Muslims, creating tension with vesting sovereignty in an individual or institution; second is the nature of authority in *fiqh* residing not over territory, as in the state that originated in Europe, but rather over people. This second point highlights a divergence with dominant notions of sovereignty in IR.

The distinction between rule over people and rule over territory has little resonance in the contemporary world; Muslim states, by definition, work within the framework of states and territory. The importance of sovereignty, however, becomes apparent when looking at the notion of God as sovereign; Muslim rulers try, in a variety of ways, to display their adherence with this principle to their citizens as a way to shore up legitimacy for their regimes. It is this problem then, which I will now explore, that is, the notion of God as sovereign.

The need for distinctions between Islam, political Islam and Normative Political Islam demonstrates that Islamic source texts are at best ambiguous about forms of government, Islamic or otherwise. Ambiguity does not mean that there is nothing to be gained from further analysis; Islam-as-faith needs to be refined in order to have a constructive impact in politics.

I attempt to answer the dilemma of how to refine theological guidance by outlining the *other* parts of the Islamic message, namely mysticism and rationalism.[5] I argue that this is exactly the method used in Iran to develop a

Shi'a Islamic State. Doing so in that instance relied heavily on a gnostic and mystic philosophy that has a prominent role in Shi'a tradition.[6] That being true, I posit that many of the reasons Sunni Islam struggles with a coherent notion of Islamic rule in the mould of Iran is because unlike Shi'ism, gnostic philosophy is marginal in Sunni Islam, resting primarily with Sufi orders. Therefore, I will look at the ways in which exoteric, rationalist philosophy, which has a long, if currently maligned tradition in Sunni Islam, might develop and refine the nature of Islam's role in politics.

After tracing the rational tradition in Islamic philosophy, I will apply this branch of philosophy to resolving the question of maintaining the sovereignty of God in a world of nation-states. Abu Zayd Abdu al-Rahman ibn Muhammed ibn Khaldun al-Hadrami, hereafter referred to as Ibn Khaldun, was a prominent historian, sociologist and philosopher in the fourteenth century. He applied the rational tradition in his study of Muslim politics and history, and I will be using his work to access a theory of sovereignty. In addition to the theological guidance explored in the introductory chapter of the book, here I will build upon a theory of sovereignty that is centred on a dual agreement, as propounded by Khadduri.[7]

Khadduri's dual contract, in brief, claims that Muslims, by virtue of their declaration of faith, agree to the moral precepts of the *shari'a*, and in doing so respect the sovereignty of God. A second agreement with a temporal authority is also established, but in order for the polity to be considered 'Islamic' as per Normative Political Islam, the temporal authority must also respect that same commitment to the first agreement. The implications of this are twofold: First, a Muslim is perfectly capable of adhering to the first contract in territories that do not govern in accordance with the declaration of faith. In other words, respect for God's sovereignty, given the ambiguous guidance on politics in religious source texts, does not imply a government wherein God is sovereign; secondly, the agreement that relates directly to the temporal world is one that is based on rationalism and human ingenuity (which I will show to currently be a 'silent' partner of contemporary political Islam), so escaping the need to derive all models and theories of politics from theological sources.

I will begin with an overview of political Islam as it relates to the state, exploring the differing epistemologies of various theoretical positions, all of which rely on *kalam* (theology) as their means of deriving knowledge of the world. I will then discuss two other strands of the Islamic message and the ways in which these relate to politics: the philosophy of mysticism will be discussed primarily in relation to the politics of Ayatollah Khomeini and the philosophy of rationalism will be discussed in the Arab Sunni Muslim world. After this, I will explore the rational tradition, as expounded by Ibn Khaldun, and I will posit a theory of sovereignty that satisfies obedience to both transcendental and temporal authorities. I am employing the two-stage conceptual framework outlined in the previous chapter. First I propose to break down existing notions of Islamic sovereignty, and identify in those existing notions areas of knowledge that have been neglected. I employ the second part of the conceptual framework in the drawing together of the aforementioned neglected components of the Islamic message (rationalism and mysticism) to form a notion of sovereignty that can be taken forward into the following chapters, which will deal specifically with Normative Political Islam in the international sphere. Resolving the issue of sovereignty for Normative Political Islam is a fundamental step in understanding the way in which that polity might behave in IR.

POLITICAL ISLAM AND THE STATE

Despite the fluctuations and metamorphoses of the international sphere in the last century, widely referred to as the process of globalisation, the state endures as a dominant locus of politics in the international sphere (even as the distinction between international and local is challenged). How political Islam might interact with the state has been a key debate ever since Muslim majority countries began to win independence from their former colonial masters. Claims that Islam 'offers a single vision for uniting the individual quest for virtue with the social goods of justice and solidarity'[8] do not recognise the nuance and the differing visions that spin out of the singular message of Islam-as-faith. John Esposito elucidates this point when he writes that '[t]hough often described in monolithic terms as "the Islamic alternative" or "the system of Islam," a diverse and prolific assortment of Islamic ideologies, actors, political parties, and organizations have reemerged in Muslim politics, grouped under the umbrella of Islam'.[9] Here Esposito reminds us of the distinction which was made in the introduction, regarding Islam-as-faith and Islam-as-politics. Accepting this distinction, I will move on to highlighting the many ways in which political Islam interacts with the state.

The famous student of Muhammed Abduh, Rashid Rida, saw a place for nationalism and the state in Islamic politics. Living through the dissolution of the Ottoman Empire, Rida warned that while a national spirit is compatible with a Muslim's faith, care must be taken to maintain priorities:

> In his [a Muslim's] service of his homeland and his people he must not, however, neglect Islam which has honoured him and raised him up by making him a brother to hundreds of millions of Muslims in the world. He is a member of a body greater than his people, and his personal homeland is part of the homeland of his religious community. He must be intent on making the progress of the part a means for the progress of the whole.[10]

In this summation there is a political Islam that happily works with the state system, as long as Muslim states working within that system do not put their own needs above the needs of the wider Muslim community. The Organisation of Islamic Cooperation (OIC) ostensibly carries out the role of ensuring Muslim solidarity comes before the needs of individual states; the second statement in the OIC's charter states that its purpose is 'promoting and consolidating the unity and solidarity among the Member States in securing their common interests at the international arena'.[11] However, while it holds regular meetings at a variety of levels, it 'has tended over the years to become identified more with the rhetoric rather than the practical implementation of Islamic unity'.[12]

The notion of Islam working within and as part of the state, what I will refer to as the 'Islamic state', is a novel idea initially propagated by Rida after the collapse of the Ottoman Empire.[13] In contrast, Nazih Ayubi in fact sees all Islamic theories of government as a novel rather than traditional theory[14] as in his summation: 'although Islam is a religion of collective morals, it is not a particularly political religion'.[15] Marking a break from Rashid Rida and others,[16] scholars like Ayubi 'attach more importance to the religious relationship with the absolute of God than to the vehement demonstrations of political movements'.[17] This articulation of political Islam is important; it is defined by the *lack* of the political. Or perhaps, if there is a political element to the faith, it is to be defined and implemented by human beings rather than divine and otherworldly direction. Such a position is especially prevalent with Muslim scholars dealing with issues of human rights and democracy, such as Abdullahi An-Na'im[18] and S. M. Zafar.[19]

A third orientation of political Islam is heavily inspired by Maududi, and sees political Islam working within the state system as before, but rather than the state and Islamic considerations being two different concerns in a hierarchical relationship, for Maududi the Islamic state would be a natural symbiosis of politics and religion. As Roy Jackson puts it, 'Maududi's Islamic society is completely in line with nature. In fact, it *is* nature'.[20] Maududi places Allah as legal and political sovereign in his state, and talks of laws as divine creations.[21] Maududi then, takes a step closer to the *din wa dawla* position of brooking no separation between Islam-the-faith and Islam-as-politics. In this summation, the presence of an Islamic state is not a peripheral addition to one's relationship with God, but is central to it—an affirmation of faith in its own right.

The overview above is not a complete taxonomy of positions within the umbrella of political Islam, but covers the key points of difference between them. Only the third variation, that representative of Maududi's position, bears a direct effect on IR as it is commonly demarcated, for it challenges the *nature* of what a state is. Much like the debate around Iran being 'different' from or somehow 'less rational' than other states due to its religious character, Maududi's Sunni Islamic state would pose similar questions to IR scholars. The first two positions, those characterised by Rida's hierarchy of national and Islamic interests in the first instance, and Ayubi's non-political Islam in the second instance, both work within the prevailing international system and so pose far fewer questions to the discipline of IR. The former institutionalises the concepts of nation and state into an Islamic world view, while the latter takes the 'political' out of political Islam, minimising the constitutive power of believers and emphasising the divine elements of the faith.

Rather than engage with the debate on religious rationality,[22] I will now look to a form of political Islam as yet unexplored in the book, yet posing challenges to IR at least as poignant as those brought forward by Maududi's Islamic State. This strand of political Islam is transnational Islam, and it focuses on the politics of the *umma*. I will look at the ways in which the politics of the *umma* relates to Normative Political Islam, and the challenges this brings to IR.

In the decline and abolition of the Ottoman Empire, debate raged as to the correct form of Islamic politics. As Piscatori notes: 'To the question, "How should the *umma* be constructed now?" little agreement emerged, with however, the significant exception: the spiritual unity of the *umma* required political expression'.[23] Herein lays the crux of transnational (political) Islam: the notion of religious solidarity, loosely defined and centred on community, is its guiding principle. Questions around this notion and its compatibility with the state, and the depth of solidarity required of the *umma*, are widely contested. Amr Sabet is critical of the ability a heavily contested Islam, political or otherwise, has to 'illuminate, comprehend or conceptualize',[24] a position I am deeply sympathetic to. Therefore, if the *umma* is to have any analytical purchase, it is necessary to refine and in some regards define the notions of transnational Islam as related to Normative Political Islam.

The political expression of the *umma* in Normative Political Islam mirrors much of what I have stated about Normative Political Islam thus far. Within Normative Political Islam the politics of the *umma*, or transnational Islam, is less about the creation of a political union of Muslim peoples, or indeed holding such a union as an article of faith. Rather, it is about fostering a culture of unity and solidarity, as was discussed in the book's introduction. This is a distinction also made by Piscatori, where pan-Islam, 'that is, giving concrete form to the idea of Muslim political unity', and pan-Islamism, 'the ideology promoting unity' are two different, if often overlapping, phenomena.[25] For the purposes of this book, transnational Islam is representative of Piscatori's pan-Islamism. In practice, this would be much like the way in which inalienable human rights, as set out in the United Nation's Universal Declaration of Human Rights, codifies a sense of commonality with far-flung peoples who are denied these rights; so too would an *umma* under Normative

Political Islam codify a sense of commonality amongst Muslims. Likewise, the ways in which human rights are challenging the power and internal efficacy of the state, so too would the politics of the *umma*, centred round rule over people rather than rule of territory, challenge centrality of the state in IR.

Mandaville paints in broad strokes a further challenge transnational Islam presents to IR: 'By locating "the political" within the state, conventional IR theory reproduces a set of political structures unsuited to circumstances in which political identities and processes configure themselves across and between forms of political community'.[26] The state is tied to notions of political modernity whereby religion is relegated to the private sphere. Mandaville continues, '[b]y reasserting itself in public space, Islam is hence disrupting the modernity which lies at the root of the state'.[27] Hence transnational Islam 'undermines' modernity in a way that the human rights discourse, being a secular discourse, does not, despite the fact that the underlying issue is the same (rule over people versus rule over territory).

A unique way in which transnational Islam, and the various strands of political Islam more broadly, represent a departure from secular debate on the rule of the individual versus rule over territory, is the transcendental element of the Islamic message, specifically, the transcendental nature of sovereignty in political Islam. The importance of sovereignty is identified by Mandaville as the remaining challenge for Islamist parties vying for power in democratic processes;[28] the notion of power sharing with God or with the *shari'a* is still controversial in theory, even if it is circumvented in practice by many Muslim rulers.[29]

The Qur'an explicitly tells believers that all power rests with God: 'Say: "To whom belongeth all that is in the Heavens and on Earth?" Say: "To Allah!"'[30] The problem faced by any rulers in an Islamic state is that of legitimacy. If sovereignty rests with God then why are Muslim citizens obliged to obey the commands of a monarch, president or other ruler? In the Islamic Republic of Iran the Supreme Leader is believed to have a unique relationship with God, whereby he is uniquely qualified to interpret His commandments. To disagree with the supreme leader is close to, if not actual blasphemy, in the opinion of the regime. The situation in Sunni orthodoxy is somewhat different; there is no hierarchical clergy system as exists in Twelver Shi'ism. Jurisprudence in Sunni orthodoxy is 'textual authority to justify what in effect is ... interpretative license'.[31] The acknowledgement of law as being a human interpretation of God's wishes, not his actual wishes, goes some way to explaining the existence of four separate schools of thought, *madhahib*, in Sunni orthodoxy. As we will recall from chapter 2, none of the *madhahib* can claim to be as authoritative as the Qur'an, the word of God, and so they accept each other's interpretations of matters not explicitly covered in the Qur'an and hadith as equally viable (matters explicitly covered in the Qur'an and hadith have very little deviance between the *madhahib*, such as prayer, for example).

Whilst the Qur'an tells Muslims they are God's vicegerents on Earth, legitimising a first amongst equals is problematic. This is an issue where the Qur'an, beyond many explicit references to God's sovereignty, is vague in its guidance on legitimising government. On the one hand, one can find verses that seemingly justify a sort of natural law whereby some individuals are 'blessed' with more power than others,[32] while on the other hand there are verses that emphasise the equality of humanity, and necessity for popular sovereignty.[33] While Qur'anic exegesis would look at the context of these revelations to discern greater clarity from the verses and resolve any contradiction, that is not my purpose. Rather, assuming that there is no explicit guidance in the Islamic source texts on who should rule a Muslim community, I seek to supplement these texts in order to refine and better articulate a position regarding the political sovereignty of God. Theology takes us so far, it seems, but no further. To proceed in articulating sovereignty and the international relations of Normative Political Islam, the body of work I now turn to is Islamic philosophy.

ISLAMIC PHILOSOPHY AND POLITICAL ISLAM

In addition to the normative and in some regards pluralistic elements of Normative Political Islam, another marker of difference between it and other interpretations of Islamic politics is the recognition of *shari'a* as *only one component* of the Islamic revelation. Those Muslims who call for 'a return to the *shari'a*' assume that the *shari'a* can offer guidance on all aspects of life. Built into that assumption is the idea that Islam-as-faith can be extrapolated out into Islam-as-politics, much as I am attempting to do in exploring Normative Political Islam. However, *shari'a* is but one strand of Islamic knowledge, as explained by Hossein Nasr:

> Islam is hierarchic when considered in its total reality and also in the way it has manifested itself in history. The Islamic revelation possesses within itself several dimensions and has been revealed to humanity on the basic levels of *al-islam*, *al-iman*, and *al-ihsan* (submission, faith, and virtue) and from another perspective as *al-Shari'ah*, *al-Tariqah* and *al-Haqiqah* (the Law, the Path and the Truth).[34]

To cure the world's ills by 'returning to the *shari'a*' reveals an assumption that the *shari'a* represents the Islamic message. Put another way, *shari'a is Islam*. Here an inherent contradiction is revealed. How can one extrapolate *all* knowledge, specifically vis-à-vis politics, from but one strand of the Islamic revelation? This is a trend that Rahman notes when he laments the cessation of practicing *fiqh* after the eighth century AD, to simply studying and learning *fiqh* thereafter.[35]

Even within *kalam*, the chosen strand of knowledge for *din wa dawla* advocates and political Islamists more generally, which relates to faith and the *shari'a* in Nasr's above summary, one can see calls for using other elements outside of theology to inform a Muslim's life. For example, *ahadith*, which are one of four key components in Islamic *fiqh* and *shari'a*,[36] can be used to give further credence to the separate strands of the Islamic revelation. Imam Nawawi's authoritative collection of hadith shows that the trifurcation of Islamic knowledge has prophetic and transcendental weight to it wherein the Prophet Muhammed explains the difference between submission, faith and virtue[37] (*al-islam, al-iman* and *al-ihsan* in Nasr's above summary). Acknowledging this separation in the revelation gives great utility to Normative Political Islam to derive an international order from Islamic sources, distinct from those that thus far have proven ambiguous in their guidance on politics (traditional *fiqh* sources). Submission and *shari'a* are related to theology, which I have explored in this and previous chapters. Faith and the Path are related to philosophy, while virtue and the Truth are related to gnosticism and esotericism (commonly identified with Sufism). I will proceed by exploring the role philosophy and gnosticism might play in Normative Political Islam.

Gnosticism and the Shi'ism of Ayatollah Khomeini

As well as Shi'a majorities in Arab countries such as Iraq and Bahrain, Shi'ism is also the predominant faith of the people of Iran, which represents the only example of a successful Islamist revolution. The Islamic state, which functions under the stipulations of (Shi'a) *shari'a* law, provides us with information on how Islam-as-faith interacts with the modern state system and the methods used in that context to refine and make clearer the so far ambiguous guidance on politics within Islamic source texts. To do so effectively, a brief overview of Shi'ism and Shi'a *fiqh* follows.

Shi'as derive their name from *shia'at 'Ali*, the party of 'Ali. 'Ali was the fourth of the *rashidun*, the 'rightly guided Caliphs', and cousin and son-in-law to the Prophet Muhammed. At first the split was political, as the 'party of 'Ali' wanted him to become the Caliph after the Prophet's death. Shi'as argue that the only people who can legitimately be Caliph are those descended from the Prophet, through the line of 'Ali and his wife, the Prophet's daughter, Fatima. Because of this, the first three Caliphs are considered 'usurpers' by the Shi'a community.[38]

Whereas Sunni Islam has limited religious hierarchy, Shi'a Islam does have such a hierarchy. I have already mentioned that the only people worthy of exercising authority over the *umma* are the descendants of the Prophet.

Such individuals are called 'imams', a word that is also used in Sunni Islam, but to mean a leader of a *masjid* (or mosque, Muslim 'church') or localised community. In Shi'ism, specifically mainstream 'Twelver' Shi'ism, the imams are without sin, and possess an infallible understanding of the Qur'an and *sunna*, granted to them through their unique relationship with God. The term imam is also conflated with the two Supreme Leaders of the Iranian Islamic State, Ayatollahs Khomeini and Khamenei; however, neither is an imam in the sense outlined above. An imam's relationship is tied to divine intellect, the truth of which is only glimpsed through gnosticism. As Tjitze De Boer comments on this esotericism, '[t]hat which the friend of God knows intuitively, remains hidden for ever from the discursive intellect of the learned'.[39]

There are twelve imams (hence the 'Twelver' adjective), the first being the Caliph 'Ali and the last being Muhammed al-Mahdi, who disappeared in 874 AD. Shi'a faith is waiting for the return of this twelfth imam, the *mahdi* or guided one, to bring a reign of justice and establish the perfect society before the end of the world.[40] The perceived religious purity of Shi'a imams grants them a similar interpretative licence and authority to the Prophet. Being able to hold such a religious authority in a way the Sunni successors to the Islamic state were unable to do so goes some way to explaining the Iranian, Shi'a justification for that state. Such an argument only holds water if one believes that part of the Prophet's mission was political, which the founder of the current Iranian order, Ayatollah Ruhollah Khomeini, firmly believed. Khomeini states that '[j]ust as the Prophet was charged by God to execute holy decrees and establish Islamic order, and obedience to him was indispensable, the just *foqaha* must be both leaders and governors, executing decrees and establishing the Islamic social order'.[41] However, recalling al-Raziq's thesis on the separate sources of authority the Prophet Muhammed drew upon, the 'kingly' and the 'prophetic', Khomeini's assertions are less than self-evident. I will continue the section by exploring the theoretical justifications of the Shi'a state.

Shi'a *fiqh* differs only slightly in its basic principles next to Sunni *fiqh*, with the issue of *hadith* and *ijma'* (consensus) being contentious. Beyond this, the difference between Sunni and Shi'a law is in details only.[42] Concerning *hadith*, unlike the Sunni *fiqh* of the four *madhahib*, Shi'ism only accepts *ahadith* that are transmitted in the first instance by the Prophet's family. In addition, Shi'ism has incorporated the *ahadith* of the twelve imams into its source of *fiqh* and such *ahadith* are elevated to the same status as those of the Prophet.[43] In development of this body of *fiqh*, *ijma'* was far less important, 'its place is taken by the authority of the Imam'.[44] It is this lack of *ijma'* that makes Shi'a *fiqh* so noticeably distinct from the Sunni variety. Returning to the founder of the Iranian Islamic state, Khomeini is unabashedly dismissive of those who claim that Islam has little to say on governance. He writes:

> They have said that Islam has no relationship whatsoever with organizing life and society or with creating a government of any kind and that it only concerns itself with the rules of menstruation and child birth. It may contain some ethics. But beyond this, it has no bearing on issues of life and of organizing society.[45]

His contempt for such a viewpoint is almost palpable, yet the evidence he gives to support his view is simply that the Qur'an and *hadith* books are superior to theses written by religious legists and commentators. This is considered an orthodox opinion of the source texts, as demonstrated earlier, but it does not diminish the fact that these texts need interpreting, and such interpretations are human, fallible endeavours. Khomeini's argument that '[t]he belief that Islam came for a limited period and for a certain place violates the essentials of the Islamic beliefs',[46] is a just one. However, the answer does not have to mean, as Khomeini advocates, that Islam has prescribed a form of government for all peoples for all time. Instead, as Abdul-Karim Soroush argues, the principles contained in the source texts, if continually reinterpreted, can yield different and differing answers to modern-day problems.[47]

Above all else, it is the Prophet's authority that gives birth to Iran's Islamic state. This authority could not be replicated in Sunni Islam but has been successfully co-opted by the Shi'a imams. Khomeini states that the Prophet 'was appointed ruler on earth by God so that he may rule justly and not follow whims'.[48] It is the imam who takes over this function in the absence of the Prophet. Khomeini himself elucidates, '[t]o the Shi'i the Imam is a virtuous man who knows the laws and implements them justly and who fears nobody's censure in serving God'.[49] In essence, one man's interpretation of the source text (the imam's) becomes canon and so, if he is looking for evidence of Islamic government and finds it, no one can dispute his finding. Theologically speaking, such a method of interpretation, while making use of *qiyas* (analogy), has no limits placed on it, limits that early Sunni thinkers had developed by way of *ijma'*. While the power of the imam is ostensibly explained due to his singular ability to interpret the source texts, the case of the Iranian political Islam is not akin to Sunni varieties, which unwittingly equate *shari'a* with the totality of Islam-as-faith; Shi'a Iran in fact uses a second strand of Islamic knowledge, *al-ihsan* (virtue/gnosticism), to help construct its method of politics. This was glimpsed when briefly discussing the Shi'a imams' unique and esoteric relationship with God, and I will now explore this further through the example of Ayatollah Khomeini, who in many respects was the architect (or arbiter) of the fusion of religion and politics at the inception of the Iranian republic.

In Khomeini's thought, 'there are two essential qualities of leadership: first, knowledge of Islamic law; second, justice'.[50] Already a divergence from Sunni political Islam appears, wherein knowledge of Islamic law *is* knowledge of justice, or the route to that knowledge. For Khomeini, though, these are two, separate wisdoms. The first, Islamic law, relates to *al-islam*, the second, knowledge of justice, relates to *al-ihsan*. Ayatollah Khomeini strove to acquire knowledge of justice and *al-ihsan* through mysticism and gnosis. These disciplines fall broadly under the banner of *hekmat* (literally 'wisdom') and had found refuge in Persia after an attack by Muslim theologians on philosophy, broadly understood, in the eleventh century AD. In this Persian context it was Mullah Sadra who came to define the study of *hekmat* and his work greatly influences Khomeini.[51]

For Khomeini, the recourse to *hekmat* was an attempt to 'transcend the standard offerings of jurisprudence and systematic theology'[52] given by the Shi'a clergy. This field of thought is very esoteric and inward looking, and Khomeini contrasts his thinking in this regard to that of 'the West' when he says: 'Let them go to Mars or anywhere they wish; they are still backward in the sphere of securing happiness to man, backward in spreading moral virtues and backward in creating a psychological and spiritual progress similar to the material progress'.[53] While he rejects rationality, that is, humanity's intellectual capacity, in his inner search for God, Khomeini uses reason extensively in his theological and formal arguments for clerical rule in Iran.[54]

In reaching beyond the traditional theological offerings of religious orthodoxy, Khomeini was able to refine and articulate the ambiguous guidance on politics found therein, and propose his take on Islamic politics. The conclusions on the content of that guidance and the veracity of his specific method will not be the subjects of my continuing enquiry. Rather, the procedures used by Khomeini point to something not tried in Sunni political Islam; they reach beyond theology and *shari'a* to inform their conception of politics, while still remaining in the Islamic tradition. Such an undertaking in the Shi'a context, and the resulting order it established, was equally 'unprecedented in the history of Shiism in Iran'.[55] Baqer Moin elucidates this novelty in Khomeini's approach when he comments on the rigidity of Shi'a orthodoxy (a claim equally applicable to Sunni orthodoxy), '[o]f the three paths to God, the only one they accept is that of total obedience and devotion. The other two, the rationalism of philosophy and the illumination of mysticism, have always been viewed as incompatible with what was revealed to the Prophet'.[56] In the following section I will examine the claim that 'the rationalism of philosophy and illumination of mysticism' have always been divergent paths from theology, *shari'a* and orthodoxy in the Sunni context. In examining this claim, I will attempt to clarify the so far ambiguous theological guidance on politics offered by Normative Political Islam by reaching beyond theology and *shari'a*, which have become synonymous with the totality of the Islamic message.

Exotericism in Sunni Islam

Having explored *al-islam* earlier in this chapter, as well as in chapter 2, and having surveyed *al-ihsan* in the preceding Shi'a example, the remaining branch of knowledge to investigate is *al-iman* (faith), related to philosophy. Here I refer explicitly to exotericism and rationalism, in contrast to the esotericism and mysticism of Khomeini's approach. The relationship between rationalism and mysticism is a complicated one in the Islamic tradition, and those familiar to philosophy as it developed in the European and broadly 'Western' context can easily, and incorrectly, define only the rational tradition as philosophy in the Islamic setting. In fact, the term *falsafah* in Arabic refers both to *hekmat*, as the tradition came to be defined by Mullah Sadra, and the rationalism of Aristotle that was the purview of the Mu'tazilite group. For me then, the term philosophy will refer to rationalism specifically, while *falsafah* will refer to both *hekmat* and rationalism in the Islamic context. When contrasting *falsafah* with *kalam*, it is important to note the ways in which these traditions have intertwined historically and have substantially co-constituted each other. Taking Hossein Nasr's overview of the subject, we can identify four or five different 'eras' of the relationship between *falsafah* and *kalam*.[57] The first is in the early ninth century AD, when the Mu'tazilite school dominated both *kalam* and *falsafah*. This period is described by Nasr as one 'of close association between *falsafah* and *kalam* in an atmosphere of more or less relative mutual respect'.[58]

During the Umayyad and Abbasid caliphates, the rise of Ash'arite theology began a gradual incorporation of certain philosophical elements into *kalam*, while at the same time separating *falsafah* from more orthodox forms of knowledge.

A third period of this relationship was near the end of the Abbasid caliphate, and was a period of intense opposition of *falsafah* by theologians, while at the same time borrowing heavily from the former.[59] This relationship is epitomised by Abu Hamed Muhammad ibn Muhammad al-Ghazali,[60] an Ash'arite theologian who wrote his *Tahafut al-Falsafah* (The Incoherence of the Philosophers) in the eleventh century AD. Even while doing so, Nasr comments that '*kalam* became even more "philosophical," employing both ideas and arguments drawn from *falsafah*'.[61]

Once the 'dominance' of *kalam* was established in the Sunni world by al-Ghazali, a more peaceful existence between *falsafah* and *kalam* continued to this day. A major development in the sixteenth and seventeenth centuries was the thought of Mullah Sadra, who represents a fifth stage in the relationship between these schools of thought. With Mullah Sadra, in the Persian setting, *falsafah* began to eclipse *kalam*, causing theology to become less important in that setting, as seen earlier in the example of Ayatollah Khomeini.

It is apparent that 'the theological movement in Islam was strongly influenced by Philosophy'.[62] What is important to emphasise here is that in reaching beyond theology to inform Normative Political Islam, I am not participating in anything alien to the Islamic tradition, for what that statement is worth. The summary provided shows that the history of theology so vehemently defended and lauded as the 'true' Islamic way by *din wa dawla* adherents is one that is not a product of immaculate, divine conception, but the result of much human endeavour and co-constitution with *falsafah*.

In previous sections and chapters I have explored an Islamic order based on gnosticism (*al-ihsan*) in Khomeini's Iran, and abstracted polities based on theology (*al-islam*) in the variations on political Islam. The third approach is that of *al-iman*, rationalism and philosophy as understood in the 'Western' context. In the Muslim world rationalism is strongly tied to the introduction of Greek philosophy, which is commonly attributed to the Mu'tazilites and personified in the person of Abu Ya'qub al-Kindi. Al-Kindi was an early Peripatetic and grappled with expressing the work of Aristotle in Arabic, as well as what would become a central problem of philosophy in the Islamic world, the 'harmonization of faith and reason'[63] (an endeavour that bears a passing resemblance to Wendt's pursued synthesis of science and interpretivism in his constructivism, a resemblance that is returned to in later chapters). Moroccan philosopher Mohammed 'Abed al-Jabri sees this mission, the exploration of faith and reason, to be key in expressing an Islamic modernity, and here I will argue that the use of philosophy and rationalism is the key to expressing a coherent concept of politics in Normative Political Islam. 'Abed al-Jabri states that in carrying out this task, '[w]e [Muslim Arabs] could thus rid our conception of tradition from that ideological and emotional charge that weighs on our conscience and forces us to perceive tradition as an absolute reality that transcends history'.[64]

The exotericism of the Mu'tazilites was to be rekindled some decades after al-Kindi by Abu Nasr Muhammad ibn Muhammad Farabi, hereafter referred to as al-Farabi.[65] Al-Farabi lived in the late ninth to early tenth century AD, a time of fragmentation of Muslim political power. As such, his philosophy is overly concerned with unity, and 'with some attempt at adaptation to the Muslim faith, he seeks to demonstrate that Plato and Aristotle harmonize with one another'.[66] In the tenth century AD Abu 'Ali al-Husayn ibn 'Abd Allah ibn Sina, hereafter referred to as Ibn Sina,[67] lived as both a rationalist and gnostic, personifying the spirit of *falsafah* in Muslim lands. De Boer claims the common perception that Ibn Sina pushed beyond al-Farabi to a 'purer' Aristotelianism is incorrect; Ibn Sina and al-Farabi differed on many metaphysical issues, specifically around the nature of the soul.[68] While both men employed reason, Ibn Sina was far more interested in mysticism than al-Farabi. When *falsafah* was criticised by theologian al-Ghazali in the Arab Middle Eastern setting, perhaps beyond repair, Ibn Sina's mix of rationalism and mysticism was the straw man used to do so.[69]

The main thrust of al-Ghazali's critique of *falsafah* was the refutation of reason as a means of understanding faith. Paraphrasing Rahman's summary of a Mu'tazilite position, while al-Farabi or Ibn Sina might say that 'God has forbidden killing because it is bad; it is not bad because God has forbidden it'[70] (and reason is the means of divining why it is bad, and thus confirms the divine message), al-Ghazali would say the opposite; for al-Ghazali, killing is bad because it is forbidden by God. However, as 'Abed al-Jabri elucidates, '[i]f indeed—as it has constantly been reiterated—philosophy never was able to recover from the blows dealt to it by Ghazali, this was only true in the case of the Arab Middle East'.[71] It is in the West of Muslim lands, in al-Andalus especially, that exoteric philosophy continued to thrive.

Al-Andalus was the refuge of the Umayyad Caliphate after its fall to the Abbasids, and the spokesperson for the cultural and ideological project of that caliphate in the eleventh century AD was Abu Muhammad 'Ali ibn Ahmad ibn Sa'id ibn Hazm. Ibn Hazm's focus on rationalism was in absolute contrast and an attempt to erase 'the imprint of Shi'ite and Sufi "illumination"'[72] from Sunni thought. Ibn Hazm is very critical of esotericism, and says that 'God's (praise be to Him) religion is purely exoteric and is by no means esoteric. It is entirely obvious and hides no latent secret. It is entirely based on proof and nothing in it is left to chance'.[73] The Almohad dynasty, some fifty years after ibn Hazm's death, carried on his exoteric doctrine in the person of Abu al-Walid Muhammad ibn Ahmad ibn Rushd,[74] who the Almohad court sponsored to compile commentaries on Aristotle.[75] Ibn Rushd was 'above all a fanatical admirer of the Aristotelian Logic',[76] and sought to show that truths are only relevant and 'true' in their own frames of reference. Therefore those conclusions of Aristotle that are not compatible with Islam can still be true, but not universal or absolute; '[t]heir veracity is conditioned by the system from which they are derived'.[77] Aristotelian rationalism is thereby conceived as compatible with the Islamic message; Ibn Rushd, in the tradition of al-Farabi, argued that '[p]hilosophy and the religion of Islam do not therefore contradict each other. They express the same truth in different forms'.[78]

Exotericism and Politics

Having outlined the tradition of exoteric thought and rationalism in the Muslim world, it now falls to operationalise the abstract notions of rationalism into a conception of politics that might inform Normative Political Islam. 'Abed al-Jabri states that the achievements of the European tradition will remain foreign to Muslims detached from their history and tradition. Referring to an Arab-Islamic future, al-Jabri is adamant that such a future must be constructed 'from our own reality, from the specificity of our history and the constituents of our personality, its historical consciousness'.[79] The importance of overviewing the lesser-drawn-upon aspects of the Islamic message, exotericism and gnosticism, which preceded this section, was to show the ways in which rationalism, gnosticism and theology are constitutive elements of an 'Islamic personality'. Given that theology and the *shari'a* provide only limited or ambiguous guidance on politics, when I proceed to look at intellectual traditions outside theology, I did not stray beyond the Islamic message (which after all is constituted by *al-islam*, *al-iman* and *al-ihsan* concurrently). I will continue by building on the exotericism of the Sunni tradition in an attempt to refine and add to the theological guidance on politics. The route I am taking into operationalising this tradition is via another who has already done so, Ibn Khaldun.

Ibn Khaldun became acquainted with the exotericism of Ibn Sina and Ibn Rushd in the court of the Marinid Sultan in Fes.[80] Ibn Khaldun wrote his treatise, the *Muqaddimah* (an Introduction to History) in the fourteenth century AD and in it acknowledges, in agreement with 'Ali al-Raziq, that the time of the Prophet was an atypical time in history with regards to politics, a rare instance where the divine played a role. With the passing of the *rashidun* it is humanity that defines politics and in this way Ibn Khaldun's theories are humanist, if not secular.[81] If political Islam 'draws much of its strength from a conviction that there is no need for a detour through the labyrinths of "Western" history, before one can arrive at a vision of the good life and a just order',[82] then I will lean heavily on Ibn Khaldun as a Muslim thinker who does not traverse such a 'labyrinth'. In fact, Khadduri, when explaining that the state (an approximation for authority in the Muslim schema) is essential for society's survival, and that without the state humanity's evil nature would ruin society, he points out that this Hobbesian position was grasped some 300 years before Hobbes, by Ibn Khaldun.[83]

Returning to the debates concerning transnational Islam, Normative Political Islam, and the sovereignty of God, I will now use the work of Ibn Khaldun to help derive a theory of Islamic sovereignty—sovereignty being the remaining impediment for Islamism in power, in Mandaville's summation. As Mandaville sees it, in circumstances where the modern nation-state model is accepted, 'the issue of shari'ah and the question of political power sharing . . . represent the sole outstanding issues that cause problems with regard to Islamist participation in democratic politics'.[84] Whether sovereignty is the *sole* impediment to Islamist participation in democratic politics is under question given the events that have transpired since the publication of Mandaville's *Global Political Islam* in 2007. Indeed, in the year after the book's publication, Hamas came to power in Gaza, four years later Tunisia's

En-Nahda party were voted into power, and five years later the Muslim Brotherhood's Mohammed Morsi came to power in Egypt.

While the world might be fluid with regards to Islamism dealing with the realities of power, the theoretical problems with regards to holding God as sovereign must still be resolved. Specifically, I have yet to explore the ways in which accepting the nation-state system might undermine or limit the ways in which the sovereignty of God might be articulated. Hamas has felt the repercussions of the incongruence between theory and practice, suspending the implementation of an Islamic state after the 2008 war with Israel, in order to deal with the aftermath of that conflict. As Max Rodenbeck and Nicolas Pelham state, 'Hamas has become captive to its own success as it struggles now to reconcile the pressing needs of day-to-day governance with the ideology it preached in opposition'.[85] To avoid the same fate for Normative Political Islam, I will be using Ibn Khaldun's exoteric method, in combination with the guidance of *kalam*, to derive a notion of sovereignty that might be more satisfactory to both *din wa dawla* advocates on the one hand, and Muslim secularists on the other. The analysis of its position vis-à-vis the discipline of IR will be left for the subsequent chapter. For now, it is enough to extrapolate a theory from the methods stated, though comparisons will be made throughout to 'Western' theories and theorists when pertinent.

IBN KHALDUN, EXOTERICISM AND SOVEREIGNTY IN ISLAM

Ibn Khaldun shows the necessity of social organisation in his explanation of human behaviour, left unchecked by external influence, in an approximate 'state of nature':

> Each [individual] will stretch out his hand for whatever he needs and (try simply to) take it, since injustice and aggressiveness are in the animal nature. The others, in turn, will try to prevent him from taking it, motivated by wrathfulness and spite and the strong human reaction when (one's own property is menaced). This causes dissention. (Dissention) leads to hostilities, and hostilities lead to trouble and bloodshed and loss of life which (in turn) lead to the destruction of the (human) species.[86]

Rather than a 'state of nature', as humanity in anarchy or without society is referred to in Social Contract Theory, Ibn Khaldun's condition ends with the destruction of humanity, and as such cannot be described as 'natural'. In this way, government or society is instead the 'natural' condition of humanity; without it we would cease to exist; as Ibn Khaldun explains, '[p]eople, thus, cannot persist in a state of anarchy'.[87]

In the liberal tradition, the impingement of the individual's rights is a central debate as the 'natural' state of being is contested; is humanity's natural state one of total freedom, where the individual will consent to only the minimum of government interference necessary to allow society to function? In the Islamic tradition transmitted by Ibn Khaldun, this is not the case. Following from the ideas of the rationalist al-Farabi, who was mentioned earlier, Khadduri sees the history of Muslim societies as group centred. The individual counts for little, as '[o]nly through the family, clan or *civtas* to which the individual belonged, could he claim the right to protection by means of custom or social mores'.[88] Considering the fundamental difference between dominant 'Western' and 'Islamic' conceptions of the natural state of humanity, the term 'state of nature' would seem to no longer apply. If used in the Islamic world view, the state of nature would imply that the destruction of the species is humanity's natural condition, when in fact it is group relations and society that is more common. Therefore, I will adapt the terminology of John Rawls, who rather than use a state of nature, employed the term 'original position'. For Rawls, individuals in the original position '[act] in ways best suited to achieving their ends',[89] and in this way were self-interested, as would coincide with Ibn Khaldun's conception of human nature. So rather than refer to Rawls's original position, I will refer to the 'Khaldunian original position' to make reference to the condition of humanity without society, in this Islamically derived world view.

The Khaldunian original position is one where humanity, in its self-interest and vice, would destroy itself. It is a condition where such anarchy is untenable, and would result in the destruction of humanity. Hence, the 'natural' position derived from that assumption is one of individuals in a societal structure,[90] rather than the atomised individuals of liberal social contract theorists. With this in mind, I will now move to construct the final part of the puzzle, as it were, for Normative Political Islam: the issue of sovereignty. I will develop this notion of sovereignty by examining the transition from the Khaldunian original position to a society based on Muslim norms.

Synthesising the Sovereignty of God and Exotericism in Normative Political Islam

The Muslims in Ibn Khaldun's study, like the ancient Greeks before them, envisioned humankind living together, as members of a society. However, as mentioned already, 'the individual's rights and obligations were always defined in terms of (though subordinate to) the community's interests'.[91] Ibn Khaldun derives his conclusions on the place of the individual in society from proto-sociological rigour; humanity, at least in the deserts of North Africa and the Arab peninsular, is unable to obtain the food necessary for survival on its own, and also cannot protect its belongings in such a condition. This leads to Ibn Khaldun's observation that '[w]hen, however, mutual co-operation exists, man obtains food for his nourishment and weapons for his defense. God's wise plan that man(kind) should subsist and the human species be preserved will be fulfilled'.[92] Hence Ibn Khaldun makes the formation of society and government an act of faith, such that proponents of the *din wa dawla* position would jump upon. However, the place of the divine is yet to be deciphered, and will be interrogated more thoroughly as this section continues.

Returning to the subject of state formation, we must ask how individuals in the Khaldunian original position *form* their societies. For while Ibn Khaldun insists that society is 'natural', such a statement provides little information on the composition of that society, or the way in which sovereignty is derived. Regarding the equality of persons in Ibn Khaldun's conception of society, the egalitarian nature of Islam is as chequered as that of political liberalism. While Islam freed people of the Middle East from the authority of kings hundreds of years before Europe did the same, it quickly reverted to hereditary royal authority. Likewise, Islam provided an unheard-of level of women's and minority rights at its inception, though these rights seem stagnant and insufficient with the advent of social or democratic liberalism. But to hold up the record of historical Islamic governance with that of modern-day liberalism is a fallacy, as liberalism, too, has its dark periods. Domenico Losurdo points out, for example, that '[s]lavery is not something that persisted despite the success of the [eighteenth and nineteenth century European and American] liberal revolutions. On the contrary, it experienced its maximum development following that success'.[93]

Political liberalism has matured over hundreds of years, yet even now is argued by Mark Duffield of having maintained large zones of exception across the world, which ensure 'our' liberties by denying 'theirs', whoever they may be,[94] much in the same way that 'exception clauses'[95] have allowed for 'liberal' slavery and 'liberal' colonialism. All the above is to say that despite the place of *dhimmis* (protected minorities) or women who were denied civic rights at various times and places in various classical Islamic polities, Islam has a strong egalitarian current that maintains that '[m]ost noble among you in God's eyes is he who fears God most'.[96] The Qur'anic verse is often used to show that there is no social distinction between Muslims, except that of piety. A more detailed analysis of the relationship between liberalism and Normative Political Islam forms the basis of the next chapter, while presently I continue with the discussion of sovereignty.

In addition to the proposed equality of persons in political Islam, Khadduri highlights another recurrent theme in Ibn Khaldun's work, that of authority. As Khadduri eloquently states, '[authority] is regarded as absolutely necessary since society without authority [is] impossible; for, though man is a social animal by nature, he is not a well-behaving animal'.[97] This much has already been demonstrated in Ibn Khaldun's thinking, but what remains to be discussed is how in a society of equals, an outcome-maximising individual might consent to be ruled by another. Further still, how does this outcome-maximising individual consent to being ruled by God, as Muslim states must come to terms with chapter 5, verse 43 of the Qur'an when it states, '[k]nowest thou not that to Allah alone belongeth the dominion of the heavens and the earth?'[98]

A Muslim sovereign, in the Sunni ideal, is constrained, to some extent, by God's *shari'a*; for the Muslim sovereign to go against the *shari'a* is to lose legitimacy, and in this limited way respects the sovereignty of God. If Normative Political Islam were to place *shari'a* in the position of natural rights and laws, perhaps in a similar way to inalienable human rights, what results is a sovereign that has the legitimacy of God, through respect of the *shari'a*. This is somewhat similar to John Locke's social contract, wherein political authority is legitimised *both* by popular consent *and* that authority's respect for the natural rights that individuals enjoyed in the state of nature.[99]

That is not to say that the sovereign, as legitimised in a Locke-style social contract, is always right in its actions. For Locke, even if a society gives their complete consent to a sovereign, it does not make the sovereign's actions right if it does not respect the natural law.[100] In effect, if individuals in a society governed by Normative Political Islam consent to actions that infringe on their natural rights (their duties interpreted through *shari'a*), then these actions are morally wrong, though that is not to say that the action cannot be carried out. The space afforded by Locke to natural rights and natural law, which is an articulation of God's will in his schema, seems to meld well with the notion of God's sovereignty in Islamic society.

Crawford Brough Macpherson's socialist critique of Locke argues that Locke's concept of human nature is intrinsically linked with capitalism. He refers to this human nature as 'possessive individualism'.[101] An Islamic notion of sovereignty is far more communitarian in nature than the asocial individualism propounded by liberal thinkers. This is alluded to in the base assumption of liberalism that humanity by natural condition is free, while in Ibn Khaldun's approach humanity by natural condition is social. Communitarianism argues that 'people's private identity really is tied to certain [communal] ends'.[102] Sunni orthodoxy's treatment of minority communities highlights the difference between the individualism practised by modern liberal states and the communitarianism of historical Islamic polities, wherein group tolerance was preferred over individual autonomy. The different minority groups in the Ottoman Empire (recognising that only the other Abrahamic faiths, the *ahl al-kitab*, were afforded such a status), for example, were 'permitted to practice their religions and earn their livelihood, as long as they deferred to Muslim authority and kept a low profile'.[103] This form of group tolerance did not respect the rights of the individual; while the group remained unmolested, the individual was not able to leave his community without being accused of apostasy, a crime punishable by death. In this regard Will Kymlicka describes the Ottoman method of rule over minorities as 'antithetical to the ideals of personal liberty'.[104]

The debate on the extent to which an Islamic society might respect individual freedoms, and beyond that an analysis of the pros and cons respect for such freedoms would yield, is not integral to the present discussion on sovereignty. However, the conclusions reached on the matter of sovereignty will have direct impact on the nature of individual rights in Normative Political Islam, and is a subject that I will return to in the next chapter. Currently, we have reached a possible solution to the first part of the puzzle: a ruler can respect the sovereignty of God by obeying the *shari'a*. As seen earlier though, the *shari'a* can be very opaque when dealing with political issues. Additionally, as *shari'a* is a result of human interpretation, it has problems with legitimacy outside any particular orthodoxy. *Shari'a* represents theology, and injunctions in the source texts in and of themselves cannot provide enough guidance to Normative Political Islam. Khomeini's political theory builds on theology *with mysticism* to develop an Islamic notion of politics. The approach of the mystics is derided by more orthodox Muslims; it vests exclusive knowledge of 'the truth' in an 'elite' or otherwise blessed few individuals, taking away from the egalitarian message of Islam. Moving beyond the sovereignty of God to justifying the sovereignty of a leader amongst equals, whilst simultaneously refining ambiguous theological guidance, is the remaining task for an Islamic exoteric method.

Deriving Political Sovereignty via an Exoteric Method

Khadduri describes a dual agreement amongst the Muslims of Medina to explain the transition of sovereignty from the Prophet Muhammed to his successors. He explains that '[u]nder Muhammad not only the executive, but also the legislative and judicial functions of Allah were united. . . . In more precise terms we may argue that only the possession of sovereignty resided with Allah, while its exercise was delegated to Muhammad'.[105] During the Prophet's lifetime, then, a single contract was needed to justify a Muslim's loyalty to him. As Muhammed's authority was synonymous with God's, granting sovereignty to one was tantamount to granting sovereignty to the other. With the death of the Prophet, those who had interpreted their contract to lie with Muhammed sought to reject the authority of Medina, the capital of the nascent Islamic polity. Those who interpreted their contract to lie with God were left to appoint a successor to Muhammed, 'entrusted with the execution of the divine commands which were still binding upon the Muslims'.[106]

Khadduri identifies the two contracts used to delineate sovereignty in the period of the *rashidun* and beyond to be:

1. A contract between the Muslims, and God and Muhammed, represented by submission to Islam, the declaration of faith, *shahada*.
2. A contract between the Muslims and the Caliph (or approximate leader), the Muslims empowering the Caliph to enforce the divine law.[107]

Related to the use of dual contracts to resolve the issue of God's sovereignty next to the sovereignty of a temporal ruler, Maududi identified a distinction between a 'Muslim' and 'Islamic' state.[108] These two concepts fall on the same lines as Khadduri's two contracts, but Maududi articulated them in the form of two different kinds of sovereignty, political and legal. 'Political sovereignty thus naturally means ownership of the authority of enforcing legal sovereignty'.[109] Here Maududi has introduced a hierarchy to the dual contract. The one, pertaining to legal sovereignty, is superior to the second, pertaining to political sovereignty. Legal sovereignty is also referred to as the 'Divine Code' by Maududi, and in this way he finds space for God, through the *shari'a*, to legislate in the Islamic State. The political sovereignty he describes is that of a 'vicegerent of God' and therefore, 'the scope of its activities will naturally be restricted within the limits ordained by the Almighty Himself'.[110] In this way he does not contradict the Qur'anic injunction in chapter 2, verse 229, '[t]hese are the limits ordained by God; so do not transgress them'.[111] Such a stalwart belief in the *shari'a*, however, does not acknowledge the fact that it is created through human interpretation, not divine creation, as Maududi would believe.

If Muslims, by virtue of their *shahada*, automatically abide by the first contract with God and the Prophet Muhammed, then does this reinforce the arguments of *din wa dawla* proponents? For such ideologues, the inseparability of politics from religion would mean no second contract is necessary, as adherence to the laws of God and His Messenger is all that is needed to form an Islamic state. Eickelman and Piscatori's assumptions as to the nature of 'sacred authority' are of great utility in the present discussion. The two assumptions the authors make are: First, sacred authority is one kind of authority amongst others. As not all authority is based on religion, then religious authority is not all-encompassing, as *din wa dawla* proponents argue; and secondly, that sacred authority does not assume religion and politics are independent spheres of activity. They are separable and intersect according to context.[112] The dual Islamic contract relies on the separation of religious and other forms of authority to function, but that will not do to silence *din wa dawla* ideologues.

Ibn Khaldun, as alluded to earlier, also linked the formation of society and government to religious duty, though for him this was done in an attempt to incorporate the rule of Muhammed and the *rashidun* into his work; Lenn Evan Goodman claims that Ibn Khaldun 'cheerfully admits that Muhammad does not fit within his model of leadership'[113] when in fact much of Ibn

Khaldun's argument applies *solely* to the Prophet Muhammed and his immediate successors. In Ibn Khaldun's description of the early years of Islam and the Islamic polity, a large emphasis is placed on religion. In this era, people had what Ibn Khaldun described as a 'restraining' influence within themselves. He talks about the asceticism of early Islam, and the *rashidun* in particular, as a key to the self-restraint that was indicative of this early caliphate. For Ibn Khaldun, then, the predominance of the faith in the early period of Islam was the reason only one contract, the first *shahada* contract, was needed to form government at that time. Such is not the situation today, and the *shahada* does not bind the Muslim community in the way it once might have. The authority of the *rashidun* was 'indistinguishable from the public body'[114] in their time, but under the Umayyad dynasty of the seventh and eighth centuries, authority became distanced from civil society. The death of the Prophet and an end to direct access to divine guidance meant the need for a second contract to legitimise authority in the Islamic polity was evident. This recognition of changing social and religious conditions in the story of Muhammed and the *rashidun* is what separates Ibn Khaldun from *din wa dawla* advocates. As Ibn Rushd's rationalist tradition dictates, 'truths' for the *rashidun* and Muhammed, the need for one pact with society to legitimise sovereignty, do not transfer to social situations distinct from the one those 'truths' were conceived from. Therefore, for those without direct access to the divine message, a feat achieved in Khomeini's conception of Shi'ism, a second contract, while breaking from the tradition of the Prophet and the *rashidun*, becomes necessary.

The second contract is an explicitly political contract when compared to the first, which being related to the Muslim's declaration of faith can be described as explicitly religious in nature. The second contract relates to life in the temporal world. The distinction between the temporal and the transcendental is one that recurs in Islamic discourse, and as recalled in chapter 2, much of the ambiguity about political guidance in Islamic source texts centres on temporal and transcendental aspects of the *shari'a*. For Ibn Khaldun an Islamic government, by which he is using the Caliphal paradigm of government, is a substitute for the role of Muhammed, 'in as much as it serves, like him, to preserve the religion and to exercise (political) leadership of the world'.[115] Therein lie the two aspects of Islamic leadership, which equate to the two contracts between government and the individual. The first is grounded in religion, and is an authority that 'will be useful for life in both this and the other world'.[116] The second is an authority that is based on an 'intellectual (rational) basis',[117] and is only of benefit to this temporal world. When my theoretical Muslim contractors agree to the second contract, they are agreeing primarily to prevent anarchy, which would lead to the demise of humanity. As a secondary concern, they are empowering the Caliph to enforce the divine law as agreed in the first contract.

This second contract is built on the first, in the hierarchy that Maududi alludes to. The first, *shahada* contract binds Muslims to the law, and in the words of Ibn Khaldun, '[t]he law ... precedes the state: it provides the basis of the state'.[118] But does this law, presumably the *shari'a*, restrict the ability of the polity to function? In adhering to the first contract, adhering to the tenets of Islam, the fear is that an Islamic state might behave in ways that could be perceived as irrational (not self-serving), or be compelled to break the peace in ways a secular state could avoid. Khadduri's historical account of the Islamic polity would seem to reinforce this view. He states that '[t]he nature of such a [universal, Islamic] state is entirely exclusive; it does not recognize, by definition, the co-existence of a second universal state. While Islam tolerated Christianity and Judaism as religions, Islamdom and Christendom, as two universal states, could not peacefully coexist'.[119] Piscatori puts this point of view regarding religion and politics succinctly, a position he is not an advocate of, writing, 'religious zealotry of all kinds demands enemies to be eliminated'.[120] I will refute the above view of religion and politics, as well as critiques of a political contract being somehow secondary to a religious contract, in three ways.

First, I argue that in certain circumstances my fictional Muslim contractor, in agreeing to the second political contract, is not necessarily agreeing to the enforcement of divine law. In such circumstances the political authority has perhaps succumbed to the evils that can result from it, 'such as tyranny, injustice, and pleasure-seeking'.[121] If such a case was not possible, then for what reason does Ibn Khaldun expound upon a taxonomy of the various authorities in Muslim lands? In fact, there is a difference between a caliph (or imam, which Ibn Khaldun uses as an approximate term) and a sultan or *mulk* (king). The former satisfy *both* contracts with the Muslims, the latter only the second in its purely temporal nature. Both are possible, and it is possible for Muslims to consent to both types of authority.

If Muslims are able to practice their faith, then the first contract is upheld. That the second contract is not used to its full advantage, to uphold and enforce Islamic values in a given territory, does not mean that its lesser function, that of maintaining government, is not of value. Upholding government is necessary for Muslims to practise their faith, and functionally necessary to avoid the destruction of the species.

A second argument countering the admonition of religion blended with politics is that of historical precedence. Piscatori uses Qur'anic verse and historical precedent to show how Islam endorses a pluralistic political life, thereby nullifying the universalism of the *faith* in the realm of the *political*. Among many verses used by Piscatori to this end,[122] the most poignant is chapter 42, verse 8, which states: 'If God had so willed, He would have made them one community'.[123] This verse lays the foundations for ideological and political divisions in Muslim territory and perhaps, even, territorial divisions.

On historical precedent, Piscatori references the pacts made by Muhammed with the Jews of Medina, the Christians of Aqaba and the polytheists of Mecca. After the period of the *rashidun* he points to the Umayyad relationship with the Byzantines, where one Caliph established truce and tribute with the Byzantines, another accepted aid from them to decorate the Prophet's Mosque and the Great Mosque in Damascus. 'The Abbasids rather more routinely concluded treaties with foreigners',[124] and during the Crusades several formal treaties were established between the Muslims and the European, Christian kings.[125] Piscatori concludes that, against the perceived universality of Islamic politics, 'Muslim rulers found no difficulty at all in having formal diplomatic dealings with non-Muslims when it was necessary to do so'.[126] So, if the Sunni Islamic social contract does not *always* demand that political authority support the cause of Islam-as-faith, as long as that authority does not impinge on the Muslims, and the ideological, political and territorial universality of Islam are not as universal as once believed, there is one final reason to contest the idea that religion and politics cannot mix (in the case of Islam).

For this final point I turn to Arkoun, who makes reference to 'secular religions' like Marxism and Fascism, and believes that secularism and religion have common features.[127] John Gray talks further on these common features, and comments on the similarities between the religious fundamentalism of al-Qaeda and other 'Western', secular, political ideologies. It is not, for Gray, religion that is a cause of what is considered 'irrational' behaviour, rather the characteristics of political modernity. Al-Qaeda's assertion that they can create a perfect order on earth is a peculiar myth shared by Nazism, Communism and Positivism.[128] The only difference between religious brutality in the past and contemporary religious or ideological brutality is that previously damage was done to individuals and society for the sake of life after death, whereas now it is done for the sake of some idealised utopia that can be realised in the here and now.[129] There is nothing inherent in religion, and specifically in Normative Political Islam as I have defined it, that should be feared as 'irrational' in the international sphere.

CONCLUSIONS

In this chapter I sought to engage Normative Political Islam with transnational Islam, which was identified to be the articulation of political Islam that exposes the most poignant sites of conflict with IR. The foremost challenge transnational Islam poses to IR was argued to be sovereignty, specifically the sovereignty of God.

Having demonstrated that the guidance in the Qur'an on politics is ambiguous, and building on the recognition of 'kingly' and 'prophetic' rule by al-

Raziq outlined in chapter 1, here I refined and supplemented this theological guidance, to arrive at a notion of Islamic politics. This was achieved by looking outside theology, to philosophy and mysticism. In the exploration of mysticism I discussed the ways in which Ayatollah Khomeini utilised *hekmat* to give credence to the notion of a privileged knowledge of God and truth by Shi'a imams. This esoteric knowledge allows for one person's interpretation of religious texts to become *the* interpretation of that subject. In Sunni Islam it was established that one of the roots of law, *ijma'*, is used to prevent just such an appropriation of interpretative licence, explaining the reason that there is such theological resistance to the idea of one 'true' Islamic path in Sunni orthodoxy.

Despite the resistance of religious scholars, Islamists show more and more their insistence that all guidance on politics can be derived from the *shari'a*, if correctly interpreted. I looked then to the last strand of Islamic knowledge, philosophy, to supplement religious guidance on politics much in the same way Khomeini attempted with mysticism. Tracing the exoteric, rational and demonstrative tradition in Sunni Islam, from al-Kindi through to al-Farabi, Ibn Sina, Ibn Hazm and Ibn Rushd, I arrived at Ibn Khaldun's *Muqaddimah* as a means to operationalise the abstract notions of rationalism to the domain of politics and sovereignty.

I concluded that a theory of sovereignty that is centred on a dual agreement, as propounded by Khadduri,[130] adequately resolves the need for Muslims to recognise God's sovereignty as well as the sovereignty of temporal leaders. My Muslim contractors, by virtue of their declaration of faith, agree to the moral precepts of the *shari'a*, and in doing so respect the sovereignty of God. A second agreement with a temporal authority is also established, but in order for the polity to be considered 'Islamic' as per Normative Political Islam, the temporal authority must also respect that same commitment to the first agreement.

I explored two major implications of this dual agreement. First was the notion that a Muslim is perfectly capable of adhering to the first contract in territories that do not govern in accordance with the declaration of faith. In other words, respect for God's sovereignty, given the ambiguous guidance on politics in religious source texts, does not imply a government wherein God is sovereign. Such a conclusion respects the differentiation between rule over territory and rule over people; if Muslims are bound by God's commandments with respect to Islam-as-faith, then that is true regardless of the territory in which the Muslim lives. Secondly, the agreement that relates directly to the temporal world is one that is based on human ingenuity, and so the need to derive all models and theories of politics from theological sources is avoided. Such a method answers the pleas of Moroccan philosopher 'Abed al-Jabri, who calls for a return of Aristotelian logic to Arab and Islamic thought.

The ways in which this notion of sovereignty might interact with the international system remains unexplored, and is the subject of the next chapter. In it, I will investigate what the focus on community, rather than the individual, might mean in the context of IR. The notion of communitarianism that has been touched upon in this chapter will be more thoroughly explored and related to the concept of political modernity and the idea of 'multiple modernities'. In such ways, I will be dealing primarily with questions around the *umma*, bringing it into a dialogue with the concept of state, to better grasp what both concepts do well, and what they cannot achieve.

NOTES

1. Dale Eickelman and James Piscatori, *Muslim Politics* (Princeton: Princeton University Press, 1996), 56.
2. L. Carl Brown, *Religion and State: The Muslim Approach to Politics* (New York: Columbia University Press, 2000), 175.
3. Talal Asad, *Formations of the Secular: Christianity, Islam, Modernity* (Stanford: Stanford University Press, 2003), 11.
4. *The Holy Qur'an* (Dublin, OH: Ahmadiyya Anjuman Ishaat Islam), 5:45. See also 3:26, 5:40, 5:120 and 6:12.
5. By rationalism I am referring to Aristotelian logic and rationalism, as distinct from Kantian rationalism, for example.
6. In Arabic gnosis, *erfan*, is a sub-field of *hekmat*, literally 'wisdom'. I refer to gnosis in English but will use the Arabic for *hekmat*, as this has no clear equivalent in the English language.
7. Majid Khadduri, *War and Peace in the Law of Islam* (Baltimore: Johns Hopkins Press, 1955), 9–12.
8. Andrew March, 'Islamic Foundations for a Social Contract in Non-Muslim Liberal Democracies', *American Political Science Review* 101, no. 2 (2007): 236.
9. John Esposito, *Islam and Politics*, 4th ed. (New York: Syracuse University Press, 1998), 312.
10. Rashid Rida, 'Patriotism, Nationalism, and Group Spirit in Islam', in *Islam in Transition: Muslim Perspectives*, ed. John Donohue and John Esposito, 2nd ed. (Oxford: Oxford University Press, 2007), 47.
11. Organisation of Islamic Cooperation, 'Charter of the Organisation of Islamic Cooperation', accessed on 24.08.2012, http://www.oic-oci.org/page_detail.asp?p_id=53.
12. Peter Mandaville, *Global Political Islam* (London: Routledge, 2007), 287.
13. Nazih Ayubi, *Political Islam: Religion and Politics in the Arab World* (London: Routledge, 1991), 64.
14. Ibid., 146.
15. Ibid., 120.
16. Such ideas are classically attributed to Jamal al-Din al-Afghani, Muhammed Abduh, Rashid Rida and Hasan al-Banna.
17. Mohammed Arkoun, 'Rethinking Islam Today', in *Liberal Islam: A Sourcebook*, ed. Charles Kurzman (Oxford: Oxford University Press, 1998), 205.
18. Abdullahi An-Na'im, '*Shari'a* and Basic Human Rights Concerns', in *Liberal Islam: A Sourcebook*, ed. Charles Kurzman (Oxford: Oxford University Press, 1998), 222–38.
19. S. M. Zafar, 'Accountability, Parliament and Ijtihad', in *Liberal Islam: A Sourcebook*, ed. Charles Kurzman (Oxford: Oxford University Press, 1998), 67–72.
20. Roy Jackson, *Mawlana Mawdudi and Political Islam: Authority and the Islamic State* (London: Routledge, 2008), 86.

21. Abu A'la Maududi, *First Principles of the Islamic State*, 2nd ed. (Lahore: Islamic Publications, 1960), 22–25.

22. For more on the debate on religious rationality see Erin Wilson, *After Secularism: Rethinking Religion in Global Politics* (Basingstoke: Palgrave Macmillan, 2012), and Elizabeth Hurd, *The Politics of Secularism in International Relations* (Princeton: Princeton University Press, 2008).

23. James Piscatori, 'Imagining Pan-Islam: Religious Activism and Political Utopias', *Proceedings of the British Academy* 131 (2005): 427.

24. Amr Sabet, *Islam and the Political: Theory, Governance and International Relations* (London: Pluto, 2008), 183.

25. Piscatori, 'Imagining Pan-Islam', 426.

26. Peter Mandaville, *Transnational Muslim Politics: Reimagining the Umma* (London: Routledge, 2001), 5.

27. Ibid., 14.

28. Mandaville, *Global Political Islam*, 335.

29. The interplay between sacred and secular authority is explored in the context of Saudi Arabia in Eickelman and Piscatori, *Muslim Politics*, 60.

30. *Holy Qur'an*, 6:12. For more verses on the sovereignty of God see 13:26, 15:43, and 15:20.

31. Eickelman and Piscatori, *Muslim Politics*, 54.

32. *Holy Qur'an*, 6:165.

33. Ibid., 7:10.

34. Hossein Nasr, *Islamic Philosophy from its Origin to the Present: Philosophy in the Land of Prophecy* (New York: State University of New York Press, 2006), 31.

35. Fazlur Rahman, *Islam* (Chicago: University of Chicago Press, 1979), 102.

36. Joseph Schacht, *The Origins of Muhammadan Jurisprudence* (Oxford: Oxford University Press, 1950), 1.

37. Imam an-Nawawi, *The Complete Forty Hadith* (London: Ta-Ha, 2000), 16–25.

38. Albert Hourani, *A History of the Arab Peoples* (London: Faber and Faber, 1991), 181–84.

39. Tjitze De Boer, *The History of Philosophy in Islam* (New York: Dover, 1967), 167.

40. Hourani, *History of the Arab Peoples*, 181–82.

41. Khomeini in Mehdi Moslem, *Factional Politics in Post-Khomeini Iran* (New York: Syracuse University Press, 2002), 13.

42. Rahman, *Islam*, 174–75.

43. Hourani, *History of the Arab Peoples*, 183.

44. Rahman, *Islam*, 173.

45. Ruhullah Khumayni, 'Islamic Government', in *Islam in Transition: Muslim Perspectives*, ed. John Donohue and John Esposito, 2nd ed. (Oxford: Oxford University Press, 2007), 333.

46. Ibid., 334.

47. Abdul-Karim Soroush, 'The Evolution and Devolution of Religious Knowledge', in *Liberal Islam: A Sourcebook*, ed. Charles Kurzman (Oxford: Oxford University Press, 1998), 245–46.

48. Khumayni, 'Islamic Government', 335.

49. Ibid., 337.

50. Jacqueline Ismael and Tarek Ismael, 'Social Change in Islamic Society: The Political Thought of Ayatollah Khomeini', *Social Problems* 27, no. 5 (1980): 614.

51. Baqer Moin, *Khomeini: Life of the Ayatollah* (London: I.B. Tauris, 1999), 40–41.

52. Shahrough Akhavi, 'Islam, Politics and Society in the Thought of Ayatullah Khomeini, Ayatullah Taliqani and Ali Shariati', *Middle Eastern Studies* 24, no. 4 (1988): 404.

53. Khomeini in Ismael and Ismael, 'Social Change in Islamic Society', 616.

54. Akhavi, 'Islam, Politics and Society', 428.

55. Mehdi Moslem, *Factional Politics in Post-Khomeini Iran* (New York: Syracuse University Press, 2002), 14.

56. Moin, *Khomeini*, 46.

57. Nasr, *Islamic Philosophy from its Origin to the Present*, 49–51.
58. Ibid., 49.
59. De Boer, *History of Philosophy in Islam*, 154.
60. In Latin al-Ghazali is known as Algazel.
61. Nasr, *Islamic Philosophy from its Origin to the Present*, 50.
62. De Boer, *History of Philosophy in Islam*, 154.
63. Nasr, *Islamic Philosophy from its Origin to the Present*, 109.
64. Mohammed 'Abed al-Jabri, *Arab-Islamic Philosophy: A Contemporary Critique* (Austin, TX: Center for Middle Eastern Studies, 1999), 2–3.
65. In Latin al-Farabi is known as Alpharabius.
66. De Boer, *History of Philosophy in Islam*, 109.
67. In Latin Ibn Sina is known as Avicenna.
68. De Boer, *History of Philosophy in Islam*, 132–34.
69. 'Abed al-Jabri, *Arab-Islamic Philosophy*, 57–59.
70. Rahman, *Islam*, 104.
71. 'Abed al-Jabri, *Arab-Islamic Philosophy*, 59.
72. Ibid., 72.
73. Ibn Hazm in ibid., 76.
74. In Latin ibn Rushd is known as Averroes.
75. 'Abed al-Jabri, *Arab-Islamic Philosophy*, 82–83.
76. De Boer, *History of Philosophy in Islam*, 189.
77. 'Abed al-Jabri, *Arab-Islamic Philosophy*, 89.
78. Hourani, *History of the Arab Peoples*, 78.
79. 'Abed al-Jabri, *Arab-Islamic Philosophy*, 130.
80. Ibid., 105.
81. Ibn Khaldun, *The Muqaddimah: An Introduction to History* (New York: Pantheon, 1958), lxxiii–lxxx.
82. Bobby Sayyid, *A Fundamental Fear: Eurocentrism and The Emergence of Islamism* (London: Zed, 2003), xxii.
83. Khadduri, *War and Peace in the Law of Islam*, 6–7.
84. Mandaville, *Global Political Islam*, 335.
85. Nicolas Pelham and Max Rodenbeck, 'Which Way for Hamas', *New York Review of Books* 56, no. 17 (2009), accessed on 11/11/15, http://www.nybooks.com/articles/archives/2009/nov/05/which-way-for-hamas/.
86. Ibn Khaldun, *Muqaddimah*, 380.
87. Ibid.
88. Khadduri, *War and Peace in the Law of Islam*, 4.
89. Michael Lessnoff, *Social Contract: Issues in Political Theory* (Basingstoke: Macmillan, 1986), 132.
90. Ibn Khaldun, *Muqaddimah*, 89–90.
91. Khadduri, *War and Peace in the Law of Islam*, 3.
92. Ibn Khaldun, *Muqaddimah*, 91.
93. Domenico Losurdo, *Liberalism: A Counter-History* (London: Verso, 2011), 35.
94. Mark Duffield, *Development, Security and Unending War: Governing the World of Peoples* (Cambridge: Polity, 2007), 192.
95. Losurdo, *Liberalism*, 342.
96. *Holy Qur'an*, 49:13.
97. Khadduri, *War and Peace in the Law of Islam*, 5.
98. *Holy Qur'an*, 5:43.
99. Vicente Medina, *Social Contract Theories: Political Obligation or Anarchy?* (Lanham, MD: Rowman & Littlefield, 1990), 39.
100. Ibid., 40.
101. Crawford Brough Macpherson, *The Political Theory of Possessive Individualism*, 8th ed. (Oxford: Oxford University Press, 1979), 3.
102. Will Kymlicka, *Contemporary Political Philosophy: An Introduction*, 2nd ed. (Oxford: Oxford University Press, 2002), 240.

103. Shlomo Deshen and Walter Zenner, 'Jews among Muslims in Precolonial Times: An Introductory Survey', in *Jews among Muslims: Communities in the Precolonial Middle East*, ed. Shlomo Deshen and Walter Zenner (New York: New York University Press, 1996), 15.

104. Kymlicka, *Contemporary Political Philosophy*, 231.

105. Khadduri, *War and Peace in the Law of Islam*, 10.

106. Ibid.

107. Ibid., 9–12.

108. Ayubi, *Political Islam*, 128.

109. Maududi, *First Principles of the Islamic State*, 18.

110. Ibid., 27.

111. *Holy Qur'an*, 2:229.

112. Eickelman and Piscatori, *Muslim Politics*, 57.

113. Lenn Evan Goodman, 'Ibn Khaldun and Thucydides', *Journal of the American Oriental Society* 92, no. 2 (1972): 253.

114. Rahman, *Islam*, 79.

115. Ibn Khaldun, *Muqaddimah*, 386.

116. Ibid.

117. Ibid.

118. Khadduri, *War and Peace in the Law of Islam*, 16.

119. Ibid., 17.

120. James Piscatori, *Islam in a World of Nation-States* (Cambridge: Cambridge University Press, 1986), 148.

121. Ibn Khaldun, *Muqaddimah*, 391.

122. See *Holy Qur'an*, 49:13, 4:59 and 42:8; and Piscatori, *Islam in a World of Nation-States*, 45–46.

123. *Holy Qur'an*, 42:8.

124. Piscatori, *Islam in a World of Nation-States*, 49.

125. Ibid.

126. Ibid.

127. Arkoun, 'Rethinking Islam Today', 218.

128. John Gray, *Al Qaeda and What It Means to be Modern* (London: Faber and Faber, 2003), 1–4.

129. Ibid., 117.

130. Khadduri, *War and Peace in the Law of Islam*, 9–12.

Chapter Six

Accounting for Community

L. Carl Brown summarises the importance of community when he states that 'Islam has—for all its cultural and territorial diversity—maintained among its adherents a communal solidarity'.[1] However, this is somewhat of an idealised notion of Islamic solidarity. The self/other distinction between 'communal' Islam and 'individualistic' European or US culture is one that is pushed hard by many Islamists, most famously by Said Qutb. An Egyptian teacher, Qutb visited the Unites States and wrote afterwards about how a corrupted and overly individualistic society existed there, one that was making inroads into his native Egypt. Stalling and combating the influence of this individualistic menace is a hallmark of much Islamist rhetoric. However, such unity is just an ideal. Cleavages between Sunni and Shi'a, between violent Sunni and democratic Sunni, between the Islam of 'back home' and the Islam of diasporic communities, all betray the many lines of belonging and community that criss-cross the Muslim world. However, despite the differences I have mentioned, there is still an *urge* for some sort of unity/solidarity.[2]

Returning to Normative Political Islam, given the many forms in which the *umma* might be articulated in the international sphere,[3] it is not inevitably the state which represents the locus of friction. The state is an adjunct to and derivative of the wider processes of political modernity. Commitment to the *umma* does not *necessitate* abandoning the state in practice or in theory. While in earlier chapters I argued that the *umma* is an alternative, not equivalent, of the state, it does not follow that these alternative methods of governance (rule over territory and rule over individuals) cannot co-exist. As Sohail Hashmi argues with regards to the pan-Islamic movement, *umma* might be articulated as thick or thin. Thick conceptions are represented by *dar al-Islam* or individuals linked through transnational organisations; '[a]ccording to this vision, the *umma* has a life apart from the state or states'. Alternatively thin conceptions of *umma* see it as an internationalist enterprise, perhaps an interstate society.[4] While Hashmi is making explicit overtones to the English School of international relations, the summary is befitting the constructivist viewpoint that, if 'anarchy is what states make of it',[5] so too is the *umma* what Muslims make of it.

In this chapter I will argue that conceptions of the *umma* are constrained by the assumptions of the European Enlightenment project that spawned the concepts of political modernity, including the state. These assumptions, broadly, are linked to the insistence on abstracting individuals out of the social conditions in which they live to find a rational concept of how one should govern and consent to be governed, to find 'the good life'. In abstracting away from social realities, Enlightenment philosophy was attempting to find a universal concept of the good life, and herein is the central issue with a Normative Political Islam. Normative Political Islam finds it necessary to locate its practices in cultural values in order to account for the sovereignty of God. This was achieved using a rational, exoteric method, so that the familiar charge of theocracy would struggle to find purchase with Normative Political Islam. Rather, notions of individual liberty, as distinct to communitarian values, will challenge this conception of sovereignty specifically, and the *umma* more generally. As Mandaville puts it, 'according to conventional accounts of modernity, religion has been relegated to the domain of the private. By reasserting itself in public space, Islam is hence disrupting the modernity which lies at the root of the state'.[6] If this challenge is couched in the liberal/communitarian divide, an exploration of this schism will help us to assess whether Normative Political Islam can operate in the schema of the Enlightenment, and what the implications are if it can, or cannot. Before that, I will discuss the ways in which Islam might interact with community more thoroughly.

Acknowledging that Muslims in the Middle East represent and construct community, and relate this to faith, in different ways from Muslims in Southeast Asia, for example, we must avoid essentialising some 'Islamic' society as a unifying essence of Muslims the globe over (acknowledging that 'Arab' homogeneity is also problematic). As Sami Zubaida articulates, '[c]ulture is a process, part of the historical flux, and cultural patterns are not fixed but reproduced at every generation in relation to different situations and conjectures'.[7] Does it now follow that each different Muslim community might develop a different relationship with the international sphere (thick or thin conceptions of the *umma*, for example)? Perhaps so, and the heterogeneity of positions thus created poses important questions about the applicability of different conceptions of community co-existing in the same geographical space. For example, some British Muslim communities might associate themselves with a thin conception of *umma,* perhaps articulated through a supra-national body like the OIC, but of course the United Kingdom is not a member of the OIC. In another case, a Baluchi Sunni community in Iran might seek a thick conception of *umma* centred on transnational solidarity with scholars at Al-Azhar in Egypt. How such a community would negotiate their obligations to the state versus their obligations to transnational solidarity, and how the state might react to those obligations, are pertinent questions to ask. I will make some headway in answering these types of questions in this chapter, but that is not the main purpose of the argument presented here. Instead, it is the challenge that this particular community holds to IR that preoccupies me. It is not a specific Muslim community which I am writing about. Rather, taking a hypothetical community of Muslims, agreeing to the dual contract explained in the previous chapter—an ideal type community of Normative Political Islamists—I will show how IR struggles to account for *any* community. A similar challenge could be posed by communities in Europe, Shi'a communities, communities in Africa of numerous faiths, and others, insofar as these communities necessitate a stance on the international sphere. An international community of *Star Trek* fans, in contrast, would likely not engage in discussions on how their community should engage with IR.

ISLAM AS COMMUNITY? ISLAM AS CITIZENSHIP?

Civil society, as distinct from the political order, is described as 'voluntary associations of individuals . . . outside the realm of the state'.[8] This type of society, argues Zubaida, does not exist in Arab states. Instead, 'political society'[9] is a more appropriate term. Individuals in political society do not relate to the state as citizens, but as groups staking a claim on rights and services that the state provides, the claim being that 'in much of the Arab world, the politics of citizenship are often eclipsed by the politics of community'.[10] Ayubi refers to Hisham Sharabi's theory of neo-patriarchy to make a similar statement: '[I]n it [modern Arab society] the individual has no individuality: he/she is lost if he breaks with the family, tribe or the sect. . . . The individual's sense of morality is collectivist and applies only within his primary group but not in the larger society'.[11] Mandaville too makes a similar point when he states that Islam presents 'circumstances in which political identities and processes configure themselves across and between forms of political community'.[12] The citizen as established from the 'Western' model derives their rights and duties as a citizen by an abstracted rationality, universally applied, as opposed to being derived from the community they live in. Such a method of deriving citizenship is intimately tied to liberal epistemology and very much derived from a method and practice that is typified by the Enlightenment. This same liberal epistemology does not, I have noted, necessarily transfer seamlessly to various Muslim communities, calling into question either the nature of those communities as 'backward', or the universality of Enlightenment rationality. In the remainder of this section I will explore which of the preceding two statements can be substantiated.

The practices that constitute an Islamic community are as contested as the discussion on what might constitute an Islamic polity. On the one hand, Sabet is very critical of social theory's 'reduction' of Islam 'from a metanarrative to middle ranged categorizations based largely, though not exclusively, on what different Muslim adherents are perceived to say or do'.[13] The idea that different communities might conceive of their Islam differently is not acceptable for Sabet, who stresses that '[w]hen one talks about Islam, one is referring to the universe and cosmology of revelation as uniquely represented by primary texts and scriptures. Hence there is only one Islam, and not many Islams'.[14] A similar view, or in this case fear, about Islam's supposed 'singular vision' for society is seen in Andrew March's attempt at folding in Muslims living in liberal democracies into Rawls's ideal of liberal citizenship. March states that Islam 'offers a single vision for uniting the individual quest for virtue with the social goods of justice and solidarity'.[15] I have already argued that such positions do not sufficiently account for the agency of Muslims in interpreting what may well be static source texts. Rahman shows the relationship between Islam and community in a more dynamic way when he talks of the source texts as primarily a source of moral practices. He notes that 'Muslim law books are full of moralising themes'[16] and that this moral and religiously ethical centre, while it may struggle to be an authoritative guide to communities, is still 'alive with a keen sensitivity to right and wrong . . . [which is] in any age better for humanity than an expediently clever and effective law'.[17]

Such differing interpretations of this moral code lead to the 'diverse and prolific assortment of Islamic ideologies, actors, political parties, and organizations . . . grouped under the umbrella of Islam'.[18] This diverse range of positions might even include interpretations which deny any political meaning Islam might bring to a community; Arkoun talks of the 'silent Islam' of 'true believers who attach more importance to the religious relationship with the absolute of God than to the vehement demonstrations of political movements'.[19]

Both March and Sabet emphasise the challenge for an Islamic liberalism to consist of reconciling a liberal order 'which at the same time preserves and consolidates Islamic principles of religiosity'.[20] Conceivably this religiosity is expressed by the 'truth' these authors claim to exist in the way Islam interacts with the community. As long as nothing is metaphysically 'superior' to Islam then there is no contradiction for Muslims to accept a liberal concept of citizenship. The problem arises with the neutrality of the liberal citizen who, 'in establishing no collective goals that require adherence to a controversial metaphysical doctrine',[21] must afford an equal status to all faiths, including even, for example, Pastafarianism, a faith founded in 2005 to challenge the teaching of intelligent design in US schools.[22] Sharing the same ontological space with the Flying Spaghetti Monster (the deity of Pastafarianism) is not a matter of rhetoric, as March argues, which the state could manipulate to make sure Muslims are not 'asked to *profess* something contrary to Islam or even endure quietly the glorification of a contrary truth'.[23] Rather, it assumes a common commitment to liberal neutrality which cannot be taken for granted in all communities, Muslim or otherwise. This is teased at by Mushir Ul-Haq, who makes a separation between a secular *state*, which for him is permissible by the historical precedent of Islamic governance,[24] and secularism as a doctrine, which he considers incompatible with Islam.[25] The distinction is subtle, showing in the first instance a procedural acceptance of being neighbours with people of different faiths and avoiding conflict on account of that difference (Ul-Haq talks about faith in the case of secularism, but faith can be broadened to community for the purpose of the present discussion). The second instance, secularism as a doctrine, involves accepting a transcendental truth about the nature of all religions as uniformly equal in worth, and a distinction between the public and private spheres.[26] While subtle, this distinction between secularism as practice and secularism as doctrine proves a highly salient point.

The distinction between secularism as a doctrine and secularism as a practice rests once more on the notion of an abstracted value. Secularism as a doctrine is applicable to all peoples by virtue of its universal validity. This is in contrast to secularism as a practice, which is based in the experience of individuals embedded in a community (in this case a multi-faith community). Mine is not a unique observation. Tibi goes to great lengths to first identify a similar problem as was argued in the last chapter, namely, the decline of a rational tradition in Islamic thought, and then to argue for its revival through a wholehearted embrace of the Enlightenment project. On diagnosing the problem, Tibi states that 'the major problems of contemporary Muslim civilization are related to the eclipse of rational discourse since the decline of the Islamic rationalism of the medieval age. In this context, I reiterate the call of al-Jabri for a return to rationality as the ultimate way out of this unsatisfactory position'.[27] While the starting point is evidently similar with the current discussion, Tibi emphasises the need for Islam to reform and embrace modernity, which is viewed by him to be universally applicable and attainable.[28] Such a position belies a developmentalist and essentialist position, two positions that according to Zubaida are separate categories to analyse 'compatibility arguments' (Islam's compatibility with modernity).

Developmentalism assumes that 'there are systematic processes of historical development in stages which apply to all societies'.[29] This position is reflected in Tibi's belief in a universal concept of modernity. The essentialism perpetrated here is not one of Islam, which in fact is conceptualised in a similar way as I have presented Normative Political Islam; Tibi states that for him 'Islam is conceptualized as a cultural system that is always in flux, and is therefore placed in a historical and social context'.[30] Tibi's essentialism is related to his presentation of political and cultural modernity. The 'West' achieved some wondrous marvel in political modernity, and this is now something all other cultures can access given the right reforms. Recalling Hobson's non-reductive Orientalism presented in chapter 3, Tibi's assertion here represents the West's pioneering agency, which Tibi's 'East' does not possess. Instead, Tibi's Islamic societies are reduced to emulating the path already travelled by an enlightened 'West'. In this way, the Orientalism displayed by Tibi is not tied to racism; he is not stating that the 'East' is unable to achieve this modernity without the West's tutelage, only that the 'West' got there first (and indeed, the end point reached by the 'West' is the only legitimate end point for societies, due to the 'universal' nature of modernity). The idea that the Enlightenment and the modernity it spawned was and is contested is not in question for Tibi.

As John Gray summarises, 'Western societies are governed by the belief that modernity is a single condition, everywhere the same and always benign. . . . Being modern means realising our values—the values of the Enlightenment, as we like to think of them'.[31] Tibi's unquestioning acceptance of the existence and virtue of this singular Enlightenment modernity complements his argument that a rejection of universality cannot be compatible with Islamism, which itself is universal.[32] Here is the familiar argument that an Islamic politics is engaged in a zero-sum competition with the politics of the Enlightenment and the 'West'. In presenting such a relationship, Tibi, who earlier is so careful to avoid essentialising Islam, is forced to do so in describing the 'face of Islamism' as uniformly totalitarian. (Preceding the Islamic reform he argues is necessary for Islam to embrace modernity.)[33]

While Tibi seeks to 'modernise' Islam, Sami Zubaida's *Beyond Islam* seeks to dis-embed Islam from discussions of politics in the Middle East. While Tibi struggles to disassociate Islam-as-faith from Islam-as-politics, and in so struggling, he talks of universal Islamic politics, Zubaida makes the distinction between Islam and political Islam very prominent. He argues that 'there are many Muslim societies, and that the range of their variation is comprehensible in terms of the normal practice of social and political analysis, like any other range of societies'.[34] While Zubaida's approach seems to find a lot of resonance with Normative Political Islam, there is still the issue of modernity. For Zubaida this term is not subject to the same nuance as Muslim society, instead presented as a singular truth, much as in Tibi's work. When religion is devoid of political meaning, except that which individuals choose to place into it, Zubaida sees no impetus to engage with the notion of modernity. He insists that '[m]odernities are not alternative: they are ideologically contested',[35] implying once more the singular conception of a political future for all peoples. It follows that if a religion interacts with politics in a way constructed by that religions' adherents, as theorised with Normative Political Islam, then the same is true with a concept of political modernity. If modernity is evacuated of the Enlightenment's propensity for universalism, it too takes meaning in ways constructed by the participants of that modernity. What needs to be revived and cultivated in any discussion of Islam and political modernity is the notion of community.

As I have shown in this section, Muslim community as a referent object for deriving politics is often at odds with an abstracted and, most relevant for the discussion here, faithless individual (though that individual is also genderless, raceless, classless etc.). This is most clearly seen with regards to the state as a method of governing people and secularism as an inherent doctrine of that governance. Both instances, state and secularism, can show insensitivity to communal practices and lives, justifying that insensitivity through a belief in a universal notion of justice derived from the abstracted individual. It is at the level of analysis of the community (indicative of al-Jabri's call to Aristotelian principles) and the individual (indicative of the liberalism of the Enlightenment) that is the crux of the issue with regards to Normative Political Islam's engagement with modernity. Accounting for community seems to reaffirm al-Jabri's conclusion that '[a]s for the human legacy in general, with its universal attributes, a nation always experiences it within its own tradition and not outside it'.[36]

In the next section of the chapter I will explore the debate between liberalism and communitarianism. Doing so will highlight the ways in which modernity is not a fixed concept but one that is debated and challenged by those even within the 'West' who supposedly 'possess' this modernity. This discussion overlays with the discussion of Normative Political Islam's emphasis on values derived from specific cultural contexts—values which inevitably will impact on politics. Through the coming discussion I hope to discover if the rationality of Normative Political Islam can interact with the rationality of the Enlightenment, or if there is a zero-sum relationship between the two, as Tibi argues.

Liberalism and Communitarianism

Alasdair MacIntyre, whose powerful critique of Enlightenment philosophy I will return to later, characterises what he refers to as 'the Enlightenment project'; this project is a 'systematic attempt to discover a rational justification for morality'.[37] This rational justification of morality took the form of liberalism, and its attempt 'to identify a universal conception of human needs or human rationality, and then . . . [invoke] this ahistorical conception of the human being to evaluate existing social and political arrangements'.[38] However, to paint liberalism in such broad strokes is to do a disservice to the tradition. Richard Bellamy identifies two general liberal traditions; one is based on 'a doctrine which is neutral between different conceptions of the good', and the other 'avowedly communitarian in nature: that is, as linked to a definite type of society and presupposing a shared understanding of its values'.[39] Within both 'forks' in this liberal trajectory there are many further distinctions to be made regarding the very nature of justice, narrow and wide concepts of liberal neutrality, thick and thin conceptions of community, etc. It is not necessary here to account for a history of ideas, be they communitarian or liberal. Rather, I will adopt much the same position of Philip Pettit when he states: 'I occasionally deal in general, ideal-typical characterization of the past, as in discussing the Enlightenment and counter-Enlightenment, but I hope the lines I take will be more or less uncontroversial'.[40] It suffices for my argument, then, to talk about liberalism in reference to its universal aspirations and assumptions about neutrality, which I will explore in more detail presently.

Liberal Universalism?

Maureen Ramsay asserts that '[i]t is not an exaggeration to say that the whole of the Western political system was founded on and shaped by liberal principle and values'.[41] The pervasiveness of this ideology justifies the initial characterisation of the Enlightenment project as more than MacIntyre's rational justification for morality, but rather a *universal* rational justification for *liberal* morality. This rational universality is achieved by abstracting the individual out of her social situation in such a way that 'the liberal individual has her own independent conception of the good'.[42] This independence is a matter of contention for Normative Political Islam in much the same way it is contentious for communitarians, that is, if Islamic politics (for Normative Political Islam) or notions of justice (for communitarians) are derived from communal understandings, then there cannot be such a thing as 'universal' values. Michael Sandel, a critic of the universal liberal position, caricatures the liberal individualist perspective and it is worth quoting at length his description to grasp fully the communitarian critique of that position:

> Freed from the dictates of nature and the sanction of social roles, the human subject is installed as sovereign, cast as the author of the only moral meanings there are. As participants in pure practical reason, or as parties to the original position, we are free to construct principles of justice unconstrained by an order of value antecedently given. And as actual, individual selves, we are free to choose our purposes and ends unbound by such an order, or by custom or tradition or inherited status. So long as they are not unjust, our conceptions of the good carry weight, whatever they are, simply in virtue of our having chosen them.[43]

Here one can see the allusions to neutrality and universality tied up with the notion of an unbounded rationality, unrelated to social context. If societies and cultures do not embrace liberal values, it is because they are not 'rational' enough. The concept of rationality, and hence liberalism, is considered as value neutral. Rawls, for example, is keen to show that his famous notion of 'justice as fairness' is not dependent on certain philosophical claims, 'for example, claims to universal truth, or claims about the essential nature and identity of person'.[44]

The communitarian critique of this position sees a universal theory of justice as unattainable: '[t]here is no such thing as a perspective external to the community, no way to step outside our history and culture'.[45] Such a position has resonance with al-Jabri's claim that human legacy is experienced 'within . . . [a nation's] own tradition and not outside it'.[46] With regards to Normative Political Islam's interaction with communitarianism, an immediate concern arises in the notion of no perspective being held externally to community. Clearly, the Islamic message necessitates submission to the external will of God, and the notions of justice derived therein. Here the distinction made between Islam-as-faith (where claims of universality can be located) and Islam-as-politics (which I argued in chapters 2 and 5 to allow a plurality of competing claims), can aid the current discussion. Talk of how one should be rule and be ruled is different from how one should worship; if indeed there is a singular conception of Muslim worship, I have established that there is considerable variance in how one should be ruled in the Islamic tradition. Accepting such plurality does not diminish the ontological problem of transcendental 'truth', which is something Islam-as-faith lays a claim upon. The communitarian approach that will be expanded upon presently, and the poststructural position on ontology that I have hitherto embraced, both deny that such a truth exists. This is a problem returned to in the next chapter; for now I will continue with an analysis of communitarianism and liberalism, aware of the limitations of engaging Normative Political Islam with the former.

When discussing justice it has been noted that liberalism assumes a position whereby 'rationality' determines the goods which are to be distributed, and to whom. Communitarian positions, like liberal ones, cover a range of divergent positions on the nature of community, and respect given to communal practices. Communitarian positions, in general terms, sees autonomy as dependent on social context. More pertinent for the present discussion is the moral claim that an individual, in being a member of a community, is 'included within moral calculations',[47] as opposed to developing those considerations outside of the society in which they develop. Put another way by Emanuel Adler: 'Rationality lies less in the act of instrumental choice between alternatives on the basis of true theories than in acting in ways that "stand to reason" given people's background expectations and dispositions'.[48] It is not my purpose in this chapter to show which and what type of politics is most appropriate for Normative Political Islam. Rather, if my assumptions about the plurality of competing claims about justice, as derived from differing social contexts, is correct, then the search for 'the politics of Normative Political Islam' is a futile one. Normative Political Islam merely allows individuals and communities to construct their structures of government in ways they find appropriate for them to achieve their communal ends.

Such an approach, however, is not a justification for social conservatism or cultural relativism, a criticism often levied against communitarianism. As Michael Walzer argues, 'pluralism does not require us to endorse every proposed distributive criteria or to accept every would-be-agent'.[49] The relativism critique implies that communitarian-based politics is always contingent and contextual, whereas the rationality of liberalism is universal. Indeed, Veit Bader laments that communitarian positions dilute the meaning of morality:

> If communitarianism, for all its versions, pretends to be an identifiable position in practical philosophy, then it must mean that in all hard cases the particularist requirements of community must trump the universalist ones of justice. . . . Universalist principles and rights should not only trump prudentialist utility but also the ethics of particular communities.[50]

Bader's position clearly highlights a notion of justice that is universally applicable. Such a position is intimately tied with the ideas of 'progress' indicative of the Enlightenment. If a universalist ethic trumps communally based ones, a notion of developmentalism is introduced whereby it is acceptable to enforce a universal ethic; it is more 'advanced' than justice derived from community. I have argued that in fact the universalism of liberalism is contingent on a specific understanding of community. In addition, politics that derive from community need not be 'irrational', seen in the theory of deriving sovereignty in Normative Political Islam via an exoteric method. Universal applicability and interaction between different notions of justice is a theme I will return to later in the chapter when I overlay the present discussion upon the international sphere and Islamic IR. Before looking at communal theories of IR, I will continue by exploring what communitarianism might offer to Normative Political Islam. Such an exploration is necessary; later it will be seen that talk of community in international relations, especially in the English School, builds upon, often in an unconscious manner, the debate being presented here between liberalism and communitarianism.

Communitarianism and Normative Political Islam

Walzer's communitarian argument in *Spheres of Justice* argues for an inherent plurality in the notion, or better put, *notions* of justice; there is no set of criteria to decide on who gets what.[51] Speaking directly to the atomism of liberalism, he claims that '[w]e cannot say what is due to this person or that until we know how these people relate to one another through the things they make and distribute. There cannot be a just society until there is a society'.[52] However, Walzer's communities and societies are idealised, generally culturally homogenous and deny the historical and contemporary violence needed to create these communities.[53] There is a conspicuous lack of recognition that societal structures perpetuate themselves sometimes not through consenting agents, but rather 'mirror the balance of power of the various groups within them and the conventions and customs of the economic and political practices in which their members are engaged'.[54] Here, Bader highlights that Walzer is over-reliant on the state to provide a sense of 'closure' to his community, preventing the splintering of people into smaller and smaller groups. The state, for Walzer, is 'necessary and legitimate to defend shared meaning, values, and ways of life'.[55] Such an argument, however, 'clings to the superposition of ethnic, cultural, and national identities and citizenship'.[56]

So I have presented on the one hand liberalism's universalism, which denies cultural or 'lived' truths, while on the other hand I have presented a communitarian perspective which alludes to a community that bears little resemblance to multicultural realities. If it is true that '[j]ustice is relative to social meanings',[57] then operationalising that dictum is proving difficult. For example, when an individual considers a practice to be unjust within the community they are a part of, does that infer that the individual is no longer part of the community? Such a view would see gradual splintering of 'community' to 'a thousand petty fortresses'.[58] Normative Political Islam has avoided this problem somewhat by the emphasis on a dual contract between the individual and government.

Recalling the dual contract in the style of Khadduri,[59] one contract is between Muslim and God through the declaration of faith (*shahada*), and a second between the Muslim and a temporal authority. Such a separation of sovereignty allows for Muslims to live in non-Muslim territory, as long as the temporal authority does not impinge upon the individual's ability to fulfil the first contract. Likewise in Muslim territory, any method of government is acceptable and does not contravene God's sovereignty, insofar as the Muslim temporal power respects the commitment to the first agreement.

Connecting the discussion of liberalism and communitarianism to sovereignty derived from Normative Political Islam, let me highlight that the first agreement, between the Muslim and God, resembles the universalism of liberal notions of justice in two ways. First, just as liberalism is a broad and contested tradition, a Muslim's concept of what constitutes their agreement with God in their declaration of faith is not pre-determined in scripture. Secondly, both liberalism and the *shahada*, while contested, assume a certain agreement in what constitutes the *core* tenets of those terms. The extent of this agreement may well be thin, and certainly does not extend to separate 'doctrines', be that between the market-liberalism of Friedrich Hayek and the communitarian-liberalism of John Rawls,[60] or the Sunni-Shi'a divide. The meaning of a commitment to liberalism, or the Muslim's declaration of faith, share a universalist tendency that tries to give both concepts meaning detached from the social context in which they are used. The second of Khadduri's contracts, between the Muslim and the temporal ruler, resembles much more the communitarian commitment to deriving meaning from social context. As Muslims need not be bound by any transcendental commandments about political life (the difference between Islam-as-politics and Islam-as-faith), it is up to human ingenuity to develop a model for politics.

I have found great difficulty in trying to accommodate both the universalism of the *shahada* and the specificity of the different cultural and religious practices of Muslims. Islam-as-faith can be interpreted to rest on certain truths, though it has been argued that these do not necessarily translate to Islam-as-politics. The truths of Islam-as-faith can be broadly understood as the universal pretensions of Khadduri's first contract (with God), in other words, divine truths that exist independent of social context. On the other hand, the interpretivism of Islam-as-politics broadly maps onto the cultural specificity of communitarianism and is inherently bound to and reliant upon social context. While separating the two notions in a dual contract allows the resolution of this tension theoretically, in practice these Muslim contractors are asked to at once embrace universalism and particularism, and to keep the two conceptually separate as they go about giving life to Normative Political Islam. The incongruence between the two positions of the dual contract is one that will be repeated when the notion of communitarianism is applied to IR in the following section of the chapter. After having articulated this same problem in the international sphere, in the following chapter I will frame the problem fully and attempt to resolve this incongruence.

Having established my critique of universalism as a hallmark of rationalism, I have argued that Normative Political Islam's exoteric method is capable of constructing notions of justice that derive from or in some way reflect the societies in which that notion of justice is to hold sway. So far, I have teased at the possibilities of engaging with this debate, and foreshadowed a prominent incongruence with applying both universalism and particularism in deriving an Islamic notion of sovereignty, and now I will take a similar dialectic and apply it to IR. In doing so, I will proceed by examining the prospects for Islamically derived, communal relations on the international sphere. Thinking back on this chapter, if you consider replacing the use of the word community with the word *umma*, the possibilities for engaging the debate between communitarianism and liberalism at the international level, to give agency to the *umma*, becomes clear.

Communitarian International Relations

Communitarian international relations, according to Emanuel Adler, is a focus on knowledge 'that gives meaning to material reality and consequently helps explain the constitutive and casual mechanisms that participate in the construction of social reality'.[61] For me, such an approach is intertwined with the constructivist framework outlined previously, and the exoteric perspective of Normative Political Islam, deriving values from social contexts. However, constructivism and communitarianism might not seem entirely in synthesis with each other. While both share an emphasis on the social aspect of existence, constructivism places a focus on the individual's place in constituting their surroundings. In IR, however, referring to the community gives it actor qualities, taking away from the individual's agency in some regard. The interaction between individual and community happens at one level of analysis, identified here as the domestic level. Much of the discussion in the previous section would occur at this domestic level, discussion over the nature of justice, the place of values in relation to the individual and the community, etc. It is not my aim to resolve the multitude of questions for Normative Political Islam at the domestic level; indeed, if such questions are dependent on societal circumstance, then it is erroneous to attempt to prescribe a form of governance in an abstract sense.

At the international level, as I mentioned in earlier chapters, there is an antipathy towards the notion of religious politics. Recall van Ess's caricaturisation of popular opinion to Islamic politics as 'repellent and strange. . . . The notion commonly associated with it is the Sharia . . . which would seem to be incompatible with the rules of enlightened reason'.[62] This particular tension with Islam is exacerbated by a more general resistance to religion in the discipline, in what Hurd calls a secular bias, reviewed in chapter 4. This bias, for Hurd, reveals that '[c]onventional understandings of international relations, focused on material capabilities and strategic interaction, exclude from the start the possibility that religion could be a fundamental organizing force in the international system'.[63] Normative Political Islam must overcome both of these perceptions at the international level if it is to give agency to the notion of *umma*.

As I mentioned at the beginning of this chapter, articulating the *umma* on the international level could happen on a scale from 'thick' conceptions, between individuals transcending the state, and 'thin' conceptions, reliant on interaction between Muslim states, perhaps in a transnational organisation.[64]

It would be presumptuous to claim that it is possible to create a conception of the *umma* abstractly, and then apply this to all Muslims. Even while I have stipulated that I am working within the confines of Sunni Islam, it is up to the community (or communities) that defines itself as such to conceptualise the *umma*. What will be attempted here is not a prescriptive account of Normative Political Islam's IR, but an exploration of the two poles of thick and thin conceptions of the *umma*. In so doing I maintain my engagement with second-order IR theorising, 'making explicit and critiquing the foundational assumptions that structure research agendas'.[65]

Thin Conceptions of the Umma

Locating the *umma* within the state and in transnational interaction, as would be posited by a thin conception of the *umma*, is problematic for a number of reasons. In the first place, the *umma* does not *necessitate* any concept of the national at all, though it often includes it. Another problem rests with Muslim minorities in non-Muslim countries, who would still need to feel part of any institutionalised conception of the *umma*. Even the term 'Islamic state' is problematic for many as it is unclear who, if anyone, can authoritatively define a state as Islamic; one group's 'Islamic' credentials are utterly blasphemous to different 'Islamic' groups, as is the case, for example, between Wahhabi and Shi'a creeds. The concept of trans*nationalism* also does not sit well with the locating politics in individuals or communities, as the nation *can* be entirely left out of the schema of the *umma*. Therefore to call the *umma* a transnational organisation is somewhat of a misnomer.

At this point, then, it becomes necessary to truncate the definition of *umma* being used. As other transnational institutions, like the EU, are based upon the states that comprise it, so too would a theoretical thin *umma* be based upon Muslim states; doing so allows such a concept to work with the term transnationalism. The disadvantages of conceptualising a state-based *umma* are significant: Such a structure would not be representative of the 'whole' *umma* as it would not include substantial numbers of Muslims living as minority populations in non-Muslim states; Muslim communities not affiliated to the state, NGOs and charities, for example, are also not represented. In addition, developing criteria for what constitutes a 'Muslim' state is not easy. These are very acute problems with a state-based conception of the *umma*, certainly, but I continue the discussion, as I have so far, not looking to solve the operative problems associated with the *umma*, but here looking to explore the problems with religious-based identity in IR. In order to do this, I will proceed by placing this religious identity and the thin conception of *umma*, however arbitrarily, in the vessel of states.

Transnational institutions can engender a communal identity, for example the EU's attempts at creating a European identity. Going by the earlier appraisal of the units constituting the international system, for the EU to exist in the international sphere it must behave like a state. Turning to Ian Manners's problem with EU studies, which broadens out to IR more generally: The EU as a super-state entity is shaped by norms which lead to 'a willingness to disregard Westphalian conventions'.[66] The EU is able to disregard these conventions; unlike a state, the EU is not constituted by the Westphalian example. Returning to Manners for a concise summary of the EU's challenge to more traditional IR:

> The creative efforts of the European integration process have changes what passes for 'normal' in world politics. Simply by existing as different in a world of states and the relations between them, the European Union changes the normality of 'international relations'. In this respect the EU is a normative power: it changes the norms, standards and prescriptions of world politics away from the bounded expectations of state-centricity.[67]

Manners is not arguing that statism is undermined, but rather *changed*. It is evident that the EU is reliant upon the states that constitute it, but the relationship between states and the super-national institution that is born out of them can be related to the constructivist notion of co-constitution.

Naveed Sheikh makes a similar point regarding the changing nature of the state in IR, when commenting on the OIC. Sheikh states that 'as an intergovernmental organization, the idiosyncrasy of the OIC is categorical, for whilst adhering to the secular logic of multistate functionalism, its ... purpose is guided by a single imperative, that of ... ideational subscription to a unification, or integration, of Muslim peoples'.[68] The approach of the OIC or EU, in pursuing integration across state boundaries, seems to share a similar purpose with that of the thin *umma*; such an approach could be adopted by Muslim states to engender some form of Islamic solidarity which is currently missing from the international relations of these states,[69] representing a source of illegitimacy vis-à-vis their domestic populations.[70] It has been observed that the plans that Islamists visualise 'have not been tested by the realities of power, nor have they themselves had to organize and staff ministries, meet budgets, or implement policies'.[71] Beyond these tests of power, it is also true and perhaps more troublesome for Islamists, that they lack the theoretical framework for such religious transnationalism in the secular world of nation-states, discounting a complete and violent rejection of the state system.

How are such claims about political Islam's lack of framework substantiated when the OIC's existence is testament to the interaction between pan-Islam and the state system?[72] Indeed, Kayaoglu describes the OIC as 'a unique religious *cosmopolitan* organization',[73] insofar as it has a religion-based membership criteria and claims to represent 1.5 billion Muslims. Such uniqueness is tempered by the author, however, as 'the dynamic of 57 member states jealously guarding their sovereignty and working to advance their own interests makes it a typical inter*governmental* organization'.[74] Sheikh's study, *The New Politics of Islam*, concludes that the OIC is more an arena for states vying for power and less an instrument for achieving the politics of the *umma*. He argues that '[w]hile the very theorem for the establishment of the OIC was the transnational body of believers, the OIC remains, in fairness, a secularized association of states rather than an international society'.[75] The notion of secularism that Sheikh draws upon betrays the way in which the OIC has been socialised into existing forms of IR. The OIC, I posit, is the result of an attempt to give saliency to Islamic IR without first challenging the basis of IR as it is commonly understood.

Recalling the two-stage analysis I am employing, the OIC is an attempt at the second stage of analysis, the construction of Islamic IR, without the first stage's analysis of the unspoken assumptions in the discipline (and practice) of IR. That is not to discount the achievement of establishing a religiously based international organisation. Indeed, as Sheikh points out, the OIC's existence as an Islamic organisation is 'an ontological achievement'.[76] It is possible that in the construction of a thin *umma* in this chapter, an institution will be imagined that resembles the OIC in whole or part. However, I am not attempting to solve the OIC's operative problems. If the thin *umma* I describe here results in a resemblance to the OIC, then that will be coincidental.

The transnationalism represented by the EU is not so easily replicated in the *umma*; there is resistance to the notion of Islamic, religious solidarity, as Thomas Risse-Kappen demonstrates when he warns that 'there is no reason to assume that transnational relations regularly promote "good" causes'.[77] Unfortunately, the supporting example of a 'bad' cause for Risse-Kappen is an ill-defined Islamic fundamentalism.[78]

Recall the universal aspirations and rights-based approach to community inherent in liberalism, versus the geographical and historical specificity of community afforded by communitarian and constructivist theory. The lack of clarity with regards to the extent and nature of unity amongst Muslims resonates with this liberal/communitarian division. On the one hand, a popular and in some senses 'classical' understanding of Islamic IR, *siyar*, bears much resemblance to the universality of liberalism. Ahmed Bsoul Labeeb tries to emphasise exactly this when he states that 'Islam is a universal message and its rulings cover and refer to all people without distinction and without favouring one group or race over another. Islamic law aims to establish one society under one system'.[79]

The quintessential Islamic reformer Jamal al-Din al-Afghani also alludes to this universality, but betrays a naïvety in the power he affords religion in this instance. For al-Afghani, Islamic solidarity is at least comparable to nationalism and he believed that by being loyal to their faith, Muslims can put sectarian considerations aside in the creation of their *umma*.[80] Much as liberalism is imbued with Eurocentric allusions about the 'neutrality' of such a position, so too is al-Afghani's reference to broad Islamic universalism laden with essentialism. This is a position criticised at length by Al-Azmeh, who notes that Islamists 'claim to speak for a univocal body of legislation which is not grounded in the vast historical experience of Muslims'.[81] He argues that generalisations made about social groups in terms of religion incorrectly overwrite socio-economic factors, when in fact 'religious difference underwrites and does not overdetermine social exclusivism'.[82] In moving away from the idea that some pre-political consensus exists amongst Muslims, perhaps Al-Azmeh goes too far, denying the co-constitutive relationship of religious ideas on the behaviour of actors, instead arguing that behaviour is already determined by socio-economic factors and subsequently given legitimacy through religious discourse. Using constructivism as a middle ground, how can Normative Political Islam better relate the religious urge for some kind of Muslim solidarity, represented through the *umma*?

While the constructivist method opens space for the study of identity, the secular bias in IR identified by Hurd ensures that religious identity is under-theorised (as was noted with Barnett's and Telhami and Barnett's studies in chapter 3). Abdul Latif Tibawi pre-empted some of the conclusions of Hurd's study when he wrote in 1964 that without understanding Islam as it is understood and experienced by a believer, scholarly work is ensured to be disconnected from the realities of Muslim people.[83] As Mandaville asserts, '[e]ven if Muslim identities remain primarily nationalized, this does not mean that it is not possible for them to make common cause with co-religionists elsewhere, or to sympathise with "Muslim" issues'.[84]

Despite the problems with current constructivist study (or omission) of Islam's relation to identity, constructivism still holds much potential for theorising the *umma*. The often-heard slogan of *din wa dawla*, the inseparability of religion and politics, is again neither representative of the realities of Muslims nor an appreciation of Islamic source texts.[85] As argued previously, there is little about the faith of Islam that predisposes its believers to a specific political order; this being so, the scope for developing a framework for common identity is huge.

The problem, of course, is deciding on *what* norms are to constitute Muslim identity. 'Abdul Hamid Abu Sulayman's study into the content of an Islamic IR makes a first attempt at deciding what these norms should be. For Abu Sulayman, self-determination, justice, peace, self-exertion and a respect for and fulfilment of commitments represent the normative basis of Islamic IR,[86] which could be adapted to form the basis of Muslim transnational identity. *Which* norms constitute Muslim identity is not clearly defined; even Abu Sulayman's norms are ambiguously tied to Islamic texts. The OIC, the almost-thin-*umma* example, is testament to the problems involved in deriving 'proper' Islamic norms; rather than a consensus of opinion on the nature of Islam-as-politics, a kind of civilisational behemoth, 'the case of the OIC vividly illustrates that the dynamics of trans-national, or pan-national alignment, fall in a spectrum from utilitarianism to hedonism'.[87] But other transnational identities, such as European identity, for example, are not derived from some essential European character; there are no 'European source texts' that bind Europeans through time and space. Rather, the identity is constructed in the here and now, in a geographically and temporally specific instance. So too can Muslim identity be formed and be relevant to Muslims *now* rather than all Muslims throughout time, as is so often the urge for Muslim thinkers. Being more concerned with what binds Muslims together in the now rather than throughout time would go some way to account for the broad spectrum of positions that Muslim states take within the OIC, for example. Similarly, it is not contradictory for EU states to take differing positions on key issues; they do not betray some 'essential' European character when divergent opinions within the union appear. Rather such divergence signals the ongoing processes of delineating what being 'European' means in the international sphere. So too could a thin *umma* support divergence in the views held by its members, as part of an ongoing appraisal of what being 'Muslim' means in the international sphere.

What I have shown in theorising a thin conception of the *umma* is that the state system places considerable constraints on the nature of the community. Constructivism allows a desire for greater solidarity between Muslims to come to fruition through the mechanisms of an international organisation. However, such an organisation would have to be geographically limited by the states that constitute it, and therefore compromise much of what makes the *umma* unique and desirable for Muslims, namely, a sense of solidarity with *individual* Muslims, regardless of the territory in which they live. But as an example of religious-based identity, the state conception of the *umma* serves; indeed, the OIC is testament to the Islam-as-faith's 'secularization-resistant profile . . . in international society'.[88]

I will proceed by looking at how to move to a thicker conception of the *umma*, which would allow for a greater solidarity exclusive of territorial limits, incorporating diaspora and non-state groups.

Moving from Thin to Thick Conceptions of the Umma: The English School of International Relations

The debate with which I am engaged, between universalism and particularism, between liberal autonomy and societal values, has many similarities with a debate found in the English School of international relations, namely, the relationship between the international system, international society, and world society. Broadly reflecting Martin Wight's three traditions of IR, representative of the ideas of Hobbes, Grotius and Kant, Barry Buzan offers an explanation of each of these three key English School terms: International system 'puts structure and process of international anarchy at the centre of IR theory'; international society 'puts the creation and maintenance of shared norms, rules and institutions at the centre of IR theory'; world society 'puts transcendence of the states-system at the centre of IR theory'.[89] The terms international system, international society and world society, when used hereafter, refer to these concepts as they are explained in the English School. Further still, 'English school theory has a lot to offer those interested in developing societal understandings of international systems',[90] and I wish to avail myself of this framework as a stepping-stone for articulating community in IR.

I argue that international society represents a local or communal rationality that is representative of the *umma* and communitarian notions of deriving value from community. As Hoffman stresses about international society, it rests on notions of 'common interests and values, common rules and institutions'.[91] Insofar as international society is heavily dependent on states, so it resembles a thin conception of *umma*. World society, by contrast, resembles the universal tendencies of Islam-as-faith, or the liberalism of the Enlightenment project. The relationship between world society and universalism is made as world society implies global pacifism through globally applicable notions of justice; Andrew Linklater highlights a tension similar to that between communitarianism and liberalism when he states that '[t]he analysis of the expansion of international society [into a world society] raises large questions about the relationship between moral and legal universals and support for respect for cultural differences'.[92] Broadly speaking, the thick *umma* is engaged somewhere between the notions of international society and world society, though this is somewhat problematic, as I will now explore.

International society is 'built around the state as the defining unit',[93] justified by an empirical statement about the 'historical sociology of international relations'.[94] This emphasis on the state's neutral, yet unchallengeable place the state system poses problems very similar to the thin *umma*, expanded upon in the previous section. Indeed, the thin *umma* is quite comparable to a 'regional society' as it shares the assumptions that constitute an international society as Hedley Bull understands it, that is, 'common interests and values'.[95] However, the English School makes a distinction between society and community, reflecting the sociological categories of *gesellschaft* (society) and *gemeinschaft* (community). Society 'focuses on patterns of interaction structured by shared norms and rules', while community 'focuses on identity and "we-feeling"'.[96] The thin *umma* seems far more concerned with identity and so is more applicable to 'community' than to 'society'. However, the relationship between society and community is complicated and contested. Even among the English School, two prominent theorists of this paradigm disagree on whether community comes before the development of international society (the position of Wight), or if society is necessary to develop a sense of community (the position of John Vincent).[97] I will therefore adopt Buzan's approach of abandoning the *gesellschaft/gemeinschaft* distinction, viewing them as ideal types, intertwined in some way, though ambiguous as to the nature of their relationship.[98] Such an ambiguity allows me to talk of thin-*umma* constructions, even ones that are concerned more with identity than procedure, as regional societies or regional communities interchangeably. Regardless, the regional society of the thin *umma* is insufficient in giving the *umma* agency, as I highlighted earlier with regards to the geographical limitations of the state compromising the sense of solidarity with individual Muslims. So, can world society help develop a thick conception of the *umma*, a conception that allows for this solidarity between persons?

Hedley Bull saw some potential in the world society concept, insofar as it could be more inclusive than international society. While international society is defined by states, those who are outside the state system would never be granted equal treatment. If the move were made to a society of *peoples*, then a more inclusive order might be achievable.[99] Using the term society of peoples seems to overlap quite nicely with the concept of the *umma*. There is, however, a prominent disconnect between the two concepts: The world society is universal, linked to the universal liberal aspirations outlined earlier in the chapter, while an *umma* is demarcated by differing belief systems. However, if Islam-as-faith is believed to one day encompass the entire globe and all peoples, then the universalism thus far criticised is applicable to both world society and *umma* concepts. I can push this similarity further, as universal or not, both world society and *umma* would begin with an otherwise particular society.

It would seem then that world society has much to offer in giving credence to a thick *umma*. Unlike the thin *umma*, the world society model would revolve around people, not states, and so encompass Muslim minorities in whatever country they may live. Broadly put, while the thin *umma*, centred on the English School concept of international society, appears more congruent with the prevailing structure of IR but less congruent with traditional articulations of the *umma*, then the thick *umma*, centred on the concept of world society, is the opposite; the thick *umma* is more consistent with the *umma* (as an ideal type), but less so with the way in which IR is predominately articulated.

Articulating the thick *umma* in the mould of world society, as has been mentioned briefly already, relies on settling questions of values and justice between a diverse range of peoples. Such a move bears more than a passing resemblance to the liberal universalism critiqued earlier in the chapter, especially if the way universal human rights are used in IR is approximated to the way the thick *umma* would operate. In this way, the world society concept in the English School is based on liberal thought; Hobson explains about the English School as a whole, that 'it rests on fundamental liberal foundations comprising Lockean or Grotian liberalism (as the "pluralist" wing) and cosmopolitan liberalism (as in the "solidarist" wing)'.[100] The implication of comparing the English School and liberalism is to note the connection that the abstracted notion of rationality has with what passes for 'civilisation' in IR theory and history, as I will explore presently.

Taking the example of liberal universalism as implying a consensus of values derived abstractly, one can glimpse at the way in which this assumption is problematic in IR. David Boucher states that 'when natural law and its derivative rights are deemed to be universal, their application is often oppressive'.[101] I will come to the notion of oppression soon. For now, we need to make a link between natural law and liberal universalism, to make Boucher's criticism relevant to the present discussion. While liberal universalism does not always rest on the concept of natural laws, abstracting values and applying them to all peoples regardless of their societal circumstances can take the place of natural law in Boucher's criticism. Both the concepts of natural law or abstractly derived values imply a pre-political consensus which in actuality cannot be taken for granted. Indeed, the notion of universality implied by liberalism has changed with time, highlighting the inconsistency in claiming that it is a pre-political, abstractly defined value system. The changing universality of liberalism is illustrated in IR when we link the term 'standard of civilisation' to liberal values. Indicative of Hobson's non-reductive Orientalism, the 'standard of civilisation' is a measure of defining 'self' (civilisation) and 'other' (barbarism),[102] and I argue that liberalism is a prominent marker of that civilisation in IR. Having made this conceptual move, I can lean on Edward Keene's analysis of the changes in this 'standard of civilisation' as it has been applied in IR, to highlight its oppressive role in the history of colonialism.

For Keene the 'standard of civilisation' changes during the late nineteenth and early twentieth centuries from 'a certain level of economic, political and judicial advancement', to the idea that 'every nation has a right to self-determination'.[103] The former served to separate the international order along racial lines, justifying the imperial attitude of Europe abroad while protecting its liberal character at home. The latter became far more inclusive: 'the concept of civilization increasingly began to separate Europeans from each other, and came to be seen in terms of an ideological divide rather than a racial one'.[104] This example of the changing standard of civilisation, and the oppression that can derive from universality, serves to demonstrate the dangers of abstracted universal values, liberal values or otherwise. Rather, the liberal values claimed to be 'universal' both during the colonial era and afterwards are in fact tied to societal circumstances, which accounts for their change over time. The divergence between the universal aspirations of liberalism in IR and the non-universality of its creation and perpetuation presents an explanation for the incoherency of human rights in IR, as Boucher summarises:

> Universal rights always were, and remain, conditional and all sorts of pretexts may be invoked to suspend their application, from the promotion of better trading relations, which made world leaders quickly forget Tiananmen Square, to the desire for order over justice, in which justice is traded for truth.[105]

MacIntyre would relate this incongruence, that is, the divergent ends of pursuing order and justice at the same time, to the 'Enlightenment project', as I noted earlier in the chapter. For MacIntyre it has not been shown that an impersonal or abstract notion of morality exists,[106] so returning us once more to societally derived values in the place of this abstraction. The implications of socially derived values in IR will be examined more thoroughly in the next chapter, while presently I will relate the discussion of the 'liberal-neutral' foundation of world society to an articulation of a thick *umma*.

The thick *umma*, in relying on a pre-political consensus similar to that required by liberal universalism, shares the same problems outlined above. Piscatori argues that any search for 'proper' Islamic values, upon which a thick *umma* would be based, 'is bound to fail, even as the general idea proves to be durably attractive'.[107] Indeed, '[t]o talk of Islamic authority in the abstract would be to reify something that is largely contingent on social relations of culture, power, and history across a wide variety of contexts'.[108] The argument that Islam-as-faith does not provide enough guidance on its own to inform Islam-as-politics necessarily implies that Normative Political Islam, or indeed any articulation of political Islam, cannot rely on a prepolitical consensus on values to be the basis of the world society articulation of *umma*. My position is contrary to the OIC, for example, whose leaders claim that Islam 'is a divinely revealed comprehensive way of life that integrates all aspects of social life'.[109] A position of comprehensive/universal applicability renders the OIC's vision of Islam as comparable to the Enlightenment project/position critiqued above.

I dubbed my variant of political Islam as *Normative* Political Islam, but the norms necessary for its articulation in a thick *umma* are not coherent with the framework employed to give agency to the concept. To create space for Normative Political Islam in IR, a poststructural critique of IR was employed, which broke down various dominant claims around the discipline, such as secularism and the centrality of the state. Currently, however, if one were to embrace a thick *umma* in the mould of world society, one would need to create a series of value claims that are just as susceptible to that original poststructural critique. If the norms of Normative Political Islam are to apply to the world over, then the geographical and cultural specificity necessary to construct these norms in the first place will have to be removed. In essence this would create a paradox, similar to the problem outlined in the discussion of communitarianism and liberalism earlier in the chapter, regarding a simultaneous embrace of both universalism and particularism in the development of Islamic sovereignty. An-Na'im alludes to a similar problem in his work *Islam and the Secular State*. An-Na'im states, in much the way I have done in this chapter, that to use *shari'a* as a *universal* normative basis for Islam-as-politics is problematic. He states that 'the so-called basic objectives of Shari'a are expressed at such a high level of abstraction [to be applicable to all Muslims] that they are neither distinctly Islamic nor sufficiently specific for the purposes of public policy and legislation'.[110]

To create norms applicable to Muslims is to embrace societal and cultural specificity, but to create norms applicable to *all* Muslims in a world society is to deny the specificity required to give these norms any purchase in the first place. In this way, I claim that both liberal universalism and the thick *umma* are flawed when used to create a world society. Embracing the specificity required by Normative Political Islam, while at the same time giving credence to the idea of solidarity with co-religionists, otherwise put, to resolve the paradox outlined here, is what I will explore in depth in the following chapter.

CONCLUSIONS

Having augmented the religious (theological) guidance on Islamic politics in the previous chapter with Islamic exotericism, developing a theory of Islamic sovereignty in the process, in this chapter I have attempted to apply those ideas to the international sphere. Focusing on the articulation of the *umma* in IR, I have argued that the foundations of dominant IR interpretations upon the liberal universal legacy of the European Enlightenment prove a severe impediment to any articulation of the *umma*. Engaging with the debate between liberalism and communitarianism, I argued that liberal universalism derives its values from an individual abstracted from her societal circumstances. Accepting these abstracted values of liberalism would undermine the distinction between Islam-as-faith and Islam-as-politics. An abstracted value system would fold the two together, so that the principles that are capable of being universalised, Islam-as-faith, would override the principles derived from societal circumstance, Islam-as-politics. Alternatively, principles derived from within a specific society might retroactively be given universal appeal, resulting in one notion of Islam-as-politics overriding competing conceptions, trying to veil itself as Islam-as-faith. If a move accepting universal values in the mould of the Enlightenment project were made by Normative Political Islam, it would create a zero-sum discourse *within* ('our

Islamism is the *only* Islamism') and *outwith* (liberalism versus Islamism) the Muslim world.

Communitarianism, on the other hand, was argued to be capable of giving agency to various forms of Islam-as-politics, Normative Political Islam included. Embracing the societal basis of value systems allows one to accept the liberalism of the Enlightenment as linked to the community it was derived from, resisting the urge to apply it globally. The *umma*, then, is indicative of whatever the Muslims that constitute it will it to be. However, relating these conclusions to the dual contract method used in the previous chapter to develop a notion of sovereignty for Normative Political Islam revealed an incoherency around the simultaneous embrace of universalism and particularism. The first contract between the Muslim and God involves a commitment to the transcendental and universal aspects of Islam-as-faith, while the second contract between Muslims and temporal authority embraces the particularism of the society the Muslim might find herself in. Asking Muslim contractors to embrace both particularism and universalism, and to neatly demarcate the two in their minds as they go about deriving their version of Islam-as-politics, is a problematic expectation. The incoherence of a position embracing both universalism and particularism was also explored when moving the debate between liberalism and communitarianism to the realm of IR.

In giving agency to the *umma* in IR, I examined two extremes on a spectrum, the thin and thick *umma*. The former was argued to represent a form of solidarity vested in states, articulated by an international organisation similar to the EU. However, what I demonstrated was that investing in the state system compromises much of what makes the *umma* desirable in the first place, specifically, solidarity with *individual* co-religionists. Moving to a thick *umma* that would be located in individuals, I identified the problem in assuming too much agreement between and amongst Muslims. In essence, a thick *umma* has to make abstracted and universal claims about the nature of the connection between individuals, much in the same way liberalism does. In doing so, it begins to deny the constitutive elements of Normative Political Islam being vested in society, and instead places those constitutive elements in those abstract and universal values, presumably vested in theological guidance (though it is entirely possible these values might be based in rationalism, much as the liberal tradition is). How to resolve this problem of at once respecting the truth associated with divine revelation, however thin that truth might be, while simultaneously arguing that cultural specificity is the best method to derive Islam-as-politics, is the problem that I take up in the following chapter.

I have demonstrated in this chapter that the IR of the *umma* would entail multiple and competing notions of Islam-as-politics, Normative Political Islam representing only one approach amongst many. If Islam-as-politics is indeed embedded within societal practice, then an attempt to abstractly dictate a singular paradigm for the articulation of that politics is futile. Abandoning the idea that a singular conception of Islam-as-politics is achievable leads me to a discussion of how and to what extent can IR embrace pluralism, or, does pluralism inevitably lead to conflict between competing value systems? This is the question that guides us into the final substantive chapter of the book.

NOTES

1. L. Carl Brown, *Religion and State: The Muslim Approach to Politics* (New York: Columbia University Press, 2000), 59.
2. James Piscatori, 'Imagining Pan-Islam: Religious Activism and Political Utopias', *Proceedings of the British Academy* 131 (2005): 427.
3. Peter Mandaville, *Global Political Islam* (London: Routledge, 2007), 1–24.
4. Sohail Hashmi, 'Islam, the Middle East and the Pan-Islamic Movement', in *International Society and the Middle East*, ed. Barry Buzan and Ana Gonzalez-Pelaez (New York: Palgrave Macmillan, 2009), 170.
5. Alexander Wendt, 'Anarchy is what States Make of It: The Social Construction of Power Politics', *International Organization* 46, no. 2 (1992): 395.
6. Peter Mandaville, *Transnational Muslim Politics: Reimagining the Umma* (London: Routledge, 2001), 11.
7. Sami Zubaida, *Islam, the People & the State*, 2nd ed. (London: I.B. Tauris, 1989), 123.
8. Sami Zubaida, 'Islam and the Politics of Community and Citizenship', *Middle East Report* no. 221 (2001): 21.
9. Partha Chatterjee in ibid.
10. Ibid.
11. Nazih Ayubi, *Over-stating the Arab State: Politics and Society in the Middle East* (London: I.B. Tauris, 1996), 166.
12. Mandaville, *Transnational Muslim Politics*, 5.
13. Amr Sabet, *Islam and the Political: Theory, Governance and International Relations* (London: Pluto, 2008), 178.
14. Ibid., 187.
15. Andrew March, 'Islamic Foundations for a Social Contract in Non-Muslim Liberal Democracies', *American Political Science Review* 101, no. 2 (2007): 236.
16. Fazlur Rahman, *Islam* (Chicago: University of Chicago Press, 1979), 116.
17. Ibid.
18. John Esposito, *Islam and Politics*, 4th ed. (New York: Syracuse University Press, 1998), 312.
19. Mohammed Arkoun, 'Rethinking Islam Today', in *Liberal Islam: A Sourcebook*, ed. Charles Kurzman (Oxford: Oxford University Press, 1998), 205–6.
20. Sabet, *Islam and the Political*, 189.
21. March, 'Islamic Foundations', 251.
22. Bobby Henderson, 'Open Letter to Kansas School Board', 2005, accessed on 21.02.2013, http://www.venganza.org/about/open-letter/.
23. March, 'Islamic Foundations', 251.
24. Piscatori refers to this as ijma' al-fi'l in James Piscatori, *Islam in a World of Nation-States* (Cambridge: Cambridge University Press, 1986), 74.
25. Mushir Ul-Haq, 'Islam in Secular India', in *Islam in Transition: Muslim Perspectives*, ed. John Donohue and John Esposito, 2nd ed. (Oxford: Oxford University Press, 2007), 134.
26. Elizabeth Hurd, *The Politics of Secularism in International Relations* (Princeton: Princeton University Press, 2008), 11.
27. Bassam Tibi, *Islam's Predicament with Modernity: Religious Reform and Cultural Change* (London: Routledge, 2009), 58.

28. Ibid., 30.
29. Sami Zubaida, *Islam, the People & the State*, 2nd ed. (London: I.B. Tauris, 1989), 123.
30. Tibi, *Islam's Predicament with Modernity*, 7.
31. John Gray, *Al Qaeda and What It Means to be Modern* (London: Faber and Faber, 2003), 1.
32. Tibi, *Islam's Predicament with Modernity*, 60.
33. Ibid.
34. Sami Zubaida, *Beyond Islam: A New Understanding of the Middle East* (London: I.B. Tauris, 2011), 32.
35. Ibid., 8.
36. Mohammed 'Abed al-Jabri, *Arab-Islamic Philosophy: A Contemporary Critique* (Austin, TX: Center for Middle Eastern Studies, 1999), 129.
37. Alasdair MacIntyre, *After Virtue: A Study in Moral Theory*, 2nd ed. (London: Duckworth, 1985), 39.
38. Will Kymlicka, *Contemporary Political Philosophy: An Introduction*, 2nd ed. (Oxford: Oxford University Press, 2002), 209.
39. Richard Bellamy, *Liberalism and Modern Society* (Cambridge: Polity, 1992), 218.
40. Philip Pettit, 'Liberal/Communitarian: MacIntyre's Mesmeric Dichotomy', in *After MacIntyre: Critical Perspectives on the Work of Alasdair MacIntyre*, ed. John Horton and Susan Mendus (Cambridge: Polity, 1994), 176.
41. Maureen Ramsay, *What's Wrong with Liberalism? A Radical Critique of Liberal Political Philosophy* (London: Continuum, 2004), 1.
42. David Gauthier, 'The Liberal Individual', in *Communitarianism and Individualism*, ed. Shlomo Avineri and Avner De-Shalit (Oxford: Oxford University Press, 1992), 154.
43. Michael Sandel, 'The Procedural Republic and the Unencumbered Self', *Political Theory* 12, no. 1 (1984): 87.
44. John Rawls, 'Justice as Fairness: Political Not Metaphysical', *Philosophy & Public Affairs* 14, no. 3 (1985): 223.
45. Kymlicka, *Contemporary Political Philosophy*, 211.
46. 'Abed al-Jabri, *Arab-Islamic Philosophy*, 129.
47. Richard Shapcott, *Justice, Community, and Dialogue in International Relations* (Cambridge: Cambridge University Press, 2001), 3.
48. Emanuel Adler, *Communitarian International Relations: The Epistemic Foundations of International Relations* (London: Routledge, 2005), 21.
49. Michael Walzer, *Spheres of Justice: A Defence of Pluralism and Equality* (New York: Basic, 1983), 5.
50. Veit Bader, 'Citizenship and Exclusion: Radical Democracy, Community, and Justice. Or, What is Wrong with Communitarianism', *Political Theory* 23, no. 2 (1995): 216.
51. Walzer, *Spheres of Justice*, 4.
52. Ibid., 312–13.
53. Bader, 'Citizenship and Exclusion', 217.
54. Bellamy, *Liberalism and Modern Society*, 249.
55. Bader, 'Citizenship and Exclusion', 213.
56. Ibid.
57. Walzer, *Spheres of Justice*, 312.
58. Ibid., 29.
59. Majid Khadduri, *War and Peace in the Law of Islam* (Baltimore: Johns Hopkins Press, 1955), 9–12.
60. Bellamy, *Liberalism and Modern Society*, 218.
61. Adler, *Communitarian International Relations*, 4.
62. Josef van Ess, *The Flowering of Muslim Theology* (London: Harvard University Press, 2006), 1.
63. Hurd, *Politics of Secularism in International Relations*, 1.
64. Hashmi, 'Islam, the Middle East and the Pan-Islamic Movement', 170.
65. Alexander Wendt, 'Bridging the Theory/Meta-Theory Gap in International Relations', *Review of International Studies* 17, no. 4 (1991): 392.

66. Ian Manners, 'Normative Power Europe: A Contradiction in Terms?' *Journal of Common Market Studies* 40, no. 2 (2002): 239.

67. Ian Manners, 'The Normative Ethics of the European Union', *International Affairs* 84, no. 1 (2008): 65.

68. Naveed Sheikh, *The New Politics of Islam: Pan-Islamic Foreign Policy in a World of States* (London: RoutledgeCurzon, 2003), 16.

69. Nazih Ayubi, *Political Islam: Religion and Politics in the Arab World* (London: Routledge, 1991), 122–23.

70. For a detailed discussion on the power of Islamic discourse and symbolism in Muslim politics, see Dale Eickelman and James Piscatori, *Muslim Politics* (Princeton: Princeton University Press, 1996), 57–67.

71. Richard Bulliet, 'Twenty Years of Islamic Politics', *Middle East Journal* 53, no. 2 (1999): 196.

72. Sheikh, *New Politics of Islam*, 2.

73. Turan Kayaoglu, *The Organization of Islamic Cooperation: Politics, Problems, and Potential* (Abingdon: Routledge, 2015), 1. Original emphasis.

74. Ibid. Original emphasis.

75. Sheikh, *New Politics of Islam*, 42.

76. Ibid., 138.

77. Thomas Risse-Kappen, 'Bringing Transnational Relations Back In: Introduction', in *Bringing Transnational Relations Back In: Non-state Actors, Domestic Structures and International Institutions*, ed. Thomas Risse-Kappen (Cambridge: Cambridge University Press, 1995), 4.

78. For a concise taxonomy of Muslim groups that might be termed 'fundamentalist', see Ayubi, *Political Islam*, 67–69.

79. Ahmed Bsoul Labeeb, 'Theory of International Relations in Islam', *Digest of Middle East Studies* 16, no. 2 (2007): 72.

80. Jamal al-Din al-Afghani, 'An Islamic Response to Imperialism', in *Islam in Transition: Muslim Perspectives*, ed. John Donohue and John Esposito (Oxford: Oxford University Press, 1982), 21–23.

81. Aziz Al-Azmeh, *Islam and Modernities*, 2nd ed. (London: Verso, 1996), 11.

82. Ibid., 3.

83. Abdul Latif Tibawi, 'English-Speaking Orientalists', in *Orientalism: A Reader*, ed. Alexander Lyon Macfie (New York: New York University Press, 2000).

84. Mandaville, *Global Political Islam*, 341.

85. Eickelman and Piscatori, *Muslim Politics*, 56.

86. Perry Gledd, 'Book Review: The Islamic Theory of International Relations: New Directions for Islamic Methodology and Thought', *American Journal of Islamic Social Sciences* 9, no. 1 (1992): 124–25.

87. Sheikh, *New Politics of Islam*, 137.

88. Ibid., 139.

89. Barry Buzan, *From International to World Society? English School Theory and the Social Structure of Globalisation* (Cambridge: Cambridge University Press, 2004), 7.

90. Ibid., 1.

91. Stanley Hoffmann, 'International Society', in *Order and Violence: Hedley Bull and International Relations*, ed. John Vincent and John Miller (Oxford: Clarendon, 1990), 22.

92. Andrew Linklater, 'The English School', in *Theories of International Relations*, ed. Scott Burchill et al., 4th ed. (Basingstoke: Palgrave Macmillan, 2009), 109.

93. Buzan, *From International to World Society?*, 91.

94. Nicholas Rengger, 'A City Which Sustains All Things? Communitarianism and International Society', *Millennium: A Journal of International Studies* 21, no. 2 (1992): 360.

95. Hoffmann, 'International Society', 2.

96. Buzan, *From International to World Society?*, 110.

97. Ibid., 114–15.

98. Ibid., 116.

99. Hedley Bull, 'The Emergence of a Universal International Society', in *The Expansion of International Society*, ed. Hedley Bull and Adam Watson (Oxford: Oxford University Press, 1984), 126.

100. John Hobson, *The Eurocentric Conception of World Politics: Western International Theory, 1760–2010* (Cambridge: Cambridge University Press, 2012), 222.

101. David Boucher, *The Limits of Ethics in International Relations: Natural Law, Natural Rights, and Human Rights in Transition* (Oxford: Oxford University Press, 2009), 11.

102. Hobson, *Eurocentric Conception of World Politics*, 4.

103. Edward Keene, *Beyond the Anarchical Society: Grotius, Colonialism and Order in World Politics* (Cambridge: Cambridge University Press, 2002), 9.

104. Ibid., 121.

105. Boucher, *The Limits of Ethics in International Relations*, 358.

106. MacIntyre, *After Virtue*, 24.

107. James Piscatori, 'Islam and the International Order', in *The Expansion of International Society*, ed. Hedley Bull and Adam Watson (Oxford: Oxford University Press, 1984), 311.

108. Mandaville, *Global Political Islam*, 303.

109. Kayaoglu, *Organization of Islamic Cooperation*, 126.

110. Abdullahi Ahmed An-Na'im, *Islam and the Secular State: Negotiating the Future of Shari'a* (Cambridge, MA: Harvard University Press, 2008), 35.

Part III

Pluralism or Polarisation?
Poststructuralism and Religion

Chapter Seven

Value Pluralism and the 'International' of International Relations

After the attacks of Al-Qaeda on the United States in 2001, the world is increasingly marked by violence perpetrated in the name of 'civilisation' (humanitarian intervention) or 'religion' (Islamic terrorism), especially in the crucible of the modern Middle East. This current configuration of security/insecurity seems increasingly polarised, with both sides dehumanising the other so that there can be no negotiation with infidels/terrorists. A zero-sum situation emerges, whereby the world can only be safe/just if the other is destroyed utterly, with all the violence this entails—to the enemy and those in the crossfire. Such a world view rests on the notion of incommensurable differences—differences that cannot be reconciled. I have argued that the creation of a Muslim *umma* relies on specific understandings of (particular) communities, rather than a universal claim on the nature of peoples and justice which some have 'achieved' and others are yet to find. I have implied that such particularism might also be based on incommensurable differences (there are some things which distinguish one group from another). But I am not advocating the pessimism that leads one to think of differences in zero-sum terms. Rather, I will explore in this chapter the opposite end of the spectrum: that differences can lead to pluralism, not polarisation.

In the previous chapter I attempted to apply the principle of the *umma* in IR using a communitarian perspective, with varying degrees of success from thick to thin conceptions of Muslim solidarity. In this chapter, however, I will investigate the implications of Normative Political Islam embracing that communitarian perspective, with a specific focus on interaction with other states or communities in the international sphere. In this discussion I will establish the challenges that the concept of the *umma*, as an alternative to the state, poses to the discipline of IR.

I will begin by noting the similarity of my argument thus far with Samuel Huntington's *Clash of Civilizations*. Specifically, I will compare the way in which both the *Clash of Civilizations* and my arguments rest upon the basis of incommensurable differences in the values of different peoples. Whilst I will show that there is indeed some similarity between my position and Huntington's ideas, in the way in which conflicting values are accepted as unavoidable in IR, I will demonstrate that the considerable difference between my argument and Huntington's lies in the way in which both invoke pluralism in IR. I argue that Huntington's use of pluralism is incoherent; he embraces a multi-polar and pluralistic international order, while at the same time maintaining that different 'civilisations' are engaged in a zero-sum contest that cannot be mediated. The issue is not the zero-sum nature of conflict; indeed I embrace the idea that while values *may* be rationally reconciled they *might also* be inherently at odds with each other. The issue with Huntington is the use of pluralism in his argument. For him, I will show, pluralism is an empirical statement about diverse locations of power in the international sphere. If it is possible for values to never be reconciled, as Huntington himself argues, then the notion of pluralism is an *embrace* of this competition in humanity's relations with one another, not, as Huntington would see it, evidence that one set of values must triumph over the others as a matter of survival.

I will move on to unpack an understanding of pluralism distinct from Huntington's. Specifically, I assert the connection between poststructuralism and pluralism. This connection is made as the poststructural position on ontology removes the possibility of universal truths, including universal norms or values, to manage the international sphere (like liberalism, for example), and pluralism is an attempt to manage the competing values that result, in this instance, from a poststructural position on ontology. After demonstrating the synthesis between the two concepts I will proceed in attempting to answer two questions: (1) To what extent can one conceive of a pluralistic IR? (2) Relating the argument thus far to Normative Political Islam, can one be a postmodern Muslim? The second question was foreshadowed in the previous chapter with regards to an embrace of the universalism of Islam-as-faith at the same time as accepting the particularism of Islam-as-politics.

To answer the first question, I will further frame the discussion of pluralism in IR by looking at poststructural studies in IR as well as area studies, in an attempt to highlight the Enlightenment rationality embedded in dominant IR paradigms that insist on a singular conception of 'the good life'. I will then provide a working definition of pluralism and point to modus vivendi, agreeing to disagree, as the way to manage conflict between competing values. In applying modus vivendi to IR, I will identify English School and realist paradigms as potentially indicative of value pluralism in IR, but will note that the concept of pluralism is under-theorised in the field.

To answer the second question regarding the poststructural Muslim, I seek to resolve the inherent problem associated with a Muslim believing in absolute truth (God) and poststructuralism's rejection of meta-narrative, simultaneously. To do this, I will argue for a notion of bounded poststructuralism and bounded Islam (as-politics). As demonstrated in chapter 5, Islam's exoteric tradition places boundaries on Islam-as-politics, preventing it from becoming universally applicable. I will attempt to make a similar argument with regards to poststructuralism. Following this, I will turn once more to value pluralism as the method to 'resolve' the question of the postmodern Muslim, arguing that the two positions of poststructuralism and belief in God are rationally unresolvable. This being so, value pluralism and the management of inevitable friction is the method forwarded to 'resolve' the problem of the poststructural Muslim.

COMMUNITARIANISM AND THE CLASH OF CIVILISATIONS

Before continuing, it is worth summarising the constitutive elements of the argument thus far presented, that is, in Part II of the book, which was concerned with what forms Islamic IR might take, rather than Part I, which discussed the deficiencies, such as they are, in 'traditional' IR theory vis-à-vis Islam. During this summary I will draw attention to the similarities with Huntington's *Clash of Civilizations*.[1] Unfortunately, if the association is accurate, *Clash of Civilizations* spells some dire consequences for Normative Political Islam.

In chapter 5 I argued that Normative Political Islam builds upon the distinction between Islam-as-faith, that is, the elements of faith which concern an individual's relationship to God, and Islam-as-politics, which refers to an individual's relationship with other people. The former is transcendental; the latter is far more mundane. In explaining the virtues of detaching Islamic discussion of politics from 'the burden of history', Rashid al-Ghannoushi describes a situation which is equally applicable to the distinction between Islam-as-faith and Islam-as-politics; al-Ghannoushi explains that 'Islam is a space and not a point. You can move within this space, it is not a prison, contrary to the dominant perception among Muslims'.[2]

The boundary between Islam-as-faith and Islam-as-politics is not a solid one, and many of the ways in which a Muslim might interact with others might be argued to derive from God's commandments, as interpreted from Islamic source texts. Likewise, one might argue that the way in which government power is exercised might help bolster citizens' relationship with God. Despite the imperfection of the distinction, I established that one of the implications of making the split between Islam-as-politics and Islam-as-faith is the recognition that Islamic guidance on politics, specifically in the form of political affiliation and IR, is not explicit in the Islamic source texts. This is the 'space' that al-Ghannoushi described, within which it becomes possible for Muslims to articulate any variety of theories about the state or the international sphere. These possible articulations, like Normative Political Islam, are *Islamic* in the way in which they derive from and respect key tenets of Islam-as-faith, but cannot claim to be *Islam*; these theories do not constitute part of the faith's dogma. Alternatively, if one collapses Islam-as-faith with Islam-as-politics then this essentialises contemporary Muslim religious resurgence as somehow an indication that Muslims 'are returning to type, rejoining their transhistorical nature; and that fundamentalist Islam is a strident and bloody but adequate expression of this inherent nature'.[3]

I noted how it is possible to derive a notion of Islamic sovereignty from the exoteric and rational (as distinct from spiritual or legal),[4] aspect of the Islamic message. Such a notion of sovereignty was respectful of the doctrinal stipulations laid out in Islamic source texts regarding the sovereignty of God. What was also seen was that such a notion of sovereignty, in escaping the need to derive theories from an immutable source text, was also able to create communally sensitive conceptions of IR. The idea of communitarian articulations of IR leads inevitably to the idea that there can exist *multiple* notions of IR, each sensitive to and derived from different communities.

In chapter 6 I explored the implications of communitarian IR. The discipline of IR was argued to inherit much of its ontological and epistemological foundations from the legacy of the European Enlightenment. One such inheritance, especially with regards to political liberalism, is the notion of the abstracted individual and resulting abstract values, as distinct from communitarian values. The abstracted individual allows for some level of universalism, while communitarianism implies some limits to the applicability of values in any given society. Furthermore, the concept of the *umma* presents one of the more pressing challenges to the way in which IR is conceived by the dominant paradigms of the discipline; the *umma* is a distinct and different unit of analysis from the state. I argued that while it is possible to consider a thin conception of the *umma*, such a conception would truncate the meaning of community in such a way that it may not be acceptable to the Muslims who would seek to give meaning to the *umma* in the contemporary world. Rather, thick conceptions of the *umma* might be far more desirable for the Muslims who would constitute it, but it would truncate the importance of the state in IR. Regardless of which conception of the *umma* is more acceptable for Normative Political Islam, an important point to consider is that *both* thick and thin *ummas* find a place for religious observance and expression in IR, be it through a religious solidarity through an EU-type structure, or through a Muslim 'world society' in the context of the definitions found in the English School. With this summary in mind, I can move on to the comparison with the *Clash of Civilizations*.

Acknowledging Ken Booth's description of Huntington's work as 'the worst book on world politics I have read for a long time',[5] I have nothing to add to the many thorough critiques of the *Clash of Civilizations* offered in the years since its publication.[6] Rather, in this section I will identify those aspects of Normative Political Islam's rendering of IR that resonate with the *Clash of Civilizations*, and examine the implications thereof.

Where I have used the language of multiple communities to derive different conceptions of IR (IR as a specific component of 'the good life'), Huntington used the language of 'civilisations' to talk about *competing* notions of the good life. This competition took the shape of familiar Cold War friend/enemy distinctions.[7] It is interesting to note that 'difference', for Huntington, is equated to (violent) competition, while I have thus far used difference to point to pluralism as a political virtue, not a threat. Writing in 1993, Huntington stated that it is 'symbols of cultural identity' that will shape post–Cold War IR, symbols 'including crosses, crescents, and even head coverings, because culture counts, and cultural identity is what is most meaningful to most people'.[8] Here Huntington, like many IR scholars identified in previous chapters, equates religion with culture in such a way as to fit religion more easily into pre-existing analytical categories. Huntington states that 'religion, however, is the principal defining characteristic of civilizations'; the conflation of culture and religion into the term 'civilisation' is problematic for the reasons I outlined earlier, namely the way in which it rejects the ways believers themselves may see their faith. Nevertheless, the idea of Huntington's civilisations being religiously delineated furthers the comparison with Normative Political Islam.

Giving space to religion, even through the back door of 'civilisation', echoes the discussion of religious values permeating the erstwhile secular discipline of IR. It is not, as Huntington would have it, that with the great battle between competing secular ideologies over, religion returns to the fore. Rather, as Mona Kanwal Sheikh notes, a preoccupation with Cold War competition and secular ideologies betrays 'biased narratives representing the rejection of religion as the conditions for peace, order and even the state-system'.[9] In other words, religion was always present in the lives and narratives of the actors in IR; it never went away and so is nothing 'new' to contend with. Despite the differences in explaining the high visibility of religion in IR, what is key is that Huntington, like me, sees religion as an important factor in understanding contemporary IR.

I have argued that the values derived from within the Islamic tradition do not represent Islam in totality but represent one of many interpretations of Islamic source texts. Huntington, conversely, is fixated on broad civilisational categories which rely on singular interpretations of a cultural/religious tradition. Booth refers to this as a caricatured depiction of actors in world politics; he writes that '[o]n the one hand he [Huntington] makes them ('Western', 'African', 'Islamic', 'Sinic', 'Orthodox', etc.) more distinct and conflictual than they have been and are; on the other hand he exaggerates the degree of intra-civilisational cohesion'.[10] Huntington tries to acknowledge the disparate voices within the Islamic 'civilisation', but claims this is due to no single, strong 'core' state to steer the global Muslim population to a singular goal. At once he is finding a place for religion in IR, a very prominent place, but also essentialising and abstracting the meaning of religion from those who identify with faith. As Bilgin explains, 'when people are encouraged to find themselves solely in their religious heritage, the pluralism and power/knowledge dynamics within civilisations are often left unacknowledged'.[11] Because Libyan Shi'as are Muslim they must naturally defer to the rising 'core' state of Wahhabi Saudi Arabia; after all they are both 'Muslim'. Likewise, do Argentine Christians defer to the dictums of the Christian European or American 'core' of that 'civilisation'?

Having found a place for religion in IR, however problematically by folding religion in with the label 'culture', Huntington uncritically accepts the classification of religion being irrational. He claims that

> Differences in secular ideology between Marxist-Leninism and liberal democracy can at least be debated if not resolved. Differences in material interest can be negotiated and often settled by compromise in a way cultural issues cannot.... Cultural questions... involved a yes or no, zero-sum choice.[12]

Here too the argument of Normative Political Islam is differentiated from the *Clash of Civilizations*. Huntington is a representation of the secular bias in IR. While describing reactions to political Islam specifically, Hurd's comments on this secular bias apply to religion in IR more generally, and the point of view propounded by Huntington. In Hurd's description, 'Political Islam is interpreted . . . as a divergence and/or infringement upon neutral secular public space, as a throwback to premodern forms of Muslim political order, or as a combination of all of these features'.[13] Huntington is doing exactly that, equating religion to a kind of Enlightenment teleology wherein 'progress' is made only when religion is confined to the private sphere. The idea of an IR which is sensitive to religion is one that, according to Huntington, must also become more sensitive to conflict; religion, for him, leads us to zero-sum relations between 'civilisations'.

Huntington's description of conflict in the IR of 'civilisations' creates a curious predicament: On the one hand, Normative Political Islam has argued for a particular Islamic discourse around IR, but on the other hand, the interaction of such a model of IR with other, perhaps religious, perhaps secular conceptions of the international sphere has not been examined. In recognising religious IR or, to be specific, the IR of Normative Political Islam, is it true that different groupings are bound to conflict over the way in which they conceive the international sphere? Such conflict is integral to Huntington's conception of post–Cold War politics, and managing that conflict is the key feature of his theory. However, here is another departure between Normative Political Islam and *Clash of Civilizations*: universalism.

I have used poststructuralism's rejection of meta-narrative and universalism to critique the way in which IR is prone to making such claims over truth. These claims to truth were tied heavily to the legacy of the European Enlightenment, specifically around the ideas of secularism and liberalism. The use of poststructuralism helped me to create a 'space' for alternative theories in the discipline, specifically, religious theory. This is not a novel approach for Muslim theorists. Tamara Sonn points out that '[t]he actual process of questioning texts [of modernity], which is a hallmark of post-modernity, is something that I think contemporary Islamic thinkers have in common'.[14] Indeed, Huntington is also critical of universal pretensions: 'For the first time in human history global politics is both multipolar and multicivilizational; modernisation is distinct from Westernization and is producing neither a universal civilization in any meaningful sense nor the Westernization of non-Western societies'.[15] He continues, curiously, to invoke a type of pluralism wherein '[a]voidance of a global war of civilizations depends on world leaders accepting and cooperating to maintain the multicvilizational character of global politics'.[16] Huntington's ontological justification for this pluralism is unclear, and likely derives from empirical data, the way in which much of his argument is derived. There is an incongruence in his method, however, for while he advocates the nature of the system as multi-polar and pluralistic, he infers that the discourse between 'civilizations' is a zero-sum competition. Faiths that are engaged in a zero-sum competition are expected to put that competition aside to maintain a multi-polar world, yet how that is to be achieved is not discussed. For Normative Political Islam and its poststructural critique of Enlightenment universalism, there is ostensibly no zero-sum competition between competing values; these values are socially constructed and embedded, rather than abstractly conceived and universally applied. However, one is perfectly capable of socially constructing and justifying proselytising values. Take certain interpretations of the Islamic concept of *da'wah*, for example. Additionally, the acceptance of socially constructed values may be problematic for Muslims who would derive their social conduct from transcendental guidance rather than the other way around.

Borrowing the language of Abdul-Karim Soroush, Muslims, generally, are *certain* about the central elements of faith (Islam-as-faith), but *sceptical* about the practicalities of Muslim conduct of IR (Islam-as-politics). Normative Political Islam seemingly resolves this combination of certainty and scepticism by delineating the different spheres Islam-as-faith and Islam-as-politics, but whether this is a successful manoeuvre has yet to be argued conclusively, something that I will attempt in the remainder of this chapter. Soroush articulates this dilemma when he puts forward the question: 'Can we be certain in scepticism'?[17] As I explore the answer to this question, I will also touch upon the remaining and indeed only real comparison between Normative Political Islam and the *Clash of Civilizations*, that is, the inevitability and management of conflict between competing values. To begin, I will explore further the ramifications in synthesising an anti-universalist perspective with the IR of Normative Political Islam. This will be done by looking at a body of work that is somewhat liminal in IR, poststructuralism, and a body of work that falls outside of the disciplinary realm of IR, area studies. Both poststructuralism and area studies make similar claims about the *problem* in uncritically applying IR paradigms to 'non-Western' societies but both, as will be seen, differ from Normative Political Islam in their prescribed *solutions* to this problem. Following this groundwork, I will have a critique of IR that is somewhat in parallel with the argument put forward by Normative Political Islam. At that point I will be in a position to compare and contrast the assumptions put forward by the poststructural critique of IR, with the assumptions that underline Normative Political Islam. Doing so will hopefully shed light on whether one can be a postmodern Muslim, an individual 'certain in scepticism'.[18]

THE FOUNDATIONS OF THE 'PROBLEM' IN IR

The 'problem' described previously is the idea that 'Enlightenment rationalism and universalism appear as a metaphysically disguised Eurocentrism'.[19] This universalism, as Acharya points out, had a dark side in 'the suppression of diversity and justification of European imperialism'.[20] With regards to Islam, I have identified other symptoms of the problem, such as the fear of and rejection of religious rationality. Rejecting religion as an analytical category in IR has led to it being subsumed by other, more tangible factors. In this sense IR is also misrepresenting the realities of Muslim peoples, especially those who are sympathetic to a supra-state identity (the *umma*). Such sympathies contribute to Hinnebusch's irredentism in the Middle East, a 'dissatisfaction with the incongruity between territorial borders and "imagined communities"'.[21]

However, as I am embarked on second-order theorising on the questions and assumptions that underpin IR, I will not here dwell on the symptoms of the problem. Rather, I will analyse the foundations of the problem in order to highlight different or alternative paths in IR, not to supplant or replace existing paradigms, but rather to complement them. Taking Islam, and more broadly religion 'seriously', that is, studying it on its own merits and not subsuming it into pre-existing or convenient analytical categories, would result in greater understanding and avoid Huntington's caricature of 'Muslim bellicosity and violence'.[22] Lemke demonstrates a similar perspective when he suggests that small changes in interpretations of existing IR paradigms, specifically neo-realism, could yield increased understandings of areas of the world suffering from irredentism. In Lemke's Congolese example, he does this by shifting focus away from states, which he admits do not have the saliency in Africa that they have in other parts of the world, to 'autonomous political entities'.[23] Such a move shows reflexivity on the part of Lemke, and allows the study of African realities in IR by acknowledging that those realities do not fit neatly with the existing boundaries of IR; that Lemke's Congolese examples do not 'fit' within these boundaries does not mean that they are not 'IR material', but rather that IR in this instance needs to adjust to accommodate 'non-Western' realities. Just as I previously explored the implications of liberal universalism, in this chapter I will examine the implications of that universalism for IR.

Sadik Jalal al-'Azm argues that '[i]n the West, the historical process may be moved by economic interests, class struggles and socio-political forces. But in the East the 'prime mover' of history is Islam'.[24] How does this (problematically reductionist) dynamic apply to IR? I discussed Kayaoglu's 'Westphalian narrative' previously in the book, and it is worth returning to this concept to talk about what he describes as interpretative dualism. For Kayaoglu, the interpretative dualism stemming from the Westphalian narrative leads to the positive behaviour of an in-group (the 'West') to be attributed to the in-group's character (Protestant work ethic, separation of church and state, etc.). Conversely, the positive behaviour of the out-group (the Islamic world) is attributed to external conditions (interaction with and influence of European powers in the Ottoman Empire). The in-group's negative behaviour, however, is attributed to external conditions, while the negative behaviour of the out-group is attributed to their inherent character (Islam). That this dualism exists is not to deny that in-groups and out-groups do not interact with and constitute each other; rather, it points out that privileging one aspect of this co-constitution leads to analytical shortcomings in IR theories. It is not enough to reject the categories of 'West' and 'non-West', as Acharya advocates,[25] but to work through the problematic ways that this and other binaries have influenced our understandings of IR.

Establishing categories of self and other in IR relates to what Larry Swatuk describes as 'the scientific method'. For Swatuk, the scientific method obscures subtlety in social science; 'if it is not "true" then is must be "false"'.[26] Take as a prime example the problem the English School suffers from in struggling to account for colonialism as a consequence of the 'expansion of international society'; if international society is 'good' then its expansion must also be a 'good' thing. Acknowledging subtlety and abandoning dualisms would help establish the co-constitution of international society and would allow exploration of the darker aspects of European expansion (such as colonialism) which is currently missing, by and large, from English School literature.[27]

Tandeka Nkiwane summarises well the incoherence of liberalism's universalism when she writes, '[i]n the case of liberalism, Eurocentric assertions are too often represented as fact. This assertion as fact is used to dismiss an entire continent [Africa] as irrelevant to a theory that expounds a "universal" message'.[28] Nkiwane explains that if liberalism is forced to acknowledge African realities, it must concede that 'universal' liberalism can in fact lead to imperialism.[29] Liberals of the colonial era used a kind of social Darwinism, creating a 'superior' liberal loving society and the 'inferior' colonised peoples, a reference to the racialised 'standard of civilisation' of Hobson's non-reductive Orientalism. At the time, the killing of these peoples was considered regrettable, but justified as necessary to expand the zone of freedom.[30] Such an approach necessitates polarisation. Be it civilisation and barbarism, order and disorder, rational and irrational, poles are established to justify and explain the domination of one group over another. Does the opposite perspective, that of pluralism, prevent this domination and violence?

Pluralism may not create opposing poles, but would imply a diverse range of positions. It is conceivable that of the many positions presented, some would be entirely incompatible. In this sense, pluralism does not solve the problem of disparate and opposing positions. In-groups may still see themselves as 'civilised' and their respective out-groups as 'barbarians'. However, as pluralism necessarily denies universalism, the impetus to 'civilise' the out-group is removed. 'Progress' in this instance is not an ordering and taming of the unknown world,[31] but rather the ability to co-exist with competing value claims. That a certain set of values exists and may be considered, by those that possess them, as being superior to different values held by other groups, does not mean that these 'superior' values have any purchase in different social condition and heritages.

Pluralism satisfies my constructivist stance on the source of communal values, specifically those that constitute Islam-as-politics. Abstract universalism cannot suffer competitors, and it cannot be the case, as I have argued, that Islam-as-politics derives from a transcendental universal message (which is the domain of Islam-as-faith). However, Normative Political Islam, as one possible articulation of Islam-as-politics, does respect certain elements of the transcendental message of Islam-as-faith. To accommodate the religious world view in IR, it was necessary to 'make space' by critiquing a different universal discourse, that of secularism in IR, and other assumptions deriving from the European Enlightenment. In doing so, I embraced a poststructural position about the nature of truth, finding it necessary to be sceptical about foundational claims, instead accepting that such truths are only ever true within specific temporal and geographical limits. Accepting this post-structural position on ontology, I was able to accept that a secular discourse in IR might work for some, but there is no reason to believe that it is the *only* example of how to conduct IR, leaving space for alternatives like Normative Political Islam to develop. In the end what is left is pluralism within Islam-as-politics *and* pluralism in IR. It is becoming clear that pluralism is doing a lot of work for me, and further discussion about the substance of and operation of that pluralism is required. Specifically, I will continue my discussion of the remaining problem from the comparison with the *Clash of Civilizations*; does a position of pluralism which might still create incompatible world views avoid violent resolution of these differences?

VALUE PLURALISM AND IR

If I want to defend the communitarian position argued for in the previous chapter, I must explore how value pluralism might sustain an international order, and whether that international order would result in 'clash' based politics, as Huntington has argued. My point of departure is Huntington's reasoning for the inevitability of conflict, the idea that cultural and religious differences are zero-sum choices.[32]

The idea that zero-sum choices are inevitable when talking about values is in fact one that is entirely reasonable, expected even, when talking about value pluralism; Stuart Hampshire elucidates, '[t]he ideals of the monk and the soldier, of the revolutionary and the poet, of the aesthete and the politician, seem incurably at odds with each other, even as ideal types, and even more so when individuals of these types are inserted into a particular historical setting'.[33] For Hampshire, the difference between the virtues of a good soldier or a good monk are incompatible; at some point in an individual's life they must make a choice to become one or the other, or neither. Gray makes a similar point in stating that '[a] life of risk and adventure and a life of tranquillity and contemplation cannot both be lived by one person across an entire lifetime'.[34] When Hampshire describes 'deep-seated spiritual antagonisms' as the 'essence of humanity',[35] there is, as with Normative Political Islam, a similarity with the *Clash of Civilisations* in the inevitability of conflict. How then does pluralism propose to resolve these inevitable conflicts? Spending time developing a more specific definition of pluralism is the first step.

Susan Mendus articulates pluralism 'as a doctrine about the sources of value. It holds that those sources are many and not one and, as such, it stands in opposition to monism, or to a Platonic search for unity'.[36] Gray proposes that there is a distinction between strong and weak pluralism; both variants accept Mendus's underlying definition, but strong pluralism applies a more stringent criterion. For Gray, strong pluralism makes three claims: (1) an *'anti-reductionism about values*. The goods of human life are many. They cannot be derived from or reduced to any one value'; (2) a *'non-harmony among values'*, the idea that goods may be incompatible; (3) '[t]he diverse types of flourishing of which humans are capable are not only often uncombinable; sometimes they are rationally incomparable. Let us call this *value-incommensurability*'.[37] Of note is the final of the three claims, that of *value-incommensurability*. Accepting that competing values might not be rationally resolvable marks strong value pluralism from weaker forms, such as liberalism; liberalism acknowledges non-harmony between values, but insists that they can be rationally resolved. How does Normative Political Islam compare with these definitions of pluralism?

There is a lot of resonance between strong value pluralism and the pluralism advocated by Normative Political Islam; it does not forward any particular conception of the good, but rather represents a framework within which Muslims might construct and articulate communally derived values about IR. Such a position is necessarily pluralistic, rejecting the idea that there is a *unifying* substance to Islamic politics derived from Islamic source texts (the Platonic search for unity). That is not to claim that the substance of Normative Political Islam *is not* derived from the Islamic source texts, only that such transcendental guidance is not conclusive and *unifying* for different Muslims who might interpret those sources in different ways. In this manner, Normative Political Islam goes some way towards satisfying Gray's first strong pluralist claim, *anti-reductionism* about values. However, anti-reductionism implies that there is no unifying value from which conceptions of the good life derive. Does that mean Muslims can accept that there are other sources for deriving moral values distinct from Islamic source texts, or God in general? Yes, in some sense, in that Christian and Jewish transcendental guidance is perfectly applicable to people of those faiths, affording a tolerance to those groups (acknowledging that in practice this tolerance waxed and waned through time).[38] Beyond other Abrahamic faiths, one can point to the *ijma' al-fi'l* (consensus of action, understood as historical precedent) of Piscatori's *Islam in a World of Nation-States* to see the capacity of Muslim rulers for peaceful relations with non-Muslims.[39]

Even by pointing to these examples of toleration, theoretical or doctrinal rivalries or antagonisms have not been resolved. For example, recall the example in the previous chapter of liberal pluralism necessitating Islam and other religions to share the same ontological space as Pastafarianism and the Flying Spaghetti Monster. Such a position assumed a commitment to liberal neutrality which in practice might not be applicable in all communities. In other words, Muslim communities living in the United Kingdom, for example, might acknowledge that Islam is granted the same rights and privileges as paganism, but that does not mean they *accept*, respect or value Paganism as a source of the good. As Mendus explains, 'insofar as pluralism holds that values are many and not one . . . it is denied by many moderns, specifically by those of a religious temperament who believe that there is but one source of value—God'.[40] Does such a position towards paganism, for example, fall short of the idea, central to pluralism, that conceptions of the good cannot be reduced or derived from one value? Not when considering the second criteria of value pluralism, *non-harmony among values*. The value of submission to God, or more basic still the belief in God, central to a Muslim's conception of the good, is incompatible with, for example, Humanistic notions of the good. It is not necessary for Muslims to accept that non-belief might yield a good life for anyone, or for the Humanist to conceive of a life believing in God to be in any way fulfilling. In fact, such perspectives would undermine the notion that different values might be entirely conflicting.

While the mere existence of the divergent positions of the Humanist and Muslim lends credence to value pluralism, Gray is clear that universal religion cannot integrate with value pluralism. He states:

> Strong pluralism denies that universal values are fully realizable only in one way of life. It repudiates the central claim of universalist religions to have identified the right or best way of life for all humankind. It rejects the secularization of this claim in the universalist moralities of the Enlightenment.[41]

Gray concludes that '[s]trong pluralism is a subversive truth. It cannot coexist with the articles of faith of any universalist creed'.[42] Here a certain paradox opens up in his argument. If value pluralism represents a truth for all of humankind in a manner which Enlightenment rationality or religion cannot, then there must be an addendum to value pluralism along the lines of 'there are innumerable conceptions of the good, except those versions of the good that consider themselves applicable to all mankind'. Rather, the conflict between universal and plural values is necessarily one of the many ways in which different values are incompatible; it does not subvert the 'truth' of value pluralism; rather it affirms it in the most emphatic manner. However, what is to say that different states, operating along different conceptions of the good, say Muslim and Christian values, would not enter into conflict over these competing and, for the sake of argument, incommensurable values? Put another way, how can societally derived values, which are pluralistic in that they are multiple, non-harmonious and incommensurable, avoid conflict?

Isaiah Berlin, in the tradition of value pluralism sketched out above, is clear that such conflict *cannot* be avoided; 'But the collisions, even if they cannot be avoided, can be softened'.[43] He argues that '[t]he best that can be done, as a general rule, is to maintain a precarious equilibrium that will prevent the occurrence of desperate situations'.[44] Gray, building on the ideas of Hampshire, refers to this equilibrium as modus vivendi, the willingness to 'agree to disagree'.[45] Such a perspective is explicitly considered in IR only very marginally. The reason for this, in broad strokes, is related to the third criterion of Gray's strong value pluralism: *value-incommensurability*. The idea that values cannot be rationally compared runs against the grain of 'subject-centred reason that dominates much of "modernist" [IR] language and forms of social organization and understanding'.[46] Richard Ashley and R. B. J. Walker talk of such a perspective representing 'disciplinary standards',[47] though this is perhaps an unfair characterisation of IR, which has seen the proliferation of much interpretivist scholarship in recent years.[48] Nevertheless, the focus on rationalism and 'the progressive "ordering", or rendering knowable, of the chaotic, untamed, and previously unknown world'[49] has been a recurring feature of the theories I have engaged with, a focus which MacIntyre suggests stems from the European Enlightenment.[50] While realism and the English School paradigms in IR inherit elements of that problematic Enlightenment tradition, they might also be exemplars of value pluralism, as I will discuss briefly now, dealing first with the English School.

The English School's distinction between solidarism and pluralism in some senses mirrors the debate between value pluralism and universalism, but is deficient in two regards. Initially there is the problematic way the English School accounts for religious rationality which, as discussed in chapter 2, is a problem shared with much IR theory. If value pluralism holds true, then the critique of a secular, state-based order is not so damning as to seek to change that system in totality. Instead, it is the claims of universal applicability of that system that cannot be defended, particularly in the face of societally based, religious rationale. This much has been well stated in the current and preceding chapters. The second broad deficiency with the English School's pluralist/solidarist divide, despite its apparent similarity with the discussion of value pluralism and universalism, is that it presumes the existence of an international society, perhaps even a global one, and that the units of this society are states. This is very much related to notions of universal applicability mentioned in the first point, but the friction between religious articulation, in the form of the *umma*, and the ways in which such a conception might interact with the state system, is a less abstract example of the ways in which competing values or conceptions of the good might collide.

Regarding realism, it shares with the English School the criticisms I briefly highlighted above (indeed the English School draws much of its epistemology from realism); realism both does not deal with religion on its own merits and overemphasises the state's actor qualities in the international sphere. However, notions of power are silent on conceptions of the good, so in some way realism allows any number of socially embedded values to be articulated; a Muslim nation need not accept or respect the values of another nation to coexist and tolerate it using the virtues of *realpolitik*. Crucially, however, the idea of *realpolitik* relies on a notion of abstracted rationality, similar in its construction, if not content, to the abstract liberal rationality discussed in the previous chapter; it implies a rationality that applies to any peoples, anywhere, anytime. Such a notion runs counter to the communitarian perspective which Normative Political Islam leans on to give agency to its particular blend of the divine and the mundane. If the communitarian construction of values does not apply to the power politics of realism, which are in fact universal, what other universal value competitors might appear and justify themselves by abstract reasoning? One can argue back to premises (justice/Marxism versus survival/realism, for example), but one cannot make a moral argument about the premises; 'each premise employs some quite different normative or evaluative concept'.[51] So realism, like liberalism, might qualify as weak value pluralism, as neither endorse *value-incommensurability*; for realism and liberalism value conflicts are rationally resolvable by the yardstick of personal freedom or *realpolitik* respectively.

The 'dialogue of civilisations' is an international policy agenda which would represent at least a part of what I am arguing for in regards to pluralism in IR. As Kayaoglu explains about the agenda:

> Essentially, any idea or practice can be part of the dialogue of civilizations agenda if it accepts: (1) the value of a plurality of civilizations; (2) the necessity for an international order that accommodates the plurality of civilizations; and (3) that dialogue and goodwill among people who identify with different civilizations are essential in order to achieve peaceful coexistence.[52]

Since the 1990s, the dialogue of civilisations has been pushed forward by Muslim policy makers, to the extent that the OIC has included dialogue in its charter.[53] However, my criticisms about the inadequacy of 'civilisation' as a category of belonging remain, and I would agree with Bilgin that 'bracketing civilisation has the effect of constraining as opposed to fostering dialogue'.[54] Dialogue as a means to value pluralism is more than a policy agenda. Value pluralism entails new ways of knowing and doing IR, which moves beyond 'uncovering historical debt'.[55]

I claim that IR has not engaged sufficiently with value pluralism, though there is great potential in that concept for giving credence to concepts and peoples otherwise marginalised by Enlightenment rationality. If poststructuralism is often caricatured for its ability to deconstruct, and its inability to propose alternatives, I would suggest that more work is taken to integrate the value pluralism in IR. Chantal Mouffe has already made inroads into this debate from a poststructural perspective. She diagnoses the contemporary ills of IR when writing that

> It is the fact that we are now living in a unipolar world where there are no legitimate channels for opposing the hegemony of the United States which is at the origin of the explosion of new antagonisms which, if we are unable to grasp their nature, might indeed lead to the announced 'clash of civilizations'. The way to avoid such a prospect is to take pluralism seriously instead of trying to impose one single model on the whole world.[56]

While labelling the nature of world order as unipolar or multipolar is contentious, it does not undermine the presence of antagonisms that can be produced either in a unipolar order or an order that is transitioning to become multipolar. Referring to Mouffe's position as agonistic pluralism, Elaine Stratford et al. note that such a position 'acknowledges the productive potential of conflict',[57] and I urge that more work be done to recognise the necessity of and, hopefully, the value of conflict in society and in IR. Value pluralism presents an epistemology that synthesises well with that of poststructuralism, namely, a profound scepticism of universalism. As such, it might represent a method through which poststructuralism might construct alternative understandings of IR, much as Mouffe has demonstrated with agonistic pluralism, rather than focus on critique or fall into relativism. Jim George and David Campbell some twenty years ago referred to postmodernism as representing 'the great skepticism (but *not* cynicism) of our time'.[58] Without a focus on the constructive elements made possible by the poststructural position on ontology in IR, poststructuralism may well be considered cynical. I hope that value pluralism and Normative Political Islam relieve some of that cynicism. But even if it is accepted that poststructuralism is not the great cynicism of our time, it undoubtedly remains sceptical (of universalisms), and scepticism, as highlighted earlier in the chapter, does not sit well with the certainty of Muslim belief in God. It is here that I turn to the final question of the chapter: the conundrum of the postmodern Muslim.

CERTAIN IN SCEPTICISM? POSTMODERNISM AND ISLAM

I have highlighted that reconciling belief in the transcendental and the use of societally derived values is problematic. I then mapped this problem onto the way in which sovereignty is constructed in Normative Political Islam, namely, the dual contract method. In the first contract, explicit deference to God by way of the *shahada* was required, which was then supplemented by a second contract which built upon the split between the transcendental Islam-as-faith and the societally derived Islam-as-politics. This second contract was between the Muslim and government, but being distinct from Islam-as-faith, the nature of this government could take numerous forms. In chapter 5 I argued that the rational, exoteric tradition, much maligned in Sunni Islam, provided the tools to derive Islam-as-politics from these differing social circumstances in a way the theological guidance of Islam-as-politics was unable to do. Applying a hierarchy between the two contracts further distinguished Islam-as-politics from Islam-as-faith, but the distinction appears more and more arbitrary when considering what it is that binds individual Muslims in an *umma*. Recalling the 'paradox' offered in the last chapter, I noted that it is the transcendental fealty towards God and the Prophet that forms the basis of the solidarity between Muslims in the *umma*; at the same time, however, it is the transcendentalism in IR which was criticised in the first place to make space for alternative conceptions of IR, such as that posed by Normative Political Islam. Applying the same poststructuralist and anti-foundational critique to the transcendentalism of the *umma* and belief in an absolute God will in turn negate the argument forwarded thus far. In this final section I will attempt to resolve this problem, and ask if it is possible to be a poststructuralist Muslim.

Framing the question another way, it is necessary to quote at length Soroush when he says,

> [A]s far as I can understand and articulate, in the classical period, or in the medieval period, we had an age of the dictatorship of religion, the dictatorship of religious institution. Then in the phase of the Enlightenment, we had the age of the dictatorship of reason. That was the age of modernity, properly speaking the dictatorship of reason. Now in the post-modern era, there is no dictatorship whatsoever; there is no god, according to the post-modern philosophers. Reason has become much more humble. Religion has become much more humble, and now it is time for these two to reconcile, to be recombined, to come to terms with each other. That is the post-modern era, and that is the occasion, the opportunity to try to reconcile again a humbler reason and a humbler religion.[59]

For Soroush, the discussion should revolve around boundaries, acknowledging the limits of both religion and reason. I have already achieved this in the attempted fusion of Islamic exotericism and communitarianism. My problem is one step removed from Soroush's outline. Where Soroush identifies postmodernism, the notion that in the contemporary world one is unable to make universal claims, as the explanation for reason's 'humbling', I have instead based my argument on poststructuralism. Recalling the differentiation between postmodernism and poststructuralism made in chapter 3, the latter is not rooted in a specific time or event, but rather is an ontological statement about the nature of knowledge. For me, then, the problem is that poststructuralism does not result in a humbler religion and humbler reason, as Soroush claims postmodernism does. Rather, poststructuralism severely cripples religion's capacity to inform the behaviour of its adherents, leaving reason somewhat intact (insofar as it is reason that is 'doing' the humbling in the first place). As Turner comments, poststructuralism 'threatens to deconstruct all theological accounts of reality into mere fairy tales or mythical grand narratives'.[60]

Turner notes a similar problem with regards to competing universal religions when he asks how religions like Christianity and Islam are able to be contained in the same environment.[61] His observation needs amending as I proceed; the question is how to contain, within a single global environment, universal religious positions and pluralist positions. It is in fact value pluralism, as summarised earlier in the chapter, that is capable of containing both absolutism and particularism in the same global environment. More than a global environment, however, for me the question is how to maintain these two positions of universalism and particularism *within the same tradition*, namely, Normative Political Islam. As the discussion continues, first the incompatibility between Islam-as-faith (represented in the first contract of Normative Political Islam's notion of sovereignty) and poststructuralism must be outlined more clearly.

Tibi is emphatic that a rejection of universality cannot be compatible with Islamism; he quips that '[t]he Western cultural relativists overlook the totalitarian face of Islamism and Islamists hide their contempt for these "unbelievers". An alliance of strange bed fellows emerges'.[62] Tibi is caricaturing popular conceptions of Islamism or otherwise is grossly essentialising 'Islamism'. The idea that Islamism, what I have referred to as Islam-as-politics, is inherently totalitarian is not substantiated given the separation of Islam-as-faith and Islam-as-politics; the latter is not necessarily committed to any particular political persuasion. Islam-as-politics, if societally derived, *might* develop a totalitarian leaning, just as European political traditions emanating from the Enlightenment's 'modernity' *might* do. As Sami Zubaida states in rebuttal to such essentialism, it was not written in Germany's history that Hitler would take control of the state, and Zubaida offers similar arguments for the Russian revolution and the Iranian revolution.[63]

Sabet articulates the incompatibility with Islam-as-faith with more clarity when he states that poststructuralism 'perpetrates an act of *violence* against Islam, both in its revelatory *and* jurisprudential/thought components'.[64] Sabet believes that there can be only a singular Islam, 'referring to the universe and cosmology of revelation as uniquely represented by primary texts and scriptures'.[65] Such a position, as I have maintained throughout the book, neglects the role that human interpretation plays in the understanding of source texts. However, it is also true that the heterogeneous interpretations of these same, as Sabet describes, unique source texts, do not diminish the feeling and belief of Muslims in the singular truth of their revelation. Whether Muslims feel that they are correctly interpreting the source texts, or acknowledge that their interpretation is a fallible endeavour, the core belief is that there *is* a divine truth to be understood somewhere, somehow. To deny this my analysis is perhaps the act of violence that Sabet refers to, equivalent to accusing Muslims of believing in fairy tales and myth.

Acknowledging the Truth of Islam, or Essentialising a Diverse Tradition?

There needs to be a more nuanced take on the idea of Islam's 'truth' than the current discussion, especially of Islamism, allows for. I am not the first, and certainly will not be the last, to grapple with the truth of Islam's revelation (Islam-as-faith) versus the diverse social construction of Islam's practice (Islam-as-politics). I will therefore be drawing on the positions of many others as I proceed to my conclusion.

The guiding question here is whether one is capable of accepting the truth of Islam, or if doing so requires us to essentialise diverse readings of the faith. Otherwise put, is essentialism creating a myth of a singular Islam, a type of Orientalist understanding of the other's belief system? Turning to Zubaida once more, his definition of essentialism claims that Islamic societies share some core elements which 'determine or limit the possibilities of their social and political development'.[66] It can be observed, from the outside in, that there is certainly a 'core' element that Muslims share with each other, a kind of lowest common denominator that gets lower the wider one defines 'Muslim'. For example, the lowest common denominator amongst Sunni Muslims is not as low as the commonality between Sunni and Shi'a Muslims. Additionally it can be understood, from the inside out, that the Muslim's belief in God and the Prophet (at the very least) is a common, perhaps defining feature of Muslims.

As argued previously this 'core', however it is defined or conceived, by the believer or the analyst, is related to the transcendental elements of Islam and *not* to the political possibilities of Muslim societies or Muslim minorities. John Esposito describes positions that would claim that any such limitations exist as romanticism; he states that '[t]he sacrosanct nature of tradition in Islam, based upon a romanticized understanding of Islamic history . . . serves as an inspirational reality for traditionalists and, at times, as a major obstacle for modern reformers'.[67] Rather than any theological or divine community of believers, Zubaida asserts that 'diverse Islamic currents tend to converge, at least in sentiment, on one front: anti-imperialism, and specifically antipathy to the US'.[68] Such a cynical take on the nature of Islamic unity is capable from the analyst's point of view, from the outside looking in, so to speak. What this view does not consider is the perspective of the believer, something I will return to shortly. As far as a loosely defined 'core' of Islam historically relates to politics, Piscatori notes that such a core has not prevented ideological, communal, political and territorial divisions among the wider Muslim community.[69] In light of this historical record, one cannot assume that the likes of Tibi and Sabet can be referring to a common truth of Islam that encapsulates or limits social or political development, as per Zubaida's definition of essentialism; these arguments are easily refuted. What, then, is the 'truth' of Islam that poststructuralism commits violence against with regards to Islam?

Ali Hassan Zaidi is emphatic with regards to the question posed above, and he states that

> [E]mpirical diversity does not mean that Islam or modernity simply dissolve into a plurality of local Islams and local modernities. Despite the multiplicity of Islamic discourses and despite their polysemic origins, there remains, not an undifferentiated unity, but a holism to those discourses which, although dismissed by anti-essentialist theorists, remains palpable for believers.[70]

The notion of holism is important, and I will use the term to talk about what has until now been referred to as an ill-defined unity/truth/core/lowest common denominator of Islam. The holism that Zaidi refers to as palpable for believers is the one that he argues is incompatible with poststructuralism; it 'compels Muslims to deprive the Qur'an of its ontological status as a sacred revelation'.[71] If I have arrived at a term that refers to the truth of Islam, that is, holism as experienced by the believer, then this term now needs to be unpacked and the relationship between poststructuralism and holism needs to be examined further, to enquire as to whether they are indeed as conflictual as Zaidi argues.

If holism refers explicitly to the transcendental aspect of Islam, as it is experienced by believers, then what exactly is referred to by 'the transcendental'? Previously I have referred to the *shahada* as representative of the holism experienced by believers, that is, the declaration of belief in God and the Prophet Muhammed. God and prophethood is clearly a commitment to the transcendental, but the interpretation of that commitment is not clear. I posit that the concept that satisfies the idea of the holism, the transcendental and universal, is *moral realism*. Boucher describes moral realism as a 'point of view that maintains that there are objective standards of truth and morality, independent of what we may wish or think'.[72] In reference to Islamic holism and the *shahada*, these objective standards would derive from God and the Prophet. Moreover, however, it is not just the case with Islamic holism that there is an objective standard, but that this standard is universal. Poststructuralism, as already demonstrated, would contest this Islamic holism; the notion of universal objective standards is one I have criticised throughout this book. As Boucher goes on to conclude:

> [W]hen natural law and its derivative rights are deemed to be universal, their application is often oppressive. They are the expression of the mind of a culture, the articulation of the values, and morality expected of its member.

When applied to other cultures, their members are almost invariable likely to fall below those standards in crucial respects.[73]

The problems of oppression I elaborated on previously, with regards to universal Enlightenment rationality and its relationship to colonialism, are equally applicable to a universal natural law encapsulated in Islamic holism. However, the extent of this universality is questionable; there is a measure of interpretation needed to derive values from the Islamic source texts. There is certainly not enough in Islam-as-faith to derive Islam-as-politics without needing to turn to human ingenuity and turn away from any such holism. I argue therefore that the distinction between Islam-as-faith and Islam-as-politics remains intact. With this distinction in mind, the holism of Islam is encapsulated in Islam-as-faith, leaving Normative Political Islam and other variants of Islam-as-politics to embrace anti-foundational concepts without hesitation. Even with this being so, the paradox of the poststructural Muslim has not been escaped; I am still relying on poststructural Muslims to neatly keep their anti-foundational critiques in a separate conceptual 'box', never allowing it to meet the holism of their faith for fear of deconstructing it into fairy tale and myth.

Bounding Expectations: Islamic Rationalism and Poststructuralism

Moral realism, the objective criteria by which one measures her actions is, in the common interpretation of many Muslims, dictated by God. However, one of the major breaks I have made with a majority of other analyses of (Sunni) political Islam, is to bring rationalism *back in*. Recalling the exoteric tradition, *al-iman*, of the Islamic revelation (in conjunction with the theology of *al-islam* and the gnosticism of *al-ihsan*), which I discussed at length in chapter 5, one can glimpse a way out of this poststructural predicament.

The rationalism of Sunni Islam's exoteric tradition is an attempt, perhaps, at taking morality *out* of God's hands and away from the transcendentalism of moral realism. In this way, God's prohibition against killing, for example, is not the reason that killing is frowned upon. Rather, because killing is bad, God forbade it.[74] The implication of this move is that there are *multiple* ways to arrive at the conclusion that killing is bad, one of which could be rationalism, and another could be unquestioning adherence to God's commandments. Therefore, bringing rationalism back in undermines the position of Sabet and others who bemoan poststructuralism's act of violence against monotheistic religions. I am not denying that there is a universal notion of value. Indeed, the *shahada* says there *is* a universal value vested in the belief in God and the Prophet. Rather, by accepting the limits of human beings in *comprehending* this value, one can accept plural derivations of this singular belief. As al-Azmeh states eloquently, '[t]here is no guarantor for the validity of translation and interpretation [of Islamic source texts]'.[75] If there is no guarantor for differing interpretations (a position eerily similar to the poststructuralist perspective of morality), does this necessarily mean that there is therefore no transcendental or objective truth? In order to give credence to the believer's sense of holism, I must answer no; not having the capacity to comprehend a truth does not mean that such a truth does not exist. As An-Na'im states,

> The separation of Islam and the state [comparable to the distinction between Islam-as-faith and Islam-as-politics] does not prevent Muslims from proposing policy or legislation stemming from their religious or other belief. . . . Citizens must be able to make counterproposals through public debate without being open to charges about their religious piety.[76]

In making this move towards moral realism I have allowed for a type of Islamic holism, but this has not quite settled the paradox of the poststructural Muslim; while the Muslim is happy, the poststructuralist may well be frustrated by the concession that an objective truth can exist.

However, the poststructuralist cannot claim emphatically that no objective truth exists. To do so would in itself be a truth claim, abstracted from people's experiences. Rather, truths do exist, but are geographically and temporally limited in their applicability. The issue in accepting any notion of moral realism, in this case the Muslim's belief in God, is not the belief per se, but the idea that such belief is applicable to all peoples, universally. In bringing rationalism back into conceptions of Islam-as-politics, I am able to avoid making such grandiose claims about universal applicability; the rationalism explored in chapter 5 demanded an acceptance of societal (and therefore geographical and temporal) limitations in any construction of Islam-as-politics, Normative Political Islam included.

Here a subtle difference can be marked between the abstract level at which I have been using poststructuralism, and the more empirical level at which I invoked value pluralism to manage conflict between competing values. Belief in God and the anti-foundationalism of poststructuralism are *incommensurable values*; they are rationally unresolvable. The poststructural Muslim paradox centred on the idea that a Muslim wanting to articulate Islam-as-politics in the way done with Normative Political Islam cannot be expected to wield a poststructural critique of IR whilst not using that critique on the transcendental elements of their own faith.[77] *Embracing value pluralism is the solution to this paradox.* Poststructural critique does not mean accepting that there is one way to construct value: poststructuralism. When critiquing Enlightenment philosophy I am not stating that it is worthless, but that the worth it carries has boundaries to its applicability. Likewise, the rationality encapsulated by the Enlightenment, or the holism of Muslim belief, places boundaries on poststructuralism, preventing it from assuming the role of a meta-narrative, or a poststructural ontology. The term ontology does not fit well with poststructuralism, especially arrived at through Foucault. A poststructural ontology would imply a truth claim about the nature of knowledge, when in fact poststructuralism makes no such claim to knowledge, but rather is sceptical of any such claims. Recalling the same argument outlined in chapter 4, where 'poststructural position on ontology' was employed to avoid confusion over a poststructural ontology, here I purposefully use the term ontology to describe an unbounded poststructuralism; a poststructural ontology therefore becomes representative of Soroush's 'dictatorship of reason'.[78]

Accepting difference, however, 'cannot serve as a blanket concession to the immutability of religious sentiment';[79] to do so would be to return to 'the dictatorship of religious institution'.[80] Rather, these two positions hold each other in check. The fact that one must accept the boundaries between these different traditions is a tacit acceptance that they are not compatible with each other. As per the dictums of value pluralism, they *will* clash, and that does not mean it is unreasonable to ask Normative Political Islam to use poststructuralism to make a space for itself in IR while holding onto a belief in God. Likewise, it is not unreasonable to ask poststructuralism to hold onto an anti-foundational perspective while accepting the holism of Islam-as-faith. Both examples accept the limits of their respective claims on knowledge. That an individual can neatly demarcate between the two in their conception of the world is in fact testament to the competing values individuals hold within themselves at any one time, and by way of conclusion I will turn to Stuart Hampshire's explanation of this point:

> The perpetual clash and friction of divisive attachments and of memories and of emotions in conflict seems to me to make up the internal life of a person, and the perpetual clash and friction of ethnic loyalties and religious loyalties and cultural loyalties and class loyalties make up the life and development of societies, cities and states.[81]

CONCLUSIONS

Building upon the articulation in the previous chapter of communitarian IR and the *umma*, I have in this chapter argued that value pluralism has the capacity to manage competing value claims in the international sphere. Value pluralism escapes the pessimism of *Clash of Civilizations* and instead sees the necessity, and perhaps virtue, of conflict. If Islam-as-politics (as well as other notions of politics) is derived from societal settings, regardless of the pretensions to abstract universalism some political ideologies might have, then it is reasonable to expect some of them to conflict with each other. It is not, however, a reductionist explanation about Islam's 'violent nature' that ensures this conflict. Rather, values both outside and within different traditions will always conflict with each other.

I have argued that resolving this conflict is a false errand whereby resolution is only achieved by the dominance of one set of values at the expense of the other. Instead, I have advocated for the management of conflict and the 'softening of blows' as a more appropriate response, both for Normative Political Islam's interaction with other polities and vice versa. Such a position requires the acknowledgement not only that values might conflict, but that they are also irreconcilable by logic or rational argument. This addendum to value pluralism distinguishes it from 'softer' forms such as liberalism, wherein diversity of values is respected unless those views challenge the underlying logic of liberalism (individual autonomy provides examples that often pit the Ottoman *millet* system against modern notions of liberal tolerance).

When translating value pluralism to IR, I noted that the English School's pluralist/solidarist divide represented a similar schism as that between pluralism and universalism respectively. However, like liberalism, this is a 'soft' version of pluralism; it relies on the universalism of Enlightenment rationality, relegating religiously derived politics to some 'backward' era, as is endemic in IR theories at large. Secondly, the notion of international society which the English School leans on also universalises the institution of the state into a necessary building block of IR. Realism, like the English School, also seems placed to enact value pluralism in IR; the *realpolitik* it propounds appears somewhat 'value neutral'. However, it shares problems in much the same way that the English School does with regards to religious rationality and the primacy of states.

I have argued that poststructuralism, with its anti-foundational perspective, is well placed to overcome the shortcomings outlined above, but is often caricatured as being overly focused on critique and unable to pose alternatives. Poststructuralism is fertile ground for the enacting of and theorising about value pluralism, and it is in their combination that pluralism in IR can be developed. Mouffe's concept of agonistic pluralism was argued to encapsulate the opportunity the synthesis of poststructuralism and value pluralism hold for IR.

With all the above being so, I was left to consider the way in which the hypothetical Muslims of Normative Political Islam could possibly embrace poststructuralism in the critique of IR, while not applying the same critique to meta-narratives in their own tradition, namely, belief in God. Turning once more to value pluralism to 'resolve' this issue, I argued that it is, in fact, unresolvable. As such, the incoherence between poststructuralism and belief in God represents another example of irreconcilable values, and so synthesising the two is not a reasonable proposition. Rather, managing the friction that these conflicting positions represent is a way to keep each of them in check, preventing poststructuralism from accidentally becoming a meta-narrative in its own right; otherwise put: 'there is no truth except the truth of the fact that there is no truth'. Likewise, the conflict between poststructuralism and belief in God stops the latter from overwhelming the sensibilities of believers into forgetting the societal basis that different notions of value derive from. For these hypothetical Muslims, such a position can even affirm the Qur'anic commandment: 'Do not exceed the limits of your religion'.[82]

NOTES

1. Samuel Huntington, *The Clash of Civilizations and the Remaking of World Order* (New York: Simon and Schuster, 1996).

2. Rashid al-Ghannoushi, quoted in John Esposito, 'Summary of the Open Debate', in *Rethinking Islam and Modernity: Essays in Honour of Fathi Osman*, ed. Abdelwahab El-Affendi (Leicester: Islamic Foundation, 2001), 174.

3. Aziz al-Azmeh, 'Postmodern Obscurantism and "the Muslim Question"', in *Fighting Identities: Race, Religion and Ethno-nationalism*, ed. Leo Pantich and Colin Leys (London: Merlin, 2002), 30.

4. The intention is not to draw comparison to irrationality, but rather to the three elements of Islamic epistemology, *al-Shari'ah*, *al-Tariqah*, and *al-Haqiqah*. For more on this distinction see Hossein Nasr, *Islamic Philosophy from its Origin to the Present: Philosophy in the Land of Prophecy* (New York: State University of New York Press, 2006), 31.

5. Ken Booth, 'Huntington's Homespun Grandeur', *Political Quarterly* 68, no. 4 (1997): 425.

6. For example, see Fred Halliday, *Islam and the Myth of Confrontation* (London: I.B. Tauris, 1996); John Esposito, *The Islamic Threat: Myth or Reality*, 3rd ed. (Oxford: Oxford University Press, 1999); Michaelene Cox, John Oneal, and Bruce Russett, 'Clash of Civilizations, or Realism and Liberalism Déjà Vu? Some Evidence', *Journal of Peace Research* 37, no. 5 (2000); Gabriele Marranci, 'Multiculturalism, Islam and the Clash of Civilisations Theory: Rethinking Islamophobia', *Culture and Religion: An Interdisciplinary Journal* 5, no. 1 (2004); and Arjun Appadurai, *A Fear of Small Numbers: An Essay on the Geography of Anger* (London: Duke University Press, 2006).

7. Pinar Bilgin, 'Civilisation, Dialogue, Security: The Challenge of Post-secularism and the Limits of Civilisational Dialogue', *Review of International Studies* 38 (2012): 1103.

8. Huntington, *Clash of Civilizations*, 20.

9. Mona Kanwal Sheikh, 'How Does Religion Matter? Pathways to Religion in International Relations', *Review of International Studies* 38, no. 2 (2012), 267.

10. Booth, 'Huntington's Homespun Grandeur', 425.

11. Bilgin, 'Civilisation, Dialogue, Security', 1108.

12. Huntington, *Clash of Civilizations*, 129–30.

13. Elizabeth Hurd, *The Politics of Secularism in International Relations* (Princeton: Princeton University Press, 2008), 117.

14. Tamara Sonn, quoted in Esposito, 'Summary of the Open Debate', 153.

15. Huntington, *Clash of Civilizations*, 20.

16. Ibid., 21.

17. Esposito, 'Summary of the Open Debate', 166.

18. Ibid.

19. Peter Dews, 'Postmodernism: Pathologies of Modernity from Nietzsche to the Poststructuralists', in *The Cambridge History of Twentieth Century Political Thought*, ed. Terence Ball and Richard Bellamy (Cambridge: Cambridge University Press, 2003), 345.

20. Amitav Acharya, 'Global International Relations (IR) and Regional Worlds: A New Agenda for International Studies', *International Studies Quarterly* 58, no. 4 (2014): 649.

21. Raymond Hinnebusch, 'Introduction: The Analytical Framework', in *The Foreign Policies of Middle East States*, ed. Raymond Hinnebusch and Anoushiravan Ehteshami (Boulder: Lynne Rienner, 2002), 7.

22. Huntington, *Clash of Civilizations*, 258.

23. Douglas Lemke, 'Intra-national IR in Africa', *Review of International Studies* 37, no. 1 (2011): 69.

24. Sadik Jalal al-'Azm, 'Orientalism and Orientalism in Reverse', in *Orientalism: A Reader*, ed. Alexander Lyon Macfie (New York: New York University Press, 2000), 234.

25. Acharya, 'Global International Relations (IR) and Regional Worlds', 649.

26. Larry Swatuk, 'The Brothers Grim: Modernity and "International" Relations in Southern Africa', in *Africa's Challenge to International Relations Theory*, ed. Kevin Dunn and Timothy Shaw (Basingstoke: Palgrave Macmillan, 2001), 166.

27. Edward Keene is a notable exception when he comments that 'the adoption of a deeper historical perspective inevitably raises some awkward questions about the civilizing mission to which international order is currently dedicated, and it is not a proper response simply to pretend that those questions do not exist because the idea of human rights was only asserted in international relations after 1945, or because the idea of human rights was only asserted in international relations after 1945, or because the division of sovereignty in contemporary international organizations is an unprecedented phenomenon'. Edward Keene, *Beyond the Anarchical Society: Grotius, Colonialism and Order in World Politics* (Cambridge: Cambridge University Press, 2002), 149.

28. Tandeka Nkiwane, 'The End of History? African Challenges to Liberalism in International Relations', in *Africa's Challenge to International Relations Theory*, ed. Kevin Dunn and Timothy Shaw (Basingstoke: Palgrave Macmillan, 2001), 111.

29. Ibid., 110.

30. Domenico Losurdo, *Liberalism: A Counter-History* (London: Verso, 2011), 334.

31. Swatuk, 'Brothers Grim', 167.

32. Huntington, *Clash of Civilizations*, 130.

33. Stuart Hampshire, 'Liberalism: The New Twist', *New York Review of Books* 40, no. 14 (1993): 43.

34. John Gray, 'Where Pluralists and Liberals Part Company', *International Journal of Philosophical Studies* 6, no. 1 (2010): 22.

35. Hampshire, 'Liberalism', 43.

36. Susan Mendus, 'Saving One's Soul or Founding a State: Morality and Politics', *Philosophia* 34, no. 3 (2006): 235.

37. Gray, 'Where Pluralists and Liberals Part Company', 20. Original emphasis.

38. See for example Shlomo Deshen and Walter Zenner, 'Jews among Muslims in Precolonial Times: An Introductory Survey', in *Jews among Muslims: Communities in the Precolonial Middle East*, ed. Shlomo Deshen and Walter Zenner (New York: New York University Press, 1996).

39. James Piscatori, *Islam in a World of Nation-States* (Cambridge: Cambridge University Press, 1986), 49.

40. Mendus, 'Saving One's Soul or Founding a State', 235.

41. Gray, 'Where Pluralists and Liberals Part Company', 23.

42. Ibid., 35.

43. Isaiah Berlin, *The Crooked Timber of Humanity: Chapters in the History of Ideas*, ed. Henry Hardy (London: Pimlico, 2003), 17.

44. Ibid. 17–18.

45. Gray, 'Where Pluralists and Liberals Part Company', 17.

46. Nicholas Rengger, 'No Time like the Present? Postmodernism and Political Theory', *Political Studies* 40, no. 3 (1992): 562.

47. Richard Ashley and R. B. J. Walker, 'Conclusion: Reading Dissidence/Writing the Discipline: Crisis and the Question of Sovereignty in International Studies', *International Studies Quarterly* 34, no. 3 (1990): 373.

48. Least of which can be seen in the saliency of the constructivist approach. See for example Jeffery Checkel, 'The Constructivist Turn in International Relations Theory', *World Politics* 50, no. 2 (1998); Dale Copeland, 'The Constructivist Challenge to Structural Realism: A Review Essay', *International Security* 25, no. 2 (2000); Jim George, *Discourses of Global Politics: A Critical (Re) Introduction to International Relations* (Boulder: Lynne Rienner, 1994); Alexander Wendt, *Social Theory of International Politics* (Cambridge: Cambridge University Press, 1999).

49. Swatuk, 'Brothers Grim', 167.

50. Alasdair MacIntyre, *After Virtue: A Study in Moral Theory*, 2nd ed. (London: Duckworth, 1985), 39.

51. Ibid., 8.

52. Turan Kayaoglu, 'Constructing the Dialogue of Civilizations in World Politics: A Case of Global Islamic Activism', *Islam and Christian-Muslim Relations* 23, no. 2 (2012): 129–30.

53. Ibid., 145.

54. Bilgin, 'Civilisation, Dialogue, Security', 1108.

55. Ibid., 1110.

56. Chantal Mouffe, *On the Political* (London: Routledge, 2005), 115.

57. Elaine Stratford, Denbeigh Armstrong, and Martina Jaskolsji, 'Relational Spaces and the Geopolitics of Community Participation in Two Tasmanian Local Governments: A Case for Agonistic Pluralism?' *Transactions of the Institute of British Geographers* 28, no. 4 (2003): 469.

58. Jim George and David Campbell, 'Patterns of Dissent and the Celebration of Difference: Critical Social Theory and International Relations', *International Studies Quarterly* 34, no. 3 (1990): 280.

59. Abdul-Karim Soroush, quoted in Esposito, 'Summary of the Open Debate', 166–67.

60. Bryan Turner, *Orientalism, Postmodernism and Globalism* (London: Routledge, 1994), 92. Turner here uses the term postmodernism, which I have replaced with poststructuralism to clear up the conceptual confusion around the two terms, as outlined in chapter 4.

61. Ibid., 78

62. Bassam Tibi, *Islam's Predicament with Modernity: Religious Reform and Cultural Change* (London: Routledge, 2009), 60.

63. Sami Zubaida, *Islam, the People & the State*, 2nd ed. (London: I.B. Tauris, 1989), 138.

64. Amr Sabet, *Islam and the Political: Theory, Governance and International Relations* (London: Pluto, 2008), 181.

65. Ibid., 187

66. Zubaida, *Islam, the People & the State*, 122.

67. John Esposito, *Islam and Politics*, 4th ed. (New York: Syracuse University Press, 1998), 315.

68. Sami Zubaida, 'Islam and the Politics of Community and Citizenship', *Middle East Report* no. 221 (2001): 24.

69. Piscatori, *Islam in a World of Nation-States*, 45–46.

70. Ali Hassan Zaidi, 'A Critical Misunderstanding: Islam and Dialogue in the Human Sciences', *International Sociology* 22, no. 4 (2007).

71. Ibid., 426.

72. David Boucher, *The Limits of Ethics in International Relations: Natural Law, Natural Rights, and Human Rights in Transition* (Oxford: Oxford University Press, 2009), 1.

73. Ibid., 11.

74. Fazlur Rahman, *Islam* (Chicago: University of Chicago Press, 1979), 104.

75. Aziz al-Azmeh, *Islam and Modernities*, 2nd ed. (London: Verso, 1996), 109.

76. Abdullahi Ahmed An-Na'im, *Islam and the Secular State: Negotiating the Future of Shari'a* (Cambridge, MA: Harvard University Press, 2008), 7–8.

77. Aziz al-Azmeh laments the propensity for modern scholars to lean on incommensurable values as unscientific and even nihilistic, but I hope that the notion of scepticism sufficiently distances itself from nihilism in my pursuit for pluralism. For a more detailed critique of value incommensurability, see al-Azmeh, 'Postmodern Obscurantism and "the Muslim Question"', 31.

78. Soroush, quoted in Esposito, 'Summary of the Open Debate', 166.
79. Mustapha Kamal Pasha, 'Islam and the Postsecular', *Review of International Studies* 38, no. 5 (2012): 1049.
80. Soroush, quoted in Esposito, 'Summary of the Open Debate', 166.
81. Hampshire, 'Liberalism', 47.
82. *Qur'an*, 4:171.

Chapter Eight

Conclusion

In this book I have contributed to the debates in IR scholarship that attempt to frame 'religious resurgence' not as the problem of stubborn religions that refuse to accept 'enlightened' values, but as the problem of a discipline that arbitrarily removes religion from the realm of politics. Barak Mendelsohn summarises the above position when he writes that

> Unlike the international society, which allows for multiple 'truths' to coexist, in a religious order the course of authority is one, and it demands exclusivity, denying the existence of any other truth but its own (although religious doctrines might acknowledge that other faiths hold partial truths).[1]

While Mendelsohn is referring here to what he calls radical Islam, it can also be noted that he quite problematically asserts that international society allows for multiple truths to exist, while I have argued that there are certain truths that remain 'beyond' debate. Mendelsohn's example of distinguishing 'self' from 'other' is indicative of claiming that 'civilisation' rests in certain institutions (Westphalia), thereby delegitimising alternative voices. That is not to say that one cannot or should not criticise radical Islam. Rather, criticising radical Islam on the grounds of exclusivity is somewhat akin to holding double standards; the Westphalian system also demands exclusivity with regards to secularism and liberal individualism, only the latter are often implicitly 'good' things in IR while Islamism is not.

I have also contributed to literature on political Islam, filling a gap in regards to how political Islam might operate with regards to IR. Previous work, as noted in chapter 3, deals primarily with defining what political Islam is *not*, rather than what it is *for*. In this respect, I have examined what a nascent 'Islamic IR' might reveal about how dominant theories of IR might fall short, focusing on two primary problems in this dialogue: secularism and liberal individualism.

First, I examined the extent to which Islam can advise on matters of IR. Beginning in chapter 2, I found this Islamic theological guidance on IR to be somewhat lacking. This is not to the detriment of the Islamic source texts, which offer themselves as guides rather than hard and fast rules for behaviour. Instead, as shown in chapter 5, it would be rather unreasonable to find guidance on all aspects of life in only one aspect of revelation (theology). In this respect bringing *al-iman*, exotericism, into the analysis allows one to 'fill the gaps' of theological guidance on politics. So while the guidance in Islamic source texts is somewhat ambiguous, that guidance still finds a place in the form of the first of Khadduri's dual contracts that legitimate Muslim sovereignty. If such theological guidance is interpreted as the lowest common denominator of faith, most likely represented by the *shahada*, the declaration of faith, then this would represent the first contract, between the individual and God. The second contract uses exotericism to derive an agreement between the individual and temporal ruler/institution/constitution.

Building on these new sources of knowledge, and constructivism's ability to interpret religion as the believer might do, I developed Normative Political Islam as a metaphorical outline to hold next to the outline of IR. Comparing the two outlines, I found that there are points at which the shape of IR is different to Normative Political Islam, and vice versa. This differing shape was revealed to be the concept of community and the universality of liberal individualism.

Dealing first with community and the *umma*, in chapter 3 I scrutinised IR's treatment of religion, looking at the regions of the MENA, sub-Saharan Africa and Southeast Asia. Where religion was a factor, uniformly, these studies did not interpret religion on its own terms, but rather subsumed it into pre-existing categories of analysis. The primary problem that the politics of the *umma* represents to IR, indicative of political Islam in general, is the fact that it is explicitly religiously derived (to some degree). IR has a secular leaning which, as seen in chapter 4, stems from Enlightenment philosophy and ideas of inexorable progress. In this myth, Westphalia created the international system, and all this was the effort of European character, innate, and spontaneous, categorised as 'pioneering agency' in Hobson's non-reductive Orientalism.[2] So, when bringing alternative concepts of IR to the fore, these alternatives challenge dominant narratives in the discipline, asking that these narratives be re-evaluated. When such re-evaluation is completed, the 'immutable' nature of concepts like secularism is removed, allowing for engagement with, in this case, Normative Political Islam.

Chapter 6 gave shape to this engagement in the form of community, and here I noted the second primary challenge to IR, a second mis-match between the shapes of IR and Normative Political Islam: liberal individualism. Liberal individualism implies an abstract, universal rationality. Translated to IR, this abstract rationality sees assumptions about the nature of shared values, that is, a shared *normative* world, on the basis of *empirical* findings. For example, the fact that different states affirm and participate in the state system, for the English School, is taken as read that these states share the same values when it comes to IR. In fact states may affirm the system, even the notion of an international society, based on different assumptions, deriving from their societal circumstances; European states may want to encourage the idea of universal values in IR; this obfuscates the fact that many of these values derive from Europe's own history. At the same time, the circumstances at the end of colonialism may have led former colonies to advocate for their independence through the language of states, not because of the universal applicability of that concept, but because the language of states was the most powerful tool at the time with regards to achieving independence. After challenging universal applicability, I forwarded values that derive, not abstractly, but from within the societies which individuals live, as an alternative. Chapter 7 saw that this alternative can lead to competing values that cannot be adjudicated between. That being so, a final challenge to IR, that is, the ultimate consequence of the fact that there is a difference between the two broad outlines of IR and Normative Political Islam, is the idea of value pluralism.

Value pluralism dares IR to find purpose not in the spread of *one* form of international politics, but the management of various, *competing* value claims. In this sense communitarian, value pluralist IR resembles the pursuit of 'order/pluralism' in the schema of the English School's pluralist/solidarist divide. With all three challenges to IR put forward, secularism, liberal individualism and pluralism, I would like to emphasise that none of these are *specific* to Islam. Each challenge represents ongoing debates in IR and so Normative Political Islam, and Islam-as-politics more generally, is not an anomaly on the fringes of the discipline, but could help explore these debates as they become more central to how IR is perceived.

Throughout the book I kept returning to the similarity of poststructuralism's and political Islam's critique of IR, juxtaposed to the radically different ontological positions between the two (rejection of meta-narrative versus belief in God). I outlined the preoccupation of Islamic critique on 'modernity', during and after colonialism, in chapter 2. Accounting for what Muslim leaders increasingly viewed as the stagnation of the Islamic world led some to embrace the principles and political models of their former colonial masters, while others critiqued these principles and sought to achieve prosperous societies without embracing the principles that found their origin in the European Enlightenment. Advocating the latter of these approaches, the *umma*'s challenges to IR, secularism, universal rationality and value pluralism, as outlined above, derive from this 'Enlightenment rationality'. In this way, the discussion about political Islam, and the discussion over 'religious resurgence' more generally, stems from the contestation of what constitutes political modernity. These themes are very similar to those of poststructuralism, which also sees the truths that became embedded in society after the Enlightenment as problematic, a 'straitjacket'[3] on social science. Poststructuralism uses scepticism of meta-narrative and universal truths to argue that behind the 'universals' of the Enlightenment project lies a reliance on a specific set of values derived from specific historical and cultural traditions. What the above affirms is that there is significant synthesis in the two approaches of poststructuralism and Islamic critique; the former disregards the 'universal' philosophy of the Enlightenment, allowing the latter to articulate its notion of 'modernity' in its own way. This does not mean that engagement between competing value systems is redundant simply because they are understandably different. In fact, the acknowledgement that there exist different, legitimate value systems is the very reason engagement and dialogue are so important.

Enlightenment philosophy would claim that there is but one way for societies to develop, translating broadly to positivism in IR. Accepting a more interpretivist understanding of the world, as I have presented in this book, there must be dialogue and an attempt to *understand* the other, rather than seek to *convert* them. In this sense, chapter 7 demonstrated that the synthesis between poststructuralism and Islam comes to an end after the 'common opponent' of Enlightenment philosophy is dealt with; both have the potential to harbour a missionary zeal with regards to delegitimising the other, based on claims to universal truths (belief in God, and the insidious 'there is no truth but the fact that there is no truth'). At this point I sought out value pluralism once more, to make sense of how both positions could be held in the same theory, that is, for Normative Political Islam to use poststructural critique of the structures of the international sphere but not use that same critique on its own universal truth claims. However, given the fact that there are values that are not rationally resolvable (such as those vested in poststructuralism and Islam respectively), it is no incoherency to embrace the two simultaneously; it is in fact an *affirmation* of value competition, in the abstracted realm of second-order theory within which the book is located.

TO WHAT EXTENT IS AN ISLAMIC NOTION OF INTERNATIONAL RELATIONS TENABLE?

The IR of Normative Political Islam, as rudimentary as it may appear in the pages of this book, disturbs the equilibrium of IR in three ways: (1) it is derived from communal sources, not abstract reason; (2) it centres on rule over people, not rule over territory; (3) it blurs the boundary between sacred and profane. Moreover, the frictions I have outlined throughout the course of this book serve to reinforce the idea that what might otherwise be accepted as value-neutral propositions do in fact have a societal heritage, specifically a European/Christian heritage. I have dealt with two such propositions, secularism and liberal individualism, concepts which have been 'universalised' and are expected to find purchase in a diverse range of settings outside of the environment where those concepts were created. Secularism and liberal individualism are reflected in the way IR is conceived, and as such, limit the exploration of any alternative conceptions.

One such alternative conception is an Islamic one. To talk of 'Islam' as a political persuasion or ideology is somewhat of a misnomer. I have argued for a distinction between Islam-as-faith and Islam-as-politics, the latter being the broad umbrella under which Normative Political Islam is oriented. Accepting this distinction, Normative Political Islam was developed not from theological guidance, but by reviving the exoteric tradition of Sunni Islam. This exotericism leads to the articulation of the *umma* through communitarian principles, which found strong resonance with the exoteric tradition discussed. Embracing communitarianism in IR, however, proved more difficult than its synthesis with Normative Political Islam. Articulating community, Islamic or otherwise, challenges dominant interpretations of who the actors are in the international sphere. Such a challenge is not new, and it is not uniquely posed by the *umma*; transnationalism and debates over the EU, for example, serve to show a comparable debate about the actors in IR. However, while community can be vested in and across states in an international organisation (such as the EU or the OIC), it is not the only way to conceive of community, and indeed is not the dominant way Muslims conceive of the *umma*.

In pushing back the 'universal' concepts of liberal individualism and secularism in IR, I demonstrated that there is considerable compatibility between Islamic and poststructuralist critique. However, this compatibility is limited by the fact that these two perspectives can and will move to critique each other once the universalisms of IR are made humbler. While such competition (between Islam and poststructuralism) might be viewed as zero-sum, in that one must inevitably win out over the other, I have shown that this is not necessarily the case. Inevitable conflict is in fact a normal and expected component of one's existence, and managing these conflicts is more important that resolving them (some conflicts cannot be resolved).

The IR of Islam-as-politics, therefore, is one that is only achievable given an internal shift in Muslims who might wish to constitute it; the need to revive exotericism is paramount; it furnishes Muslims with the tools necessary in constructing notions of politics that at once abide by broad theological guidance, but can be sensitive to and take their cue from the societies they wish to represent. As such, it allows Islam-as-politics, and Normative Political Islam specifically, to abide by the 'conviction that there is no need for a detour through the labyrinths of Western history, before one can arrive at a vision of the good life and a just order'.[4] Moreover, IR practitioners require a more reflexive understanding of the ideas they use to explain 'non-Western' examples, identifying where the tools they are using are not as value neutral or 'objective' as otherwise assumed. Questioning the limits of one's own tradition helps to better appreciate the traditions of others, finding, in this instance, a more satisfactory place for religion in IR. That is not to say that every instance of religious reasoning need be accepted at face value. Rather, it must be understood when religion is playing a more substantial role than simply an articulation of 'culture' or 'socio-economic factors'. Only with this double move, one on the side of political Islamists, and the other on the side of those who try to explain their behaviour, do Islamic, or indeed any number of other alternative notions of IR, have any chance of being conceived. Once conceived though, as Normative Political Islam has been in the pages of this book, the case for articulating it is another, separate project. This separation points back to the distinction between first- and second-order theorising, for while I have made a conceptual space for Normative Political Islam, the empirical space has yet to be explored; such exploration is the task of future first-order studies.

NOTES

1. Barak Mendelsohn, 'God vs. Westphalia: Radical Islamist Movements and the Battle for Organising the World', *Review of International Studies* 38, no. 3 (2012): 596.

2. John Hobson, *The Eurocentric Conception of World Politics: Western International Theory, 1760–2010* (Cambridge: Cambridge University Press, 2012), 196.

3. Torbjorn Knutsen, *A History of International Relations Theory* (Manchester: Manchester University Press, 1997), 274.

4. Bobby Sayyid, *A Fundamental Fear: Eurocentrism and The Emergence of Islamism* (London: Zed, 2003), xxii.

Bibliography

'Abduh, Muhammed. 'Islam, Reason, and Civilisation'. In *Islam in Transition: Muslim Perspectives*, edited by John Donohue and John Esposito, 24–28. Oxford: Oxford University Press, 1982.
'Abed al-Jabri, Mohammed. *Arab-Islamic Philosophy: A Contemporary Critique*. Translated by Aziz Abbassi. Austin, TX: Center for Middle Eastern Studies, 1999.
Abou El Fadl, Khaled. 'Islam and the Theology of Power'. *Middle East Report* no. 221 (2001): 28–33.
AbuSulayman, 'AbdulHamid. *Towards an Islamic Theory of International Relations: New Directions for Methodology and Thought*. Herndon, VA: International Institute of Islamic Thought, 1993.
Acharya, Amitav. 'Global International Relations (IR) and Regional Worlds: A New Agenda for International Studies'. *International Studies Quarterly* 58, no. 4 (2014): 647–59.
Adamson, Fiona. 'Global Liberalism versus Political Islam: Competing Ideological Frameworks in International Politics'. *International Studies Review* 7, no. 4 (2005): 547–69.
Adler, Emanuel. *Communitarian International Relations: The Epistemic Foundations of International Relations*. London: Routledge, 2005.
Ahkavi, Shahrough. 'Islam, Politics and Society in the Thought of Ayatullah Khomeini, Ayatullah Taliqani and Ali Shariati'. *Middle Eastern Studies* 24, no. 4 (1988): 404–31.
Ahmed, Aijaz. 'Between Orientalism and Historicism'. In *Orientalism: A Reader*, edited by Alexander Lyon Macfie, 285–97. New York: New York University Press, 2000.
Ahmed Fauzi, Abdul Hamid. 'Religion, Secularism and the State in Southeast Asia'. In *Thinking International Relations Differently*, edited by Arlene B. Tickner and David L. Blaney, 253–74. Abingdon: Routledge, 2012.
Al-Afghani, Jamal al-Din. 'An Islamic Response to Imperialism'. In *Islam in Transition: Muslim Perspectives*, edited by John Donohue and John Esposito, 16–19. Oxford: Oxford University Press, 1982.
al-'Azm, Sadik Jalal. 'Orientalism and Orientalism in Reverse'. In *Orientalism: A Reader*, edited by Alexander Lyon Macfie, 217–38. New York: New York University Press, 2000.
Al-Azmeh, Aziz. *Islam and Modernities*. 2nd ed. London: Verso, 1996.
———. 'Postmodern Obscurantism and "the Muslim Question"'. In *Fighting Identities: Race, Religion and Ethno-Nationalism*, edited by Leo Pantich and Colin Leys, 28–50. London: Merlin, 2002.
Al-Banna, Hasan. 'The New Renaissance'. In *Islam in Transition: Muslim Perspectives*, edited by John Donohue and John Esposito, 78–83. Oxford: Oxford University Press, 1982.
Al-Raziq, 'Ali-'Abd. 'Message Not Government, Religion Not State'. In *Liberal Islam: A Sourcebook*, edited by Charles Kurzman, 29–36. Oxford: Oxford University Press, 1998.

Bibliography

Andreasson, Stefan. 'Elusive Agency: Africa's Persistently Peripheral Role in International Relations'. In *African Agency in International Politics*, edited by William Brown and Sophie Harman, 143–58. London: Routledge, 2013.
An-Na'im, Abdullahi. '*Shari'a* and Basic Human Rights Concerns'. In *Liberal Islam: A Sourcebook*, edited by Charles Kurzman, 222–38. Oxford: Oxford University Press, 1998.
An-Na'im, Abdullahi Ahmed. *Islam and the Secular State: Negotiating the Future of Shari'a*. Cambridge, MA: Harvard University Press, 2008.
an-Nawawi, Imam. *The Complete Forty Hadith*. Translated by Abdassamad Clarke. London: Ta-Ha, 2000.
Appadurai, Arjun. *A Fear of Small Numbers: An Essay on the Geography of Anger*. London: Duke University Press, 2006.
Arkoun, Mohammed. 'Rethinking Islam Today'. In *Liberal Islam: A Sourcebook*, edited by Charles Kurzman, 205–21. Oxford: Oxford University Press, 1998.
Asad, Talal. *Formations of the Secular: Christianity, Islam, Modernity*. Stanford: Stanford University Press, 2003.
ASEAN. 'The ASEAN Charter'. Accessed 13.12.2015. http://www.asean.org/images/2015/October/Charter-of-the-ASEAN-Singapore-20-November-2007/7%20ASEAN%20CHARTER%20rev.2%20update%20on%2002%20Oct15%20IJP.pdf.
Ashley, Richard, and R. B. J. Walker. 'Conclusion: Reading Dissidence/Writing the Discipline: Crisis and the Question of Sovereignty in International Studies'. *International Studies Quarterly* 34, no. 3 (1990): 367–416.
Avineri, Shlomo, and Avner De-Shalit, eds. *Communitarianism and Individualism*. Oxford: Oxford University Press, 1992.
Ayubi, Nazih. *Political Islam: Religion and Politics in the Arab World*. London: Routledge, 1991.
———. *Over-stating the Arab State: Politics and Society in the Middle East*. London: I.B. Tauris, 1996.
Bader, Veit. 'Citizenship and Exclusion: Radical Democracy, Community, and Justice. Or, What is Wrong with Communitarianism'. *Political Theory* 23, no. 2 (1995): 211–46.
Ball, Terence, and Richard Bellamy, eds. *The Cambridge History of Twentieth Century Political Thought*. Cambridge: Cambridge University Press, 2003.
Barnett, Michael. *Dialogues in Arab Politics: Negotiations in Regional Order*. New York: Columbia University Press, 1998.
Bayat, Asef, ed. *Post-Islamism: The Changing Faces of Political Islam*. Oxford: Oxford University Press, 2013.
———. 'Post-Islamism at Large'. In *Post-Islamism: The Changing Faces of Political Islam*, edited by Asef Bayat, 3–32. Oxford: Oxford University Press, 2013.
Bellamy, Richard. *Liberalism and Modern Society*. Cambridge: Polity, 1992.
Berlin, Isaiah. *Four Essays on Liberty*. Oxford: Oxford University Press, 1969.
———. *The Crooked Timber of Humanity: Chapters in the History of Ideas*, edited by Henry Hardy. London: Pimlico, 2003.
Bernstein, Richard. 'Foucault: Critique as a Philosophical Ethos'. In *Critique and Power: Recasting the Foucault/Habermas Debate*, edited by Michael Kelly. London: MIT Press, 1994, 211–41.
Bhambra, Gurminder. *Rethinking Modernity: Postcolonialism and the Sociological Imagination*. Basingstoke: Palgrave, 2007.
Bilgin, Pinar. 'Civilisation, Dialogue, Security: The Challenge of Post-Secularism and the Limits of Civilisational Dialogue'. *Review of International Studies* 38, no. 5 (2012): 1099–1115.
Bill, James A., and Robert Springborg. *Politics in the Middle East*. 5th ed. New York: Addison Wesley Longman, 1999.
Bleiker, Ronald, and Mark Chou. 'Nietzsche's Style: On Language, Knowledge and Power in International Relations'. In *International Relations Theory and Philosophy: Interpretive Dialogues*, edited by Cerwyn Moore and Chris Farrands, 8–19. London: Routledge, 2010.
Booth, Ken. 'Huntington's Homespun Grandeur'. *Political Quarterly* 68, no. 4 (1997): 425–28.

Boucher, David. *The Limits of Ethics in International Relations: Natural Law, Natural Rights, and Human Rights in Transition*. Oxford: Oxford University Press, 2009.

Boutros-Ghali, Boutros. 'An Agenda for Peace: Preventive Diplomacy, Peacemaking and Peacekeeping'. Accessed 7.5.13. http://www.unrol.org/files/A_47_277.pdf.

Brenner, Louis, ed. *Muslim Identity and Social Change in Sub-Saharan Africa*. London: Hurst & Company, 1993.

Bromley, Simon. *Rethinking Middle East Politics*. Oxford: Blackwell, 1994.

Brown, L. Carl. *Religion and State: The Muslim Approach to Politics*. New York: Columbia University Press, 2000.

Brown, William. 'Africa and International Relations: A Comment on IR theory, Anarchy and Statehood'. *Review of International Studies* 32, no. 1 (2006): 119–43.

———. 'A Question of Agency: Africa in International Politics'. *Third World Quarterly* 33, no. 10 (2012): 1889–1908.

Brown, William, and Sophie Harman, eds. *African Agency in International Politics*. London: Routledge, 2013.

Bull, Hedley. 'The Emergence of a Universal International Society'. In *The Expansion of International Society*, edited by Hedley Bull and Adam Watson, 117–26. Oxford: Oxford University Press, 1984.

Bull, Hedley, and Adam Watson, eds. *The Expansion of International Society*. Oxford: Oxford University Press, 1984.

Bulliet, Richard. 'Twenty Years of Islamic Politics'. *Middle East Journal* 53, no. 2 (1999): 189–200.

Burchill, Scott, Andrew Linklater, Richard Devetak, Jack Donnelly, Terry Nardin, Matthew Paterson, Christian Reus-Smit, and Jacqui True, eds. *Theories of International Relations*. 4th ed. Basingstoke: Palgrave Macmillan, 2009.

Butko, Thomas. 'Revelation or Revolution: A Gramscian Approach to the Rise of Political Islam'. *British Journal of Middle Eastern Studies* 31, no. 1 (2004): 41–62.

Buzan, Barry. *From International to World Society? English School Theory and the Social Structure of Globalisation*. Cambridge: Cambridge University Press, 2004.

Buzan, Barry, and Ana Gonzalez-Pelaez, eds. *International Society and the Middle East*. New York: Palgrave Macmillan, 2009.

Calhoun, Craig, Mark Juergensmeyer, and Jonathan VanAntwerpen, eds. *Rethinking Secularism*. Oxford: Oxford University Press, 2011.

Camilleri, Joseph. 'Postsecularist Discourse in an "Age of Transition"'. *Review of International Studies* 38, no. 5 (2012): 1019–39.

Chakrabarty, Dipesh. *Provincializing Europe: Postcolonial Thought and Historical Difference*. Princeton: Princeton University Press, 2000.

Chandler, David. 'Critiquing Liberal Cosmopolitanism? The Limits of the Biopolitical Approach'. *International Political Sociology* 3, no. 1 (2009): 53–70.

Checkel, Jeffery. 'The Constructivist Turn in International Relations Theory'. *World Politics* 50, no. 2 (1998): 324–48.

Copeland, Dale. 'The Constructivist Challenge to Structural Realism: A Review Essay'. *International Security* 25, no. 2 (2000): 187–212.

Cox, Michaelene, John Oneal, and Bruce Russett. 'Clash of Civilizations, or Realism and Liberalism Déjà Vu? Some Evidence'. *Journal of Peace Research* 37, no. 5 (2000): 583–608.

Cox, Robert. 'Social Forces, States and World Orders: Beyond International Relations Theory'. *Millennium: A Journal of International Studies* 10, no. 2 (1981): 126–55.

Dallmayr, Fred. 'Exit from Orientalism'. In *Orientalism: A Reader*, edited by Alexander Lyon Macfie, 365–68. New York: New York University Press, 2000.

Davidson, Roderic. 'Turkish Attitudes Concerning Christian-Muslim Equality in the Nineteenth Century'. In *The Modern Middle East: A Reader*, edited by Albert Hourani, Philip Khoury, and Mary Wilson. London: I.B. Tauris, 1993.

Dean, Mitchell. *Governing Societies: Political Perspectives on Domestic and International Rule*. Berkshire: Open University Press, 2007.

De Boer, Tjitze. *The History of Philosophy in Islam*. Translated by Edward Jones. New York: Dover, 1967.

Debrix, François. 'We Other IR Foucaultians'. *International Political Sociology* 4, no. 2 (2010): 197–99.

Delfolie, David. 'Malaysian Extroversion towards the Muslim World: Ideological Positioning for a "Mirror Effect"'. *Journal of Current Southeast Asian Affairs* 31, no. 4 (2012): 3–29.

Deshen, Shlomo, and Walter Zenner, eds. *Jews among Muslims: Communities in the Precolonial Middle East*. New York: New York University Press, 1996.

———. 'Jews among Muslims in Precolonial Times: An Introductory Survey'. In *Jews among Muslims: Communities in the Precolonial Middle East*, edited by Shlomo Deshen and Walter Zenner, 3–24. New York: New York University Press, 1996.

Dews, Peter. 'Postmodernism: Pathologies of Modernity from Nietzsche to the Post-structuralists'. In *The Cambridge History of Twentieth-Century Political Thought*, edited by Terence Ball and Richard Bellamy, 43–367. Cambridge: Cambridge University Press, 2003.

Donner, Fred. 'The Sources of Islamic Conceptions of War'. In *Just War and Jihad: Historical and Theoretical Perspectives on War and Peace in Western and Islamic Traditions*, edited by John Kelsay and James Johnson. London: Greenbridge, 1991.

Donohue, John, and John Esposito, eds. *Islam in Transition: Muslim Perspectives*. Oxford: Oxford University Press, 1982.

———, eds. *Islam in Transition: Muslim Perspectives,* 2nd ed. Oxford: Oxford University Press, 2007.

Doyle, Michael. 'Liberalism and World Politics'. *American Political Science Review* 80, no. 4 (1986): 1151–69.

Duffield, Mark. *Development, Security and Unending War: Governing the World of Peoples*. Cambridge: Polity, 2007.

Dunn, Kevin. 'Introduction: Africa and International Relations Theory'. In *Africa's Challenge to International Relations Theory*, edited by Kevin Dunn and Timothy Shaw, 1–10. Basingstoke: Palgrave Macmillan, 2001.

Dunn, Kevin, and Timothy Shaw, eds. *Africa's Challenge to International Relations Theory*. Basingstoke: Palgrave Macmillan, 2001.

Eickelman, Dale, and James Piscatori. *Muslim Politics*. Princeton: Princeton University Press, 1996.

El-Affendi, Abdelwahab, ed. *Rethinking Islam and Modernity: Essays in Honour of Fathi Osman*. Leicester: The Islamic Foundation, 2001.

Ernesto, Laclam, and Chantal Mouffe. *Hegemony and Socialist Strategy: Towards a Radical Democratic Politics*. 2nd ed. London: Verso, 2001.

Esposito, John. *Islam and Politics*. 4th ed. New York: Syracuse University Press, 1998.

———. *The Islamic Threat: Myth or Reality*. 3rd ed. Oxford: Oxford University Press, 1999.

———. 'Summary of the Open Debate'. In *Rethinking Islam and Modernity: Essays in Honour of Fathi Osman*, edited by Abdelwahab El-Affendi. Leicester: Islamic Foundation, 2001.

Fawcett, Louise, ed. *International Relations of the Middle East*. 2nd ed. Oxford: Oxford University Press, 2009.

———. 'Introduction: The Middle East and International Relations'. In *International Relations of the Middle East*, edited by Louise Fawcett, 1–16. 2nd ed. Oxford: Oxford University Press, 2009.

Foucault, Michel. *Power/Knowledge: Selected Interviews and Other Writings 1972–1977*. Harlow: Longman, 1980.

———. *Society Must Be Defended*. Translated by David Macey. London: Penguin, 2004.

Frost, Mervyn. *Ethics in International Relations: A Constitutive Theory*. Cambridge: Cambridge University Press, 1996.

Gaus, Gerald, and Chandran Kukathas, eds. *Handbook of Political Theory*. London: Sage, 2004.

Gause, Gregory. *Oil Monarchies: Domestic and Security Challenges in the Arab Gulf States*. New York: Council on Foreign Relations, 1994.

Gauthier, David. 'The Liberal Individual'. In *Communitarianism and Individualism*, edited by Shlomo Avineri and Avner De-Shalit, 151–64. Oxford: Oxford University Press, 1992.

George, Jim. *Discourses of Global Politics: A Critical (Re) Introduction to International Relations*. Boulder, CO: Lynne Rienner, 1994.

George, Jim, and David Campbell. 'Patterns of Dissent and the Celebration of Difference: Critical Social Theory and International Relations'. *International Studies Quarterly* 34, no. 3 (1990): 269–93.

Gledd, Perry. 'Book Review: The Islamic Theory of International Relations: New Directions for Islamic Methodology and Thought'. *American Journal of Islamic Social Sciences* 9, no. 1 (1992): 123–25.

Goodman, Lenn Evan. 'Ibn Khaldun and Thucydides'. *Journal of the American Oriental Society* 92, no. 2 (1972): 250–70.

Gow, James, Funmi Olonisakin, and Ernst Dijxhoorn, eds. *Militancy and Violence in West Africa: Religion, Politics and Radicalisation*. London: Routledge, 2013.

Gray, John. *Al Qaeda and What It Means to be Modern*. London: Faber and Faber, 2003.

———. 'Where Pluralists and Liberals Part Company'. *International Journal of Philosophical Studies* 6, no. 1 (2010): 17–36.

Guzzini, Stefano, and Anna Leander, eds. *Constructivism and International Relations: Alexander Wendt and His Critics*. London: Routledge, 2006.

Habermas, Jurgen. *The Philosophical Discourse of Modernity: Twelve Lectures*. Translated by Frederick Lawrence. Cambridge, MA: MIT Press, 1991.

———. *Between Naturalism and Religion: Philosophical Essays*. Cambridge: Polity, 2008.

Habermas, Jurgen, and Joseph Ratzinger. *The Dialectics of Secularization: On Reason and Religion*. San Francisco: Ignatius, 2007.

Hadiz, Vedi. 'Indonesian Political Islam: Capitalist Development and the Legacies of the Cold War'. *Journal of Current Southeast Asian Affairs* 30, no. 1 (2011): 3–38.

Haidar, Hamid Hadji. *Liberalism and Islam: Practical Reconciliation Between the Liberal State and Shiite Muslims*. New York: Palgrave Macmillan, 2008.

Halliday, Fred. *Islam and the Myth of Confrontation*. London: I.B. Tauris, 1996.

———. *The Middle East in International Relations: Power, Politics and Ideology*. Cambridge: Cambridge University Press, 2005.

———. 'The Middle East and Conceptions of "International Society"'. In *International Society and the Middle East*, edited by Barry Buzan and Ana Gonzalez-Pelaez, 1–23. New York: Palgrave Macmillan, 2009.

Hampshire, Stuart. 'Liberalism: The New Twist'. *New York Review of Books* 40, no. 14 (1993): 43–47.

Hardt, Michael, and Antonio Negri. *Empire*. Cambridge, MA: Harvard University Press, 2000.

Harman, Sophie, and William Brown. 'In from the Margins? The Changing Place of Africa in International Relations'. *International Affairs* 89, no. 1 (2013): 69–87.

Hashmi, Sohail. 'Islam, the Middle East and the Pan-Islamic Movement'. In *International Society and the Middle East*, edited by Barry Buzan and Ana Gonzalez-Pelaez, 170–200. New York: Palgrave Macmillan, 2009.

Henderson, Bobby. 'Open Letter to Kansas School Board'. Accessed 21.02.2013. http://www.venganza.org/about/open-letter/.

Herbst, Jeffrey. 'Responding to State Failure in Africa'. *International Security* 21, no. 3 (1996): 120–44.

Hewitt, Vernon. *The New International Politics of South Asia*. Manchester: Manchester University Press, 1997.

Hinnebusch, Raymond. 'Introduction: The Analytical Framework'. In *The Foreign Policies of Middle East States*, edited by Raymond Hinnebusch and Anoushiravan Ehteshami, 1–27. Boulder: Lynne Rienner, 2002.

Hinnebusch, Raymond, and Anoushiravan Ehteshami, eds. *The Foreign Policies of Middle East States*. Boulder: Lynne Rienner, 2002.

Hobson, John. *The Eastern Origins of Western Civilisation*. Cambridge: Cambridge University Press, 2004.

———. *The Eurocentric Conception of World Politics: Western International Theory, 1760–2010*. Cambridge: Cambridge University Press, 2012.

Hoffmann, Stanley. 'International Society'. In *Order and Violence: Hedley Bull and International Relations*, edited by John Vincent and John Miller, 13–37. Oxford: Clarendon Press, 1990.
The Holy Qur'an. Dublin, OH: Ahmadiyya Anjuman Ishaat Islam.
Horton, John, and Susan Mendus, eds. *After MacIntyre: Critical Perspectives on the Work of Alasdair MacIntyre*. Cambridge: Polity, 1994.
Hourani, Albert. *A History of the Arab Peoples*. London: Faber and Faber, 1991.
Hourani, Albert, Philip Khoury, and Mary Wilson, eds. *The Modern Middle East: A Reader*. London: I.B. Tauris, 1993.
Huntington, Samuel. *The Clash of Civilizations and the Remaking of World Order*. New York: Simon and Schuster, 1996.
Hurd, Elizabeth. *The Politics of Secularism in International Relations*. Princeton: Princeton University Press, 2008.
Ibn Khaldun. *The Muqaddimah: An Introduction to History*. Translated by Franz Rosenthal. New York: Pantheon, 1958.
Ismael, Jacqueline, and Tarek Ismael. 'Social Change in Islamic Society: The Political Thought of Ayatollah Khomeini'. *Social Problems* 27, no. 5 (1980): 601–19.
Jackson, Roy. *Mawlana Mawdudi and Political Islam: Authority and the Islamic State*. London: Routledge, 2008.
Jung, Dietrich. *Orientalists, Islamists and the Global Public Sphere: A Genealogy of the Modern Essentialist Image of Islam*. Sheffield: Equinox, 2011.
Kayaoglu, Turan. 'Westphalian Eurocentrism in International Relations Theory'. *International Studies Review* 12, no. 2 (2010): 193–217.
———. 'Constructing the Dialogue of Civilizations in World Politics: A Case of Global Islamic Activism'. *Islam and Christian-Muslim Relations* 23, no. 2 (2012): 129–47.
———. *The Organization of Islamic Cooperation: Politics, Problems, and Potential*. Abingdon: Routledge, 2015.
Keene, Edward. *Beyond the Anarchical Society: Grotius, Colonialism and Order in World Politics*. Cambridge: Cambridge University Press, 2002.
Kelsay, John, and James Johnson, eds. *Just War and Jihad: Historical and Theoretical Perspectives on War and Peace in Western and Islamic Traditions*. London: Greenbridge, 1991.
Kepel, Gilles. *Jihad: The Trail of Political Islam*. Harvard: Harvard University Press, 2002.
Khadduri, Majid. *War and Peace in the Law of Islam*. Baltimore: Johns Hopkins Press, 1955.
Khalaf-Allah, Muhammed. 'Legislative Authority'. In *Liberal Islam: A Sourcebook*, edited by Charles Kurzman, 37–45. Oxford: Oxford University Press, 1998.
Khan, Qamaruddin. *Political Concepts in the Qur'an*. Lahore: Islamic Book Foundation, 1982.
Khumayni, Ruhullah. 'Islamic Government'. In *Islam in Transition: Muslim Perspectives*, edited by John Donohue and John Esposito, 332–40. 2nd ed. Oxford: Oxford University Press, 2007.
Knutsen, Torbjorn. *A History of International Relations Theory*. Manchester: Manchester University Press, 1997.
Kratochwil, Fredrich, and John Ruggie. 'International Organization: A State of the Art on an Art of the State'. *International Organization* 40, no. 4 (1986): 753–75.
Kurzman, Charles, ed. *Liberal Islam: A Sourcebook*. Oxford: Oxford University Press, 1998.
Kymlicka, Will. *Contemporary Political Philosophy: An Introduction*. 2nd ed. Oxford: Oxford University Press, 2002.
Labeeb, Ahmed Bsoul. 'Theory of International Relations in Islam'. *Digest of Middle East Studies* 16, no. 2 (2007): 71–96.
Lapidus, Ira. 'The Separation of State and Religion in the Development of Early Islamic Society'. *International Journal of Middle East Studies* 6, no. 4 (1975): 363–85.
Lemke, Douglas. 'African Lessons for International Relations Research'. *Review of International Studies* 56, no. 1 (2011): 114–38.
———. 'Intra-national IR in Africa'. *Review of International Studies* 37, no. 1 (2011): 49–70.
Lessnoff, Michael. *Social Contract: Issues in Political Theory*. Basingstoke: Macmillan, 1986.
Lewis, Bernard. *The Arabs in History*. 6th ed. Oxford: Oxford University Press, 1993.

Linklater, Andrew. 'The English School'. In *Theories of International Relations*, edited by Scott Burchill, Andrew Linklater, Richard Devetak, Jack Donnelly, Terry Nardin, Matthew Paterson, Christian Reus-Smit, and Jacqui True, 86–110. 4th ed. Basingstoke: Palgrave Macmillan, 2009.

Liow, Joseph Chinyong. *Piety and Politics: Islamism in Contemporary Malaysia*. Oxford: Oxford University Press, 2009.

Losurdo, Domenico. *Liberalism: A Counter-History*. Translated by Gregory Elliot. London: Verso, 2011.

Lyotard, Jean-Francois. *The Postmodern Condition: A Report on Knowledge*. Translated by Geoff Bennington and Brian Massumi. Manchester: Manchester University Press, 1984.

Macfie, Alexander Lyon, ed. *Orientalism: A Reader*. New York: New York University Press, 2000.

MacIntyre, Alasdair. *After Virtue: A Study in Moral Theory*. 2nd ed. London: Duckworth, 1985.

Macpherson, Crawford Brough. *The Political Theory of Possessive Individualism*. 8th ed. Oxford: Oxford University Press, 1979.

Malaquias, Assis. 'Reformulating International Relations Theory: African Insights and Challenges'. In *Africa's Challenge to International Relations Theory*, edited by Kevin Dunn and Timothy Shaw, 11–28. Basingstoke: Palgrave Macmillan, 2001.

Mamdani, Mahmood. 'Good Muslim, Bad Muslim: A Political Perspective on Culture and Terrorism'. *American Anthropologist* 104, no. 3 (2002): 766–75.

Mandaville, Peter. *Transnational Muslim Politics: Reimagining the Umma*. London: Routledge, 2001.

———. *Global Political Islam*. London: Routledge, 2007.

Manners, Ian. 'Normative Power Europe: A Contradiction in Terms?'. *Journal of Common Market Studies* 40, no. 2 (2002): 235–58.

———. 'The Normative Ethics of the European Union'. *International Affairs* 84, no. 1 (2008): 65–80.

March, Andrew. 'Islamic Foundations for a Social Contract in Non-Muslim Liberal Democracies'. *American Political Science Review* 101, no. 2 (2007): 235–52.

Marranci, Gabriele. 'Multiculturalism, Islam and the Clash of Civilisations Theory: Rethinking Islamophobia'. *Culture and Religion: An Interdisciplinary Journal* 5, no. 1 (2004): 105–17.

Martin, Richard C., and Abbas Barzegar. 'Introduction: The Debate About Islamism in the Public Sphere'. In *Islamism: Contested Perspectives on Political Islam*, edited by Richard C. Martin and Abbas Barzegar, 1–13. Stanford: Stanford University Press, 2010.

———, eds. *Islamism: Contested Perspectives on Political Islam*. Stanford: Stanford University Press, 2010.

Marty, Martin, and Scott Appleby, eds. *Fundamentalisms Observed*. The Fundamentalism Project 1. London: University of Chicago Press, 1991.

Marx, Karl. 'The Eighteenth Brumaire of Louis Bonaparte'. Accessed 31.05.2013. https://www.marxists.org/archive/marx/works/1852/18th-brumaire/ch01.htm.

Maududi, Abu A'la. *First Principles of the Islamic State*. Translated by Kurshid Ahmed. 2nd ed. Lahore: Islamic Publications, 1960.

———. 'Nationalism and Islam'. In *Islam in Transition: Muslim Perspectives*, edited by John Donohue and John Esposito. Oxford: Oxford University Press, 1982.

Mavelli, Luca. *Europe's Encounter with Islam: The Secular and the Postsecular*. New York: Routledge, 2012.

Mavelli, Luca, and Fabio Petito. 'The Postsecular in International Relations: An Overview'. *Review of International Studies* 38, no. 5 (2012): 931–42.

Medina, Vicente. *Social Contract Theories: Political Obligation or Anarchy?* Lanham, MD: Rowman & Littlefield, 1990.

Mendelsohn, Barak. 'God vs. Westphalia: Radical Islamist Movements and the Battle for Organising the World'. *Review of International Studies* 38, no. 3 (2012): 589–613.

Mendus, Susan. 'Saving One's Soul or Founding a State: Morality and Politics'. *Philosophia* 34, no. 3 (2006): 233–41.

Michael, Kelly, ed. *Critique and Power: Recasting the Foucault/Habermas Debate*. London: MIT Press, 1994.
Mill, John Stuart. 'On Liberty'. In *Modern Political Thought: Readings From Machiavelli to Nietzsche*, edited by David Wootton. Cambridge: Hackett, 1996.
Moaddel, Mansoor, and Kamran Talattof. 'Contemporary Debates in Islam'. In *Modernist and Fundamentalist Debates in Islam*, edited by Mansoor Moaddel and Kamran Talattof, 1–21. Basingstoke: Palgrave Macmillan, 2002.
———, eds. *Modernist and Fundamentalist Debates in Islam*. Basingstoke: Palgrave Macmillan, 2002.
Moin, Baqer. *Khomeini: Life of the Ayatollah*. London: I.B. Tauris, 1999.
Moore, Cerwyn, and Chris Farrands, eds. *International Relations Theory and Philosophy: Interpretive Dialogues*. London: Routledge, 2010.
Moslem, Mehdi. *Factional Politics in Post-Khomeini Iran*. New York: Syracuse University Press, 2002.
Mouffe, Chantal. *On the Political*. London: Routledge, 2005.
Munson, Henry. *Islam and Revolution in the Middle East*. New Haven: Yale University Press, 1988.
Naseer, Aruri, ed. *Middle East Crucible*. Wilmette: Medina University Press, 1975.
Nasr, Hossein. *Islamic Philosophy from its Origin to the Present: Philosophy in the Land of Prophecy*. New York: State University of New York Press, 2006.
Nietzsche, Friedrich. *Human, All Too Human*. London: University of Nebraska Press, 1984.
Nkiwane, Tandeka. 'The End of History? African Challenges to Liberalism in International Relations'. In *Africa's Challenge to International Relations Theory*, edited by Kevin Dunn and Timothy Shaw, 103–11. Basingstoke: Palgrave Macmillan, 2001.
Nonneman, Gerd, ed. *Analyzing Middle East Foreign Policies and the Relationships with Europe*. London: Routledge, 2005.
———. 'Analyzing the Foreign Policies of the Middle East and North Africa: A Conceptual Framework'. In *Analyzing Middle East Foreign Policies and the Relationships with Europe*, edited by Gerd Nonneman, 6–18. London: Routledge, 2005.
———. 'Introduction'. In *Analyzing Middle East Foreign Policies and the Relationships with Europe*, edited by Gerd Nonneman, 1–5. London: Routledge, 2005.
Noor, Farish. 'The Malaysian General Elections of 2013: The Last Attempt at Secular-inclusive Nation-building'. *Journal of Current Southeast Asian Affairs* 32, no. 2 (2013): 89–104.
O'Fahey, R. S. 'Islamic Hegemonies in the Sudan: Sufism, Mahdism and Islamism'. In *Muslim Identity and Social Change in Sub-Saharan Africa*, edited by Louis Brenner, 21–35. London: Hurst & Company, 1993.
Onuf, Nicholas. *World of Our Making: Rules and Rule in Social Theory and International Relations*. Columbia: University of South Carolina Press, 1989.
Organisation of Islamic Cooperation. 'Charter of the Organisation of Islamic Cooperation'. Accessed 24.08.2012. http://www.oic-oci.org/page_detail.asp?p_id=.
Osman, Sulastri. 'Jemaah Islamiyah: Of Kin and Kind'. *Journal of Current Southeast Asian Affairs* 29, no. 2 (2010): 157–75.
Otayek, René, and Benjamin F. Soares. 'Introduction: Islam and Muslim Politics in Africa'. In *Islam and Muslim Politics in Africa*, edited by Benjamin F. Soares and René Otayek, 1–26. Basingstoke: Palgrave Macmillan, 2007.
Owen, Roger. *State, Power and Politics in the Making of the Modern Middle East*. 3rd ed. New York: Routledge, 2004.
Pantich, Leo and Colin Leys, eds. *Fighting Identities: Race, Religion and Ethno-nationalism*. London: Merlin, 2002.
Pasha, Mustapha Kamal. 'Islam and the Postsecular'. *Review of International Studies* 38, no. 5 (2012): 1041–56.
Pelham, Nicolas, and Max Rodenbeck. 'Which Way for Hamas'. *New York Review of Books* 56, no. 17 (2009). Accessed 19.06.2010. http://www.nybooks.com/articles/archives/2009/nov/05/which-way-for-hamas/.
Pella, John Anthony. *Africa and the Expansion of International Society: Surrendering the Savanah*. London: Routledge, 2015.

Pettit, Philip. 'Liberal/Communitarian: MacIntyre's Mesmeric Dichotomy'. In *After MacIntyre: Critical Perspectives on the Work of Alasdair MacIntyre*, edited by John Horton and Susan Mendus, 176–86. Cambridge: Polity, 1994.
Piscatori, James. 'Islam and the International Order'. In *The Expansion of International Society*, edited by Hedley Bull and Adam Watson, 309–22. Oxford: Oxford University Press, 1984.
———. *Islam in a World of Nation-States*. Cambridge: Cambridge University Press, 1986.
———. 'Imagining Pan-Islam: Religious Activism and Political Utopias'. *Proceedings of the British Academy* 131 (2005): 421–42.
Quayle, Linda. *Southeast Asia and the English School of International Relations: A Region-Theory Dialogue*. Basingstoke: Palgrave Macmillan, 2013.
Rahman, Fazlur. *Islam*. Chicago: University of Chicago Press, 1979.
Ramadan, Tariq. *Western Muslims and the Future of Islam*. Oxford: Oxford University Press, 2004.
Ramsay, Maureen. *What's Wrong with Liberalism? A Radical Critique of Liberal Political Philosophy*. London: Continuum, 2004.
Rawls, John. 'Justice as Fairness: Political Not Metaphysical'. *Philosophy & Public Affairs* 14, no. 3 (1985): 223–51.
Renders, Marleen. 'Global Concerns, Local Realities: Islam and Islamism in a Somali State under Construction'. In *Islam and Muslim Politics in Africa*, edited by Benjamin F. Soares and René Otayek, 43–63. Basingstoke: Palgrave Macmillan, 2007.
Rengger, Nicholas. 'A City Which Sustains All Things? Communitarianism and International Society'. *Millennium: A Journal of International Studies* 21, no. 2 (1992): 353–69.
———. 'No Time like the Present? Postmodernism and Political Theory'. *Political Studies* 40, no. 3 (1992): 561–70.
Rida, Rashid. 'Patriotism, Nationalism, and Group Spirit in Islam'. In *Islam in Transition: Muslim Perspectives*, edited by John Donohue and John Esposito, 41–43. 2nd ed. Oxford: Oxford University Press, 2007.
Risse-Kappen, Thomas. 'Bringing Transnational Relations Back In: Introduction'. In *Bringing Transnational Relations Back In: Non-State Actors, Domestic Structures and International Institutions*, edited by Thomas Risse-Kappen, 3–36. Cambridge: Cambridge University Press, 1995.
———, ed. *Bringing Transnational Relations Back In: Non-State Actors, Domestic Structures and International Institutions*. Cambridge: Cambridge University Press, 1995.
Roy, Olivier. *The Failure of Political Islam*. London: I.B. Tauris, 1994.
Sabet, Amr. *Islam and the Political: Theory, Governance and International Relations*. London: Pluto Press, 2008.
Said, Edward. 'Shattered Myths'. In *Middle East Crucible*, edited by Aruri Naseer, 410–27. Wilmette: Medina University Press, 1975.
———. 'Arabs, Islam and the Dogmas of the West'. In *Orientalism: A Reader*, edited by Alexander Lyon Macfie, 104–5. New York: New York University Press, 2000.
Sandel, Michael. 'The Procedural Republic and the Unencumbered Self'. *Political Theory* 12, no. 1 (1984): 81–96.
Sayyid, Bobby. *A Fundamental Fear: Eurocentrism and The Emergence of Islamism*. London: Zed, 2003.
Schacht, Joseph. *The Origins of Muhammadan Jurisprudence*. Oxford: Oxford University Press, 1950.
Schwarzmantel, John. *Ideology and Politics*. London: Sage, 2008.
Shani, Giorgio. 'De-colonizing Foucault'. *International Political Sociology* 4, no. 2 (2010): 210–12.
Shapcott, Richard. *Justice, Community, and Dialogue in International Relations*. Cambridge: Cambridge University Press, 2001.
Sheikh, Faiz. 'Two Sides of the Same Coin? The Muslim Umma and the European Union'. *Politics, Religion and Ideology* 14, no. 3 (2014): 422–55.
Sheikh, Mona Kanwal. 'How Does Religion Matter? Pathways to Religion in International Relations'. *Review of International Studies* 38, no. 2 (2012): 365–92.

Sheikh, Naveed. *The New Politics of Islam: Pan-Islamic Foreign Policy in a World of States*. London: RoutledgeCurzon, 2003.
Soares, Benjamin F., and René Otayek, eds. *Islam and Muslim Politics in Africa*. Basingstoke: Palgrave Macmillan, 2007.
Soroush, Abdul-Karim. 'The Evolution and Devolution of Religious Knowledge'. In *Liberal Islam: A Sourcebook*, edited by Charles Kurzman, 244–54. Oxford: Oxford University Press, 1998.
Stratford, Elaine, Denbeigh Armstrong, and Martina Jaskolsji. 'Relational Spaces and the Geopolitics of Community Participation in Two Tasmanian Local Governments: A Case for Agonistic Pluralism?' *Transactions of the Institute of British Geographers* 28, no. 4 (2003): 461–72.
Suganami, Hidemi. 'Wendt, IR, and Philosophy: A Critique'. In *Constructivism and International Relations: Alexander Wendt and His Critics*, edited by Stefano Guzzini and Anna Leander, 57–92. London: Routledge, 2006.
Swatuk, Larry. 'The Brothers Grim: Modernity and 'International' Relations in Southern Africa'. In *Africa's Challenge to International Relations Theory*, edited by Kevin Dunn and Timothy Shaw, 163–85. Basingstoke: Palgrave Macmillan, 2001.
Taylor, Ian. 'Blind Spots in Analyzing Africa's Place in World Politics'. *Global Governance* 10, no. 4 (2004): 411–17.
———. *The International Relations of Sub-Saharan Africa*. London: Continuum, 2010.
Taylor, Ian, and Paul Williams, eds. *Africa in International Politics: External Involvement on the Continent*. London: Routledge, 2004.
———. 'Introduction: Understanding Africa's Place in World Politics'. In *Africa in International Politics: External Involvement on the Continent*, edited by Ian Taylor and Paul Williams, 1–22. London: Routledge, 2004.
Telhami, Shibley, and Michael Barnett, eds. *Identity and Foreign Policy in the Middle East*. Ithaca: Cornell University Press, 2002.
———. 'Introduction: Identity and Foreign Policy in the Middle East'. In *Identity and Foreign Policy in the Middle East*, edited by Shibley Telhami and Michael Barnett, 1–25. Ithaca: Cornell University Press, 2002.
Tibawi, Abdul Latif. 'English-Speaking Orientalists'. In *Orientalism: A Reader*, edited by Alexander Lyon Macfie, 57–76. New York: New York University Press, 2000.
Tibi, Bassam. *The Challenge of Fundamentalism: Political Islam and the New World Disorder*. London: University of California Press, 1998.
———. *Islam's Predicament with Modernity: Religious Reform and Cultural Change*. London: Routledge, 2009.
———. *Islam in Global Politics: Conflict and Cross-civilizational Bridging*. Abingdon: Routledge, 2012.
Tickner, Arlene B., and David L. Blaney, eds. *Thinking International Relations Differently*. Abingdon: Routledge, 2012.
Trimingham, J. Spencer. *The Influence of Islam upon Africa*. London: Longmans, Green, 1968.
Turner, Bryan. *Orientalism, Postmodernism and Globalism*. London: Routledge, 1994.
Ul-Haq, Mushir. 'Islam in Secular India'. In *Islam in Transition: Muslim Perspectives*, edited by John Donohue and John Esposito, 133–35. 2nd ed. Oxford: Oxford University Press, 2007.
van Ess, Josef. *The Flowering of Muslim Theology*. London: Harvard University Press, 2006.
Vincent, John, and John Miller, eds. *Order and Violence: Hedley Bull and International Relations*. Oxford: Clarendon Press, 1990.
Voll, John. 'Fundamentalism in the Sunni Arab World: Egypt and the Sudan'. In *Fundamentalisms Observed*, edited by Martin Marty and Scott Appleby, 345–402. The Fundamentalism Project 1. London: University of Chicago Press, 1991.
Walzer, Michael. *Spheres of Justice: A Defence of Pluralism and Equality*. New York: Basic, 1983.
Wendt, Alexander. 'Bridging the Theory/Meta-Theory Gap in International Relations'. *Review of International Studies* 17, no. 4 (1991): 383–92.

———. 'Anarchy Is What States Make of It: The Social Construction of Power Politics'. *International Organization* 46, no. 2 (1992): 391–425.

———. *Social Theory of International Politics*. Cambridge: Cambridge University Press, 1999.

———. 'Social Theory as Cartesian Science: An Auto-critique from a Quantum Perspective'. In *Constructivism and International Relations: Alexander Wendt and His Critics*, edited by Stefano Guzzini and Anna Leander, 181–219. London: Routledge, 2006.

Wilson, Erin. *After Secularism: Rethinking Religion in Global Politics*. Basingstoke: Palgrave Macmillan, 2012.

Wootton, David, ed. *Modern Political Thought: Readings from Machiavelli to Nietzsche*. Cambridge: Hackett, 1996.

Zafar, S. M. 'Accountability, Parliament and Ijtihad'. In *Liberal Islam: A Sourcebook*, edited by Charles Kurzman, 67–72. Oxford: Oxford University Press, 1998.

Zaidi, Ali Hassan. 'A Critical Misunderstanding: Islam and Dialogue in the Human Sciences'. *International Sociology* 22, no. 4 (2007): 411–34.

Zubaida, Sami. *Islam, the People & the State*. 2nd ed. London: I.B. Tauris, 1989.

———. 'Islam and the Politics of Community and Citizenship'. *Middle East Report* no. 221 (2001): 20–27.

———. *Beyond Islam: A New Understanding of the Middle East*. London: I.B. Tauris, 2011.

Index

African exceptionalism, 52
Africa in international relations, 50–53, 53
ancient Greek philosophy, 110, 111
Aristotelianism, 110
Ash'arite theology, 109
Association of Southeast Asian Nations, 55, 56, 60
Ayatollah Khomeini, 99, 104; and mysticism, 107–108

al-Banna, Hasan, 75

citizenship, 129
civilisation, 161
civil society, 129
Clash of Civilisations, 80, 158
Cold War, 57
colonialism, 147
communitarianism, 37, 133; and international relations, 139, 160, 186; and rationality, 135; and the social contract, 116
community: and Islam, 127; and the state, 137
constructivism, 37, 42–44, 83; and agency, 84; and identity, 142; and pluralism, 166; and universalism, 84
critical theory. *See* meta-theory

D-8 Organization of Economic Cooperation, 56

Darul Islam, 57
developmentalism, 131
dialogue of civilisations, 171
din wa dawla, 5, 17, 97, 101; and exceptionalism, 24; and shari'a, 104; and taqlid, 20

East/West dichotomy, 78, 87
English School, 47–48, 56, 144; conception of pluralism/solidarism, 56; and religion, 57
The Enlightenment. *See* modernity
epistemological scepticism, 163
essentialism, 52
Eurocentrism, 164, 166. *See also* Westphalian narrative
European Union, 58, 140
exotericism. *See* rationalism

fiqh, 105
foreign policy analysis (fpa), 37, 46

al-Ghazali, 109, 111
global international relations, 1, 40, 52, 62
Gnosticism. *See* mysticism

hadith, 106
Hamas, 36, 71, 113
Hobbes, Thomas, 112
holism, 175, 176, 178

identity, 140; and community, 145. *See also* constructivism
al-ihsan. *See* mysticism
ijtihad, 86
al-iman. *See* rationalism
international relations: and community, 128; and the state, 86
international society and civilisation, 60
Iran, 105; and mysticism, 98
irredentism, 49
al-islam. *See* theology
Islam, 27; and doctrinal difference, 24; and exceptionalism, 23; golden age of, 71; in international relations, 35–36, 70; and interpretation, 107; in the Middle East and North Africa, 82; and minority rights, 115; and norms, 149; and orthopraxy, 26; as protest, 30; and shari'a, 26; in sub-Saharan Africa, 50, 54; and transnationalism, 46, 140; and truth, 79, 135; and unity, 41, 175. *See also* religion in international relations
Islamic international relations, 54, 142. *See also* siyar
Islamic fundamentalism, 18
Islamic liberalism, 130
Islamic philosophy, 122
Islamic state, 5; and shari'a, 120
Islamisation, 56
Islamism. *See* political Islam
Islamology, 82

kalam. *See* theology
ibn Khaldun, 99, 111; and authority, 115; and government, 119; and Social Contract Theory, 113
Khaldunian original position, 114

liberal individualism, 86
liberalism, 37, 55, 61; and Christianity, 188; and the English School, 146; and exceptionalism, 115; and rationality, 135
logocentrism, 60

Marx, Karl, 40
Marxism, 37, 40–42
material-discursive divide, 37, 84
Maududi, Mawlana, 101; and shari'a, 27

meta-theory, 38, 70
modernity, 55, 60, 71, 75, 103; and epistemology, 74; and political Islam, 163; and postcolonialism, 76; and rationalism, 164; and secularism, 80; and umma, 128; and universalism, 132
modus vivendi, 158
Mohamad, Mahathir, 56
moral realism. *See* holism
Muslim Brotherhood, 71, 75
Muslim community. *See* umma
Muslim states, 58
Mu'tazilites, 20, 110
mysticism, 98, 104, 107

En-Nahda party, 71
nationalism, 100
negative liberty, 62
neo-patriarchy, 129
neo-realism, 59. *See also* realism
non-reductive Orientalism, 78; and pioneering agency, 131, 186
Normative Political Islam, 27, 97; and communitarianism, 188; and constructivism, 186; and international relations, 98; and Islam, 159; and poststructuralism, 148, 172; and the social contract, 116; and sovereignty, 112, 120; and umma, 102; and universalism, 132; and value pluralism, 168
norms, 143

ontological scepticism, 173
Organisation of Islamic Cooperation, 56, 101, 128, 141, 171
Orientalism, 87; and Said, Edward, 77. *See also* non-reductive Orientalism
Ottoman Empire, 102, 116

pan-Islam, 47, 102
Pastafarianism, 130
Philosophy, 104
pluralism, 187; in international relations, 158, 160; and Islam, 130; and justice, 135
political Islam, 17; and constructivism, 9, 85; and international relations, 64, 101; and liberalism, 8; as opposition, 21, 56;

and modernity, 75; and secularism, 82; and the state, 100; and universalism, 6
positive liberty, 62
positivism, 188
post-Islamism, 17
postmodernism. *See* poststructuralism
postsecularism, 81
poststructuralism, 73–74; and constructivism, 83; and Foucault, 72; and Islam, 69, 79, 158, 180; and ontology, 158, 178; and political Islam, 187

al-Qaeda, 121
Qur'an, 4, 103

rashidun, 118
rationalism, 98, 104, 109
al-Raziq, Ali Abd, 22
realism, 37, 48–49
realpolitik, 170
The Reformation, 97
regime change, 36
relativism, 136
religion in international relations, 37, 69, 161, 162. *See also* secular bias; Islam in international relations
religious resurgence, 185
Rida, Rashid, 101

salafism, 97
second order theory. *See* meta-theory
secular bias, 81, 139, 161
secular religion, 121
Secularism, 69, 103, 130; laicist variant, 81; and liberalism, 62; Judeo-Christian variant, 81, 188; in Southeast Asia, 57, 58
self/other dichotomy, 52, 53, 62, 64, 147, 165, 166
Shi'ism, 105
ibn Sina, 110
social contract: and Islam, 186; and the Prophet Muhammed, 118; and sovereignty, 99
Somalia, 37
Southeast Asia in international relations, 55–56

sovereignty: and God, 104; and Iran, 103; and Islam, 98; and shari'a, 116
standard of civilisation, 147
state-centrism, 60
Structural Adjustment Programmes, 53
structure/agency, 83
Sufism, 105

theology, 98, 99, 104; and philosophy, 110
transnational Islam, 102; and shari'a, 103. *See also* political Islam
transnationalism and religion, 141
Treaty of Westphalia, 60. *See also* Westphalian narrative

umma, 7, 28–29, 37, 58, 59, 61, 102; as an alternative to the state, 28; and heterogeneity, 128; in international relations, 150, 160, 186, 187; and Malaysia, 56; and regional society, 145; and solidarity, 144; and the state, 127; as thickly conceptualised, 146, 148; as thinly conceptualised, 140; and world society, 145
Universal Declaration of Human Rights, 102
universalism, 189; and the Enlightenment, 128; and international relations, 51, 186; and Islam, 130, 138, 142, 174, 175, 177; and liberalism, 134, 147; and rationality, 135; and shari'a, 148

value-incommensurability, 167, 169, 178
value pluralism, 158, 179; and the English School, 170; and epistemology, 172; and international relations, 171, 180; and realism, 170; and secularism, 168; and zero-sum conflict, 167. *See also* poststructuralism

War on Terror, 87
Westphalian narrative, 6, 165. *See also* Treaty of Westphalia

zero-sum conflict, 157, 163